A BOOK OF
NARRATIVE VERSE

A BOOK OF
NARRATIVE VERSE

A BOOK OF
NARRATIVE VERSE

Compiled by

V. H. COLLINS

With Remarks on Narrative Poetry by

EDMUND BLUNDEN

OXFORD   NEW YORK

OXFORD UNIVERSITY PRESS

Oxford University Press, Walton Street, Oxford OX2 6DP

Oxford New York Toronto
Delhi Bombay Calcutta Madras Karachi
Petaling Jaya Singapore Hong Kong Tokyo
Nairobi Dar es Salaam Cape Town
Melbourne Auckland
and associated companies in
Beirut Berlin Ibadan Nicosia

Oxford is a trade mark of Oxford University Press

A Book of Narrative Verse *was first published in 1930,
and reprinted in 1931 (twice), 1932 (twice), 1936, 1937
(twice), 1942, 1945, 1946, 1947, 1948, and 1950. Reset in
1954 and reprinted in 1955, 1956, 1958, 1959, 1960, 1961.
Reprinted with revisions in 1963 (three times), 1966, 1968,
1969, 1970, 1972, 1976, 1978, 1980, 1981, 1982, 1983, 1986

ISBN 0–19–250350–2

Printed in Great Britain by
The Thetford Press Limited
Thetford, Norfolk

Preface

FOR much valuable help in the selection the editor is indebted to several friends, especially to Mrs. Thomas, who placed unreservedly at his service a scheme for an anthology of narrative verse drawn up provisionally in 1914 by her husband, Edward Thomas, who was killed before he could complete it; and to Dr. J. C. Smith, who, in addition to various other suggestions, selected the passages from Spenser and Milton.

V. H. C.

ACKNOWLEDGEMENTS are due to Messrs. William Heinemann for A. C. Swinburne's 'St. Dorothy'; to Mr. A. T. A. Dobson for Austin Dobson's 'The Ballad of "Beau Brocade"'; to the Executors of Thomas Hardy and Messrs. Macmillan & Co. for 'The Sacrilege'; to Sir Henry Newbolt for 'A Ballad of John Nicholson' (from *Collected Poems 1897–1907*); to Laurence Binyon for 'The Battle of Stamford Bridge'; to Messrs. Burns, Oates, & Washbourne for 'Lepanto' (from G. K. Chesterton's *Collected Poems*); to Mr. John Masefield for 'The Rider at the Gate' (from *Collected Poems* published by Messrs. William Heinemann); to Mr. Alfred Noyes and Messrs. William Blackwood & Sons for 'The Highwayman' (from *Collected Poems*); and to Messrs. Methuen & Co. for 'Tomlinson' (from Rudyard Kipling's *Barrack-Room Ballads and Other Verse*).

Contents

viii   *Contents*

Contents

Remarks on Narrative Poetry

A GOOD narrative poem is a long strain of music accompanying a designed movement of human lives and passions, various in volume, in harmony, in time; its charm is not quite that of the drama, with its stir and grasp and interrogation, nor of the novel, vigorous in direct action and multitudinous in characters and conversations. It is romance in closest relation to the ways of existence, and asking no strange, sudden transcendings of the imagination. The lyric and the ballad (so far as we may use these or any terms with a sense of limits) require of us an immediate sublimity of our own. If we hear how

> Arethusa arose
> From her couch of snows
> In the Acroceraunian mountains,

we are probably surprised rather than illuminated, and it may be some time before we too are on those marvellous mountains, swift with that swiftness, having eyes and ears for those phantasms. The narrative poem habitually makes the ascent in less precipitous fashion, and, though its world is not the world we face, seems to open a region where the same principles and proportions reign. The reflection is enriched and tranquillized.

If realism without refinement could be the parent of narrative poetry fit to live, we might have inherited a great deal of verse on the plan of the *Rejected Addresses*, and our anthology would be composed of it:

> John Richard William Alexander Dwyer
> Was footman to Justinian Stubbs, Esquire;
> But when John Dwyer listed in the Blues,
> Emanuel Jennings polish'd Stubbs's shoes.
> Emanuel Jennings brought his youngest boy
> Up as a corn-cutter—a safe employ;

In Holywell Street, St. Pancras, he was bred }
  (At number twenty-seven, it is said), }
Facing the pump, and near the Granby's Head. }

The novelist might be pleased to write, 'Just as these thoughts were passing in his mind, a drowsy, slatternly charwoman, in an old black straw bonnet and grey bedgown, opened one of the shutters, and threw up the sash of the window by where Mr. Sponge sat, disclosing the contents of the apartment. The last wax-light was just dying out in the centre of a splendid candelabra on the middle of a table scattered about with claret-jugs, glasses, decanters, pine-apple tops, grape-dishes, cakes, anchovy-toast plates, devilled-biscuit racks—all the concomitants of a sumptuous entertainment. "Sir Harry at home?" asked Mr. Sponge, making the woman sensible of his presence, by cracking his whip close to her ear. "No," replied the dame gruffly, at the same time commencing an assault upon the nearest chair with a duster. "Where is he?" asked our friend. "Bed, to be sure," replied the woman, in the same tone. "Bed, to be sure," repeated Mr. Sponge.' It is correct narrative. But the narrative poet would not use those circumstances, or colloquialisms, notwithstanding that he is not denied the art of caricature and comedy. Chaucer has his broad humour and his minute and homely detail; and yet he tells us his tale with a brightness of idea over all, and through all.

Among the numerous volumes of narrative poetry which have been published in English since Chaucer, I take up one which illustrates the failure of attempts to be literal in this form of writing. The author of 'Abide with me' was a poet beyond question. When will the next utterance of such command over the souls of men and women be made? Lyte in his younger days, under the influence of *Endymion* and George Crabbe, issued a set of *Tales in Verse*. It is worth finding. In a lucky moment, you see the poet there:

> He banqueted on music; and his taste
> Was quick to all of beautiful and chaste.
> He looked on nature with a painter's eye,
> And caught the soul of speaking poesy.

But usually Lyte is recording, with an exactitude creditable by itself, matters like these:

> Her husband had his avocations too:
> He kept, I've said, a garden, where he grew
> The earliest peas in all the country round,
> And fruit for size and flavour far renowned;
> To bud and graft, he was supremely skilled,
> And aye a pruning knife his pocket filled.

In more recent times, we have seen the extraordinary rise, and the subsequent obscuration, of Mr. Masefield's daring narrative poems. Here again, we encounter a poet, a rich sensibility, an exemplary humanity. Mr. Masefield's scenery should have been ideally ready for actions and characters that would not fade. But the intention to make them look like life itself was the old fallacy at work anew. The police-report and the foul language, the broken mugs and the silver cigarette-cases would not endure the atmosphere of the true tale in verse.

Particularly during the eighteenth century, a kind of rhyming episode-poem was well written, and, obviously seeking no higher mark than that of the witty private letter somewhat generalized, deserved the popularity that it earned. The value of a definite metre and an expected rhyme, with the changes that can be rung upon these, for the lively anecdote or amusing incident, was well known to Swift and Prior and Gay and those who followed. Their age understood that the business of literature is not incessantly to tear the soul of the reader asunder; it would have asked of our age, why this eternal long face?

> Methinks of late you are too much i' the frown.

A separate anthology is needed for the familiar stories in verse of the days when the earth was *terra firma*; and Swift, clearest, surest, keenest of narrators, for ever leads the way with 'Baucis and Philemon'. It is too long to be printed here as an invitation to the kindlier moods of English verse, and the comfort for the mind that dexterous art can give in plain iambics.

Of all the poetical story-tellers who have approached the world and characteristics of the novel, the prince, or Lord Chief Justice, was and is George Crabbe. It is desirable, therefore, that we should be conscious of his views on the subject of narrative poetry, as he expressed them (for example) in introducing his volume of *Tales* in 1812. He was defending himself against the charge that he was really writing prose: 'In whatever degree I may venture to differ from any others in my notions of the qualifications and character of the true Poet, I most cordially assent to their opinions who assert, that his principal exertions must be made to engage the attention of his readers; and further, I must allow that the effect of poetry should be to lift the mind from the painful realities of actual existence, from its everyday concerns, and its perpetually-occurring vexations, and to give it repose by substituting objects in their place which it may contemplate with some degree of interest and satisfaction: but what is there in all this, which may not be effected by a fair representation of existing character? nay, by a faithful delineation of those painful realities, those every-day concerns, and those perpetually-occurring vexations themselves, provided they be not (which is hardly to be supposed) the very concerns and distresses of the reader? for when it is admitted that they have no particular relation to him, but are the troubles and anxieties of other men, they excite and interest his feelings as the imaginary exploits, adventures, and perils of romance;—they soothe his mind, and keep his curiosity pleasantly awake; they appear to have enough of reality to engage his sympathy, but possess not interest sufficient to create painful sensations.

'Fiction itself, we know, and every work of fancy,

must for a time have the effect of realities; nay, the very enchanters, spirits, and monsters of Ariosto and Spenser must be present in the mind of the reader while he is engaged by their operations, or they would be as the objects and incidents of a nursery tale to a rational understanding, altogether despised and neglected: in truth, I can but consider this pleasant effect upon the mind of a reader as depending neither upon the events related (whether they be actual or imaginary), nor upon the characters introduced (whether taken from life or fancy), but upon the manner in which the poem itself is conducted; let that be judiciously managed, and the occurrences actually copied from life will have the same happy effect as the inventions of a creative fancy.'

But whence does it arise that the poet, chronicling *what everybody knows, what happens,* does not produce the objects, the talk, the turns of the tale that are natural in the novel? There is, I believe, a primitive and ineradicable instinct in the breasts of men, which lays down the law on this head. In spite of the epitaphs and poets' corners which are not disliked by the mass of Englishmen (they are merely institutions), an element of sublimity is expected when a man stands forth under the form of a poet. He must have something out of the ordinary ruck for our attention, or he would address us in the ordinary manner. He is a Druid, emerging from prophetic glades; and Druids do not spend their time in chewing American gums. The least poetical atmosphere in the world is perhaps to be found in an army hut, but let a budding poet appear there with a narrative poem seriously displaying the trivial round, and he will at once find a vigorous criticism. Everything in its place. 'Why wasn't you on parade?' is in its order nothing to laugh at; indeed, it has an imperial suggestion; but if it occurred in an attempt at narrative poetry, it would be the occasion of considerable amusement:

Heaven was not kind to Private William Grieg,
He clicked for a gas-cylinder fatigue,
Thinking of her the while; and oft the tear
Fell almost into his thin Belgian beer;
Through his sad vision and the midnight shade,
Rang the hoarse call, 'Why wasn't you on parade?'
He hobbled on through wildly roaring gloom,
Still fancying Daisy in her youthful bloom,
And haunted by the morrow's Orderly Room.

The grand insight, equity, courage, knowledge, utterance of Crabbe have done much to sustain his poetical character through the frequent pettinesses of reported detail or speech in his *Tales*. His characters and settings are like Trollope's. That is to say, you would not believe them ghosts if they walked into your room; you cannot put your hand through them. Nor is all that trivial in him which at a hasty glance looks so. But even Crabbe would have been a greater poet had his 'conduct' of his tales remained more mysterious, less explicit, less gramophonic. A tincture of the luxuriousness of Keats, or the high sorrowfulness of that 'picture-writing young poet', would have relieved his works from dry and thin passages. By a paradoxical dispensation, Crabbe, gifted with a marvellous power of conciseness, often spent much time and art on description and dialogue which a few phrases would have sufficed to communicate; and the author of 'Peter Grimes' and 'Sir Eustace Grey' is seen exerting himself to portray insipidity and to memorize chatter.

Of all English narrative poems, 'Peter Grimes' is probably the sternest, and in movement and appeal one of the completest. The characters pass in and out, facts are recorded, left behind—and Peter goes on with his nets, and his ghosts, until solitude turns into a harder master than he was himself. The action is simple at first, but how wonderfully Crabbe has conceived the transformation of the incidents that first occurred into the expanding hell of the mind! The full and inimitably observed study of the mud-flats, with all their slow, grey, sultry, recurrent business, is well fitted to encompass the transition from brutality to vacancy and horror. Crabbe especially sees that description, borne on strong feeling, is itself dramatic and fascinating; the pathos, the pleasure, the fear with which a narrative poem is concerned reaches its height when it is diffused into the air, the sea and the sky. We look through the eyes of the persons imagined, and our sensations are vivid for and from things which in the ordinary course would not be our concern, and which description would seem tediously to catalogue.

Remembering the large audience that awaited Crabbe's *Tales*, I am tempted to point out how often a narrative poet has won a great name among us. If one excludes all those compositions of which the better classification would be the epic, the allegory, the satire, the autobiography, or the pastoral, there remains a profusion of extensive narrative poems, some still holding their place and spirit, others at any rate associated with former glories and the history of the race. Chaucer, unfolding many-coloured life with the ease of the intellectual aristocrat, is still 'alive and hale'. No one in England since his day has discovered so simple and comprehensive a method of telling stories, in verse or prose, to the utmost of his own wish and enjoyment. The *Canterbury Tales* are narratives within narrative. The poems of Shakespeare include the most fervent and deep-lighted pageant-narratives of our verse, unless indeed *Venus and Adonis* be outsplendoured by the *Hero and Leander* begun by Marlowe and completed by Chapman. Ben Jonson called that astonishing river of imagery 'fitter for admiration than for parallel'.

In later days Dryden, refashioning Chaucer and Boccaccio with his own strong fruitfulness of wisdom and art, achieved permanence as a poetic teller of tales; Pope did the same, 'a masker bold,' in *The*

Rape of the Lock. After names like those it will sound odd, perhaps worthy of a note in some new *Dunciad*, that the luckless sailor William Falconer should be recalled for his poem *The Shipwreck*. Yet it was read and re-read for sixty or seventy years, and there was a reason: it was unusual and essentially truthful. The nineteenth century harvested a rare crop of narrative poems—besides Crabbe's. 'To CHARLES LAMB, ESQ. My Dear Friend,—When I sent you, a few weeks ago, the Tale of *Peter Bell*, you asked "why *The Waggoner* was not added?"' So wrote Wordsworth, author of those and other narratives, short and long. In spite of Hazlitt, who called the author of *The Lady of the Lake* a 'mere narrative and descriptive poet, garrulous of the old time', Scott has his worshippers today as much for his verse, with its great scenery and chivalrous heartbeat, as for his prose romances.

Hazlitt also damned the *Lalla Rookh* of Tom Moore, and nobody seems disposed to undertake the defence; but what that performance of bulbuls and lovers' lutes meant to the period is best implied in Moore's remark (1818), 'The young Bristol lady who inclosed me three pounds after reading "Lalla Rookh" had very laudable ideas on the subject; and if every reader of "Lalla Rookh" had done the same I need never have written again.' Thirty years later Messrs. Longman were still printing new editions. Thomas Campbell, with *Gertrude of Wyoming*, Leigh Hunt with *The Story of Rimini*, and Samuel Rogers with *Italy*, commanded a great deal of critical and general notice a century since. The lines which charm me most in the easy-going medley of Rogers are these:

> Had I thy pencil, Crabbe (when thou hast done,
> Late may it be ... it will, like Prospero's staff,
> Be buried fifty fathoms in the earth)
> I would portray the Italian.

If none of those new minstrels satisfied, was there not Byron? *The Bride of Abydos, The Corsair, Parisina,*

Mazeppa, and still others—what can Hollywood do to equal that series of thrilling spectacles?

> 'List!—'tis the bulge'—Juan shrilly blew—
> 'One kiss—one more—another—Oh! Adieu!'

Many of the ardent spirits who had marked the margins of Byron's tales with excited approval lived to travel westward in fancy, hardly less strenuous and exhilarating, when (in 1855) *The Song of Hiawatha* made an American poet the most popular English poet of the nineteenth century. But it is time that these desultory remarks should come to an end, with many a name not to be forgotten in the history of our narrative poetry—Keats, Shelley, Browning, Tennyson, Arnold, Patmore, Morris—barely mentioned. 'Forgive, blest shades—.' Mr. Hardy, too, was a great inventor of stories in verse, and hewed out his own channels of metrical expression for them. He has been known to advise a beginner in the art of poetry to 'tell stories', and the following selections will not weaken the force of that hint from a narrator equally celebrated for his novels and for his poems.

EDMUND BLUNDEN

GEOFFREY CHAUCER

1340–1400

The Nonne Preestes Tale

A povre widwe, somdel stape in age,
Was whylom dwelling in a narwe cotage,
Bisyde a grove, stonding in a dale.
This widwe, of which I telle yow my tale,
Sin thilke day that she was last a wyf,　　　　　5
In pacience ladde a ful simple lyf,
For litel was hir catel and hir rente;
By housbondrye, of such as God hir sente,
She fond hir-self, and eek hir doghtren two.
Three large sowes hadde she, and namo,　　　10
Three kyn, and eek a sheep that highte Malle.
Ful sooty was hir bour, and eek hir halle,
In which she eet ful many a sclendre meel.
Of poynaunt sauce hir neded never a deel.
No deyntee morsel passed thurgh hir throte;　　15
Hir dyete was accordant to hir cote.
Repleccioun ne made hir never syk;
Attempree dyete was al hir phisyk,
And exercyse, and hertes suffisaunce.
The goute lette hir no-thing for to daunce,　　20
N'apoplexye shente nat hir heed;
No wyn ne drank she, neither whyt ne reed;
Hir bord was served most with whyt and blak,
Milk and broun breed, in which she fond no lak,
Seynd bacoun, and somtyme an ey or tweye,　　25
For she was as it were a maner deye.
　　A yerd she hadde, enclosed al aboute
With stikkes, and a drye dich with-oute,
In which she hadde a cok, hight Chauntecleer,
In al the land of crowing nas his peer.　　　　30
His vois was merier than the mery orgon
On messe-dayes that in the chirche gon;

Wel sikerer was his crowing in his logge,
Than is a clokke, or an abbey orlogge.
By nature knew he ech ascencioun   35
Of equinoxial in thilke toun;
For whan degrees fiftene were ascended,
Thanne crew he, that it mighte nat ben amended.
His comb was redder than the fyn coral,
And batailed, as it were a castel-wal.   40
His bile was blak, and as the leet it shoon;
Lyk asur were his legges, and his toon;
His nayles whytter than the lilie flour,
And lyk the burned gold was his colour.
This gentil cok hadde in his governaunce   45
Sevene hennes, for to doon al his plesaunce,
Which were his sustres and his paramours,
And wonder lyk to him, as of colours.
Of whiche the faireste hewed on hir throte
Was cleped faire damoysele Pertelote.   50
Curteys she was, discreet, and debonaire,
And compaignable, and bar hir-self so faire,
Sin thilke day that she was seven night old,
That trewely she hath the herte in hold
Of Chauntecleer loken in every lith;   55
He loved hir so, that wel was him therwith.
But such a Ioye was it to here hem singe,
Whan that the brighte sonne gan to springe,
In swete accord, 'my lief is faren in londe.'
For thilke tyme, as I have understonde,   60
Bestes and briddes coude speke and singe.
    And so bifel, that in a daweninge,
As Chauntecleer among his wyves alle
Sat on his perche, that was in the halle,
And next him sat this faire Pertelote,   65
This Chauntecleer gan gronen in his throte,
As man that in his dreem is drecched sore.
And whan that Pertelote thus herde him rore,
She was agast, and seyde, 'O herte dere,
What eyleth yow, to grone in this manere?   70
Ye been a verray sleper, fy for shame!'

And he answerde and seyde thus, 'madame,
I pray yow, that ye take it nat a-grief:
By god, me mette I was in swich meschief
Right now, that yet myn herte is sore afright.   75
Now god,' quod he, 'my swevene recche aright,
And keep my body out of foul prisoun!
Me mette, how that I romed up and doun
Withinne our yerde, wher-as I saugh a beste,
Was lyk an hound, and wolde han maad areste   80
Upon my body, and wolde han had me deed.
His colour was bitwixe yelwe and reed;
And tipped was his tail, and bothe his eres,
With blak, unlyk the remenant of his heres;
His snowte smal, with glowinge eyen tweye.   85
Yet of his look for fere almost I deye;
This caused me my groning, doutelees.'
    'Avoy!' quod she, 'fy on yow, herteleesl
Allas!' quod she, 'for, by that god above,
Now han ye lost myn herte and al my love;   90
I can nat love a coward, by my feith.
For certes, what so any womman seith,
We alle desyren, if it mighte be,
To han housbondes hardy, wyse, and free,
And secree, and no nigard, ne no fool,   95
Ne him that is agast of every tool,
Ne noon avauntour, by that god above!
How dorste ye seyn for shame unto your love,
That any thing mighte make yow aferd?
Have ye no mannes herte, and han a berd?   100
Allas! and conne ye been agast of swevenis?
No-thing, god wot, but vanitee, in sweven is.
Swevenes engendren of replecciouns,
And ofte of fume, and of complecciouns,
Whan humours been to habundant in a wight.   105
Certes this dreem, which ye han met to-night,
Cometh of the grete superfluitee
Of youre rede *colera*, pardee,
Which causeth folk to dreden in here dremes
Of arwes, and of fyr with rede lemes,   110

Of grete bestes, that they wol hem byte,
Of contek, and of whelpes grete and lyte;
Right as the humour of malencolye
Causeth ful many a man, in sleep, to crye,
For fere of blake beres, or boles blake,   115
Or elles, blake develes wole hem take.
Of othere humours coude I telle also,
That werken many a man in sleep ful wo;
But I wol passe as lightly as I can.

    Lo Catoun, which that was so wys a man,   120
Seyde he nat thus, ne do no fors of dremes?
Now, sire,' quod she, 'whan we flee fro the bemes,
For Goddes love, as tak som laxatyf;
Up peril of my soule, and of my lyf,
I counseille yow the beste, I wol nat lye,   125
That bothe of colere and of malencolye
Ye purge yow; and for ye shul nat tarie,
Though in this toun is noon apotecarie,
I shal my-self to herbes techen yow,
That shul ben for your hele, and for your prow;
And in our yerd tho herbes shal I finde,   131
The whiche han of hir propretee, by kynde,
To purgen yow binethe, and eek above.
Forget not this, for goddes owene love!
Ye been ful colerik of compleccioun.   135
Ware the sonne in his ascencioun
Ne fynde yow nat replect of humours hote;
And if it do, I dar wel leye a grote,
That ye shul have a fevere terciane,
Or an agu, that may be youre bane.   140
A day or two ye shul have digestyves
Of wormes, er ye take your laxatyves,
Of lauriol, centaure, and fumetere,
Or elles of ellebor, that groweth there,
Of catapuce, or of gaytres beryis,   145
Of erbe yve, growing in our yerd, that mery is;
Pekke hem up right as they growe, and ete hem in.
Be mery, housbond, for your fader kin!
Dredeth no dreem; I can say yow na-more.'

'Madame,' quod he, '*graunt mercy* of your lore.
But nathelees, as touching daun Catoun,   151
That hath of wisdom such a greet renoun,
Though that he bad no dremes for to drede,
By god, men may in olde bokes rede
Of many a man, more of auctoritee   155
Than ever Catoun was, so mote I thee,
That al the revers seyn of his sentence,
And han wel founden by experience,
That dremes ben significaciouns,
As wel of Ioye as tribulaciouns   160
That folk enduren in this lyf present.
Ther nedeth make of this noon argument;
The verray preve sheweth it in dede.

    Oon of the gretteste auctours that men rede
Seith thus, that whylom two felawes wente   165
On pilgrimage, in a ful good entente;
And happed so, thay come into a toun,
Wher-as ther was swich congregacioun
Of peple, and eek so streit of herbergage,
That they ne founde as muche as o cotage,   170
In which they bothe mighte y-logged be.
Wherfor thay mosten, of necessitee,
As for that night, departen compaignye;
And ech of hem goth to his hostelrye,
And took his logging as it wolde falle.   175
That oon of hem was logged in a stalle,
Fer in a yerd, with oxen of the plough;
That other man was logged wel y-nough,
As was his aventure, or his fortune,
That us governeth alle as in commune.   180

    And so bifel, that, longe er it were day,
This man mette in his bed, ther-as he lay,
How that his felawe gan up-on him calle,
And seyde, "allas! for in an oxes stalle
This night I shal be mordred ther I lye.   185
Now help me, dere brother, er I dye;
In alle haste com to me," he sayde.
This man out of his sleep for fere abrayde;

But whan that he was wakned of his sleep,
He turned him, and took of this no keep; 190
Him thoughte his dreem nas but a vanitee.
Thus twyës in his sleping dremed he.
And atte thridde tyme yet his felawe
Cam, as him thoughte, and seide, "I am now slawe;
Bihold my blody woundes, depe and wyde! 195
Arys up erly in the morwe-tyde,
And at the west gate of the toun," quod he,
"A carte ful of dong ther shaltow see,
In which my body is hid ful prively;
Do thilke carte aresten boldely. 200
My gold caused my mordre, sooth to sayn;"
And tolde him every poynt how he was slayn,
With a ful pitous face, pale of hewe.
And truste wel, his dreem he fond ful trewe;
For on the morwe, as sone as it was day, 205
To his felawes in he took the way;
And whan that he cam to this oxes stalle,
After his felawe he bigan to calle.

The hostiler answered him anon,
And seyde, "sire, your felawe is agon, 210
As sone as day he wente out of the toun."
This man gan fallen in suspecioun,
Remembring on his dremes that he mette,
And forth he goth, no lenger wolde he lette,
Unto the west gate of the toun, and fond 215
A dong-carte, as it were to donge lond,
That was arrayed in the same wyse
As ye han herd the dede man devyse;
And with an hardy herte he gan to crye
Vengeaunce and Iustice of this felonye:— 220
"My felawe mordred is this same night,
And in this carte he lyth gaping upright.
I crye out on the ministres," quod he,
"That sholden kepe and reulen this citee;
Harrow! allas! her lyth my felawe slayn!" 225
What sholde I more un-to this tale sayn?
The peple out-sterte, and caste the cart to grounde,

And in the middel of the dong they founde
The dede man, that mordred was al newe.
    O blisful god, that art so Iust and trewe!   230
Lo, how that thou biwreyest mordre alway!
Mordre wol out, that see we day by day.
Mordre is so wlatsom and abhominable
To god, that is so Iust and resonable,
That he ne wol nat suffre it heled be;   235
Though it abyde a yeer, or two, or three,
Mordre wol out, this my conclusioun.
And right anoon, ministres of that toun
Han hent the carter, and so sore him pyned,
And eek the hostiler so sore engyned,   240
That thay biknewe hir wikkednesse anoon,
And were an-hanged by the nekke-boon.
    Here may men seen that dremes been to drede.
And certes, in the same book I rede,
Right in the nexte chapitre after this,   245
(I gabbe nat, so have I Ioye or blis,)
Two men that wolde han passed over see,
For certeyn cause, in-to a fer contree,
If that the wind ne hadde been contrarie,
That made hem in a citee for to tarie,   250
That stood ful mery upon an haven-syde.
But on a day, agayn the even-tyde,
The wind gan chaunge, and blew right as hem leste.
Iolif and glad they wente un-to hir reste,
And casten hem ful erly for to saille;   255
But to that oo man fil a greet mervaille.
That oon of hem, in sleping as he lay,
Him mette a wonder dreem, agayn the day;
Him thoughte a man stood by his beddes syde,
And him comaunded, that he sholde abyde,   260
And seyde him thus, "if thou to-morwe wende,
Thou shalt be dreynt; my tale is at an ende."
He wook, and tolde his felawe what he mette,
And preyde him his viage for to lette;
As for that day, he preyde him to abyde.   265
His felawe, that lay by his beddes syde,

Gan for to laughe, and scorned him ful faste.
"No dreem," quod he, "may so myn herte agaste,
That I wol lette for to do my thinges.
I sette not a straw by thy dreminges,   270
For swevenes been but vanitees and Iapes.
Men dreme al-day of owles or of apes,
And eke of many a mase therwithal;
Men dreme of thing that never was ne shal.
But sith I see that thou wolt heer abyde,   275
And thus for-sleuthen wilfully thy tyde,
God wot it reweth me; and have good day."
And thus he took his leve, and wente his way.
But er that he hadde halfe his cours y-seyled,
Noot I nat why, ne what mischaunce it eyled,   280
But casuelly the shippes botme rente,
And ship and man under the water wente
In sighte of othere shippes it byside,
That with hem seyled at the same tyde.
And therfor, faire Pertelote so dere,   285
By swiche ensamples olde maistow lere,
That no man sholde been to recchelees
Of dremes, for I sey thee, doutelees,
That many a dreem ful sore is for to drede.
    Lo, in the lyf of seint Kenelm, I rede,   290
That was Kenulphus sone, the noble king
Of Mercenrike, how Kenelm mette a thing;
A lyte er he was mordred, on a day,
His mordre in his avisioun he say.
His norice him expounded every del   295
His sweven, and bad him for to kepe him wel
For traisoun; but he nas but seven yeer old,
And therefore litel tale hath he told
Of any dreem, so holy was his herte.
By god, I hadde lever than my sherte   300
That ye had rad his legende, as have I.
Dame Pertelote, I sey yow trewely,
Macrobeus, that writ th'avisioun
In Affrike of the worthy Cipioun,
Affermeth dremes, and seith that they been   305

Warning of thinges that men after seen.
   And forther-more, I pray yow loketh wel
In the olde testament, of Daniel,
If he held dremes any vanitee.
Reed eek of Ioseph, and ther shul ye see   310
Wher dremes ben somtyme (I sey nat alle)
Warning of thinges that shul after falle.
Loke of Egipt the king, daun Pharao,
His bakere and his boteler also,
Wher they ne felte noon effect in dremes.   315
Who-so wol seken actes of sondry remes,
May rede of dremes many a wonder thing.
   Lo Cresus, which that was of Lyde king,
Mette he nat that he sat upon a tree,
Which signified he sholde anhanged be?   320
Lo heer Andromacha, Ectores wyf,
That day that Ector sholde lese his lyf,
She dremed on the same night biforn,
How that the lyf of Ector sholde be lorn,
If thilke day he wente in-to bataille;   325
She warned him, but it mighte nat availle;
He wente for to fighte nathelees,
But he was slayn anoon of Achilles.
But thilke tale is al to long to telle,
And eek it is ny day, I may nat dwelle.   330
Shortly I seye, as for conclusioun,
That I shal han of this avisioun
Adversitee; and I seye forther-more,
That I ne telle of laxatyves no store,
For they ben venimous, I woot it wel;   335
I hem defye, I love hem never a del.
   Now let us speke of mirthe, and stinte al this;
Madame Pertelote, so have I blis,
Of o thing god hath sent me large grace;
For whan I see the beautee of your face,   340
Ye ben so scarlet-reed about your yën,
It maketh al my drede for to dyen;
For, also siker as *In principio*,
Mulier est hominis confusio;

Madame, the sentence of this Latin is—   345
Womman is mannes Ioye and al his blis.
For whan I fele a-night your softe syde,
Al-be-it that I may nat on you ryde,
For that our perche is maad so narwe, alas!
I am so ful of Ioye and of solas   350
That I defye bothe sweven and dreem.'
And with that word he fley doun fro the beem,
For it was day, and eek his hennes alle;
And with a chuk he gan hem for to calle,
For he had founde a corn, lay in the yerd.   355
Royal he was, he was namore aferd;
He fethered Pertelote twenty tyme,
And trad as ofte, er that it was pryme.
He loketh as it were a grim leoun;
And on his toos he rometh up and doun,   360
Him deyned not to sette his foot to grounde.
He chukketh, whan he hath a corn y-founde,
And to him rennen thanne his wyves alle.
Thus royal, as a prince is in his halle,
Leve I this Chauntecleer in his pasture;   365
And after wol I telle his aventure.

Whan that the month in which the world bigan,
That highte March, whan god first maked man,
Was complet, and [y]-passed were also,
Sin March bigan, thritty dayes and two,   370
Bifel that Chauntecleer, in al his pryde,
His seven wyves walking by his syde,
Caste up his eyen to the brighte sonne,
That in the signe of Taurus hadde y-ronne
Twenty degrees and oon, and somwhat more;   375
And knew by kynde, and by noon other lore,
That it was pryme, and crew with blisful stevene.
'The sonne,' he sayde, 'is clomben up on hevene
Fourty degrees and oon, and more, y-wis.
Madame Pertelote, my worldes blis,   380
Herkneth thise blisful briddes how they singe,
And see the fresshe floures how they springe;
Ful is myn herte of revel and solas.'

But sodeinly him fil a sorweful cas;
For ever the latter end of Ioye is wo.   385
God woot that worldly Ioye is sone ago;
And if a rethor coude faire endyte,
He in a cronique saufly mighte it wryte,
As for a sovereyn notabilitee.
Now every wys man, lat him herkne me;   390
This storie is al-so trewe, I undertake,
As is the book of Launcelot de Lake,
That wommen holde in ful gret reverence.
Now wol I torne agayn to my sentence.

   A col-fox, ful of sly iniquitee,   395
That in the grove hadde woned yeres three,
By heigh imaginacioun forn-cast,
The same night thurgh-out the hegges brast
Into the yerd, ther Chauntecleer the faire
Was wont, and eek his wyves, to repaire;   400
And in a bed of wortes stille he lay,
Til it was passed undern of the day,
Wayting his tyme on Chauntecleer to falle,
As gladly doon thise homicydes alle,
That in awayt liggen to mordre men.   405
O false mordrer, lurking in thy den!
O newe Scariot, newe Genilon!
False dissimilour, O Greek Sinon,
That broghtest Troye al outrely to sorwe!
O Chauntecleer, acursed be that morwe,   410
That thou into that yerd flough fro the bemes!
Thou were ful wel y-warned by thy dremes,
That thilke day was perilous to thee.
But what that god forwoot mot nedes be,
After the opinion of certeyn clerkis.   415
Witnesse on him, that any perfit clerk is,
That in scole is gret altercacioun
In this matere, and greet disputisoun,
And hath ben of an hundred thousand men.
But I ne can not bulte it to the bren,   420
As can the holy doctour Augustyn,
Or Boece, or the bishop Bradwardyn,

Whether that goddes worthy forwiting
Streyneth me nedely for to doon a thing,
(Nedely clepe I simple necessitee);　　　　　　425
Or elles, if free choys be graunted me
To do that same thing, or do it noght,
Though god forwoot it, er that it was wroght;
Or if his witing streyneth nevere a del
But by necessitee condicionel.　　　　　　430
I wol not han to do of swich matere;
My tale is of a cok, as ye may here,
That took his counseil of his wyf, with sorwe,
To walken in the yerd upon that morwe
That he had met the dreem, that I yow tolde.　　　435
Wommennes counseils been ful ofte colde;
Wommannes counseil broghte us first to wo,
And made Adam fro paradys to go,
Ther-as he was ful mery, and wel at ese.
But for I noot, to whom it mighte displese,　　　440
If I counseil of wommen wolde blame,
Passe over, for I seyde it in my game.
Rede auctours, wher they trete of swich matere,
And what thay seyn of wommen ye may here.
Thise been the cokkes wordes, and nat myne;　　　445
I can noon harm of no womman divyne.
　　Faire in the sond, to bathe hir merily,
Lyth Pertelote, and alle hir sustres by,
Agayn the sonne; and Chauntecleer so free
Song merier than the mermayde in the see;　　　450
For Phisiologus seith sikerly,
How that they singen wel and merily.
And so bifel that, as he caste his yë,
Among the wortes, on a boterflye,
He was war of this fox that lay ful lowe.　　　455
No-thing ne liste him thanne for to crowe,
But cryde anon, 'cok, cok,' and up he sterte,
As man that was affrayed in his herte.
For naturely a beest desyreth flee
Fro his contrarie, if he may it see,　　　460
Though he never erst had seyn it with his yë.

This Chauntecleer, whan he gan him espye,
He wolde han fled, but that the fox anon
Seyde, 'Gentil sire, allas! wher wol ye gon?
Be ye affrayed of me that am your freend?   465
Now certes, I were worse than a feend,
If I to yow wolde harm or vileinye.
I am nat come your counseil for tespye;
But trewely, the cause of my cominge
Was only for to herkne how that ye singe.   470
For trewely ye have as mery a stevene
As eny aungel hath, that is in hevene;
Therwith ye han in musik more felinge
Than hadde Boece, or any that can singe.
My lord your fader (god his soule blesse!)   475
And eek your moder, of hir gentilesse,
Han in myn hous y-been, to my gret ese;
And certes, sire, ful fayn wolde I yow plese.
But for men speke of singing, I wol saye,
So mote I brouke wel myn eyen tweye,   480
Save yow, I herde never man so singe,
As dide your fader in the morweninge;
Certes, it was of herte, al that he song.
And for to make his voys the more strong,
He wolde so peyne him, that with both his yën   485
He moste winke, so loude he wolde cryen,
And stonden on his tiptoon ther-with-al,
And strecche forth his nekke long and smal.
And eek he was of swich discrecioun,
That ther nas no man in no regioun   490
That him in song or wisdom mighte passe.
I have wel rad in daun Burnel the Asse,
Among his vers, how that ther was a cok,
For that a preestes sone yaf him a knok
Upon his leg, whyl he was yong and nyce,   495
He made him for to lese his benefyce.
But certeyn, ther nis no comparisoun
Bitwix the wisdom and discrecioun
Of youre fader, and of his subtiltee.
Now singeth, sire, for seinte Charitee,   500

Let see, conne ye your fader countrefete?'
This Chauntecleer his winges gan to bete,
As man that coude his tresoun nat espye,
So was he ravisshed with his flaterye.

Allas! ye lordes, many a fals flatour   505
Is in your courtes, and many a losengeour,
That plesen yow wel more, by my feith,
Than he that soothfastnessse unto yow seith.
Redeth Ecclesiaste of flaterye;
Beth war, ye lordes, of hir trecherye.   510

This Chauntecleer stood hye up-on his toos,
Strecching his nekke, and heeld his eyen cloos,
And gan to crowe loude for the nones;
And daun Russel the fox sterte up at ones,
And by the gargat hente Chauntecleer,   515
And on his bak toward the wode him beer,
For yet ne was ther no man that him sewed.
O destinee, that mayst nat been eschewed!
Allas, that Chauntecleer fleigh fro the bemes!
Allas, his wyf ne roghte nat of dremes!   520
And on a Friday fil al this meschaunce.
O Venus, that art goddesse of plesaunce,
Sin that thy servant was this Chauntecleer,
And in thy service dide al his poweer,
More for delyt, than world to multiplye,   525
Why woldestow suffre him on thy day to dye?
O Gaufred, dere mayster soverayn,
That, whan thy worthy king Richard was slayn
With shot, compleynedest his deth so sore,
Why ne hadde I now thy sentence and thy lore,
The Friday for to chyde, as diden ye?   531
(For on a Friday soothly slayn was he.)
Than wolde I shewe yow how that I coude pleyne
For Chauntecleres drede, and for his peyne.

Certes, swich cry ne lamentacioun   535
Was never of ladies maad, whan Ilioun
Was wonne, and Pirrus with his streite swerd,
Whan he hadde hent king Priam by the berd,
And slayn him (as saith us *Eneydos*),

As maden alle the hennes in the clos,   540
Whan they had seyn of Chauntecleer the sighte.
But sovereynly dame Pertelote shrighte,
Ful louder than dide Hasdrubales wyf,
Whan that hir housband hadde lost his lyf,
And that the Romayns hadde brend Cartage;   545
She was so ful of torment and of rage,
That wilfully into the fyr she sterte,
And brende hir-selven with a stedfast herte.
O woful hennes, right so cryden ye,
As, whan that Nero brende the citee   550
Of Rome, cryden senatoures wyves,
For that hir housbondes losten alle hir lyves;
Withouten gilt this Nero hath hem slayn.
Now wol I torne to my tale agayn: —
    This sely widwe, and eek hir doghtres two,   555
Herden thise hennes crye and maken wo,
And out at dores sterten they anoon,
And syen the fox toward the grove goon,
And bar upon his bak the cok away;
And cryden, 'Out! harrow! and weylaway!   560
Ha, ha, the fox!' and after him they ran,
And eek with staves many another man;
Ran Colle our dogge, and Talbot, and Gerland,
And Malkin, with a distaf in hir hand;
Ran cow and calf, and eek the verray hogges   565
So were they fered for berking of the dogges
And shouting of the men and wimmen eke,
They ronne so, hem thoughte hir herte breke.
They yelleden as feendes doon in helle;
The dokes cryden as men wolde hem quelle;   570
The gees for fere flowen over the trees;
Out of the hyve cam the swarm of bees;
So hidous was the noyse, a! *benedicite!*
Certes, he Jakke Straw, and his meynee,
Ne made never shoutes half so shrille,   575
Whan that they wolden any Fleming kille,
As thilke day was maad upon the fox.
Of bras thay broghten bemes, and of box,

Of horn, of boon, in whiche they blewe and pouped,
And therwithal thay shryked and they houped;
It seemed as that heven sholde falle.   581
Now, gode men, I pray yow herkneth alle!
    Lo, how fortune turneth sodeinly
The hope and pryde eek of hir enemy!
This cok, that lay upon the foxes bak,   585
In al his drede, un-to the fox he spak,
And seyde, 'sire, if that I were as ye,
Yet sholde I seyn (as wis god helpe me),
Turneth agayn, ye proude cherles alle!
A verray pestilence up-on yow falle!   590
Now am I come un-to this wodes syde,
Maugree your heed, the cok shal heer abyde;
I wol him ete in feith, and that anon.'—
The fox answerde, 'in feith, it shal be don,'—
And as he spak that word, al sodeinly   595
This cok brak from his mouth deliverly,
And heighe up-on a tree he fleigh anon.
And whan the fox saugh that he was y-gon,
'Allas!' quod he, 'O Chauntecleer, allas!
I have to yow,' quod he, 'y-doon trespas,   600
In-as-muche as I maked yow aferd,
Whan I yow hente, and broghte out of the yerd;
But, sire, I dide it in no wikke entente;
Com doun, and I shal telle yow what I mente.
I shal seye sooth to yow, god help me so.'   605
'Nay than,' quod he, 'I shrewe us bothe two,
And first I shrewe my-self, bothe blood and bones,
If thou bigyle me ofter than ones.
Thou shalt na-more, thurgh thy flaterye,
Do me to singe and winke with myn yë.   610
For he that winketh, whan he sholde see,
Al wilfully, god lat him never thee!'
'Nay,' quod the fox, 'but god yeve him meschaunce,
That is so undiscreet of governaunce,
That Iangleth whan he sholde holde his pees.'   615
    Lo, swich it is for to be recchelees,
And necligent, and truste on flaterye.

But ye that holden this tale a folye,
As of a fox, or of a cok and hen,
Taketh the moralitee, good men.   620
For seint Paul seith, that al that writen is,
To our doctryne it is y-write, y-wis.
Taketh the fruyt, and lat the chaf be stille.
   Now, gode god, if that it be thy wille,
As seith my lord, so make us alle good men;   625
And bringe us to his heighe blisse. Amen.

The Pardoners Tale

In Flaundres whylom was a companye
Of yonge folk, that haunteden folye,
As ryot, hasard, stewes, and tavernes,
Wher-as, with harpes, lutes, and giternes,   4
They daunce and pleye at dees bothe day and night,
And ete also and drinken over hir might,
Thurgh which they doon the devel sacrifyse
With-in that develes temple, in cursed wyse,
By superfluitee abhominable;
Hir othes been so grete and so dampnable,   10
That it is grisly for to here hem swere;
Our blissed lordes body they to-tere;
Hem thoughte Iewes rente him noght y-nough;
And ech of hem at othere sinne lough.
And right anon than comen tombesteres   15
Fetys and smale, and yonge fruytesteres,
Singers with harpes, baudes, wafereres,
Whiche been the verray develes officeres
To kindle and blowe the fyr of lecherye,
That is annexed un-to glotonye;   20
The holy writ take I to my witnesse,
That luxurie is in wyn and dronkenesse.
   Lo, how that dronken Loth, unkindely,
Lay by his doghtres two, unwitingly;
So dronke he was, he niste what he wroghte.   25
   Herodes, (who-so wel the stories soghte,)
Whan he of wyn was replet at his feste,

Right at his owene table he yaf his heste
To sleen the Baptist Iohn ful giltelees.
   Senek seith eek a good word doutelees;   30
He seith, he can no difference finde
Bitwix a man that is out of his minde
And a man which that is dronkelewe,
But that woodnesse, y-fallen in a shrewe,
Persevereth lenger than doth dronkenesse.   35
O glotonye, ful of cursednesse,
O cause first of our confusioun,
O original of our dampnacioun,
Til Crist had boght us with his blood agayn!
Lo, how dere, shortly for to sayn,   40
Aboght was thilke cursed vileinye;
Corrupt was al this world for glotonye!
   Adam our fader, and his wyf also,
Fro Paradys to labour and to wo
Were driven for that vyce, it is no drede;   45
For whyl that Adam fasted, as I rede,
He was in Paradys; and whan that he
Eet of the fruyt defended on the tree,
Anon he was out-cast to wo and peyne.
O glotonye, on thee wel oghte us pleyne!   50
O, wiste a man how many maladyes
Folwen of excesse and of glotonyes,
He wolde been the more mesurable
Of his diete, sittinge at his table.
Allas! the shorte throte, the tendre mouth,   55
Maketh that, Est and West, and North and South,
In erthe, in eir, in water men to-swinke
To gete a glotoun deyntee mete and drinke!
Of this matere, o Paul, wel canstow trete,   59
'Mete un-to wombe, and wombe eek un-to mete,
Shal god destroyen bothe,' as Paulus seith.
Allas! a foul thing is it, by my feith,
To seye this word, and fouler is the dede,
Whan man so drinketh of the whyte and rede,
That of his throte he maketh his privee,   65
Thurgh thilke cursed superfluitee.

The apostel weping seith ful pitously,
'Ther walken many of whiche yow told have I,
I seye it now weping with pitous voys,
That they been enemys of Cristes croys,   70
Of whiche the ende is deeth, wombe is her god.'
O wombe! O bely! O stinking cod,
Fulfild of donge and of corrupcioun!
At either ende of thee foul is the soun.
How greet labour and cost is thee to finde!   75
Thise cokes, how they stampe, and streyne, and
    grinde,
And turnen substaunce in-to accident,
To fulfille al thy likerous talent!
Out of the harde bones knokke they
The mary, for they caste noght a-wey   80
That may go thurgh the golet softe and swote;
Of spicerye, of leef, and bark, and rote
Shal been his sauce y-maked by delyt,
To make him yet a newer appetyt.
But certes, he that haunteth swich delyces   85
Is deed, whyl that he liveth in tho vyces.
      A lecherous thing is wyn, and dronkenesse
Is ful of stryving and of wrecchednesse.
O dronke man, disfigured is thy face,
Sour is thy breeth, foul artow to embrace,   90
And thurgh thy dronke nose semeth the soun
As though thou seydest ay 'Sampsoun, Sampsoun';
And yet, god wot, Sampsoun drank never no wyn.
Thou fallest, as it were a stiked swyn;
Thy tonge is lost, and al thyn honest cure;   95
For dronkenesse is verray sepulture
Of mannes wit and his discrecioun.
In whom that drinke hath dominacioun,
He can no conseil kepe, it is no drede.
Now kepe yow fro the whyte and fro the rede,   100
And namely fro the whyte wyn of Lepe,
That is to selle in Fish-strete or in Chepe.
This wyn of Spayne crepeth subtilly
In othere wynes, growing faste by,

Of which ther ryseth swich fumositee,   105
That whan a man hath dronken draughtes three,
And weneth that he be at hoom in Chepe,
He is in Spayne, right at the toune of Lepe,
Nat at the Rochel, ne at Burdeux toun;   109
And thanne wol he seye, 'Sampsoun, Sampsoun.'

But herkneth, lordings, o word, I yow preye,
That alle the sovereyn actes, dar I seye,
Of victories in th'olde testament,
Thurgh verray god, that is omnipotent,
Were doon in abstinence and in preyere;   115
Loketh the Bible, and ther ye may it lere.

Loke, Attila, the grete conqueror,
Deyde in his sleep, with shame and dishonour,
Bledinge ay at his nose in dronkenesse;
A capitayn shoulde live in sobrenesse.   120
And over al this, avyseth yow right wel
What was comaunded un-to Lamuel—
Nat Samuel, but Lamuel, seye I—
Redeth the Bible, and finde it expresly
Of wyn-yeving to hem that han justyse.   125
Na-more of this, for it may wel suffyse.

And now that I have spoke of glotonye,
Now wol I yow defenden hasardrye.
Hasard is verray moder of lesinges,
And of deceite, and cursed forsweringes,   130
Blaspheme of Crist, manslaughtre, and wast also
Of catel and of tyme; and forthermo,
It is repreve and contrarie of honour
For to ben holde a commune hasardour.
And ever the hyër he is of estaat,   135
The more is he holden desolaat.
If that a prince useth hasardrye,
In alle governaunce and policye
He is, as by commune opinioun,
Y-holde the lasse in reputacioun.   140

Stilbon, that was a wys embassadour,
Was sent to Corinthe, in ful greet honour,
Fro Lacidomie, to make hir alliaunce.

And whan he cam, him happede, par chaunce,
That alle the grettest that were of that lond, 145
Pleyinge atte hasard he hem fond.
For which, as sone as it mighte be,
He stal him hoom agayn to his contree,
And seyde, 'ther wol I nat lese my name;
Ne I wol nat take on me so greet defame, 150
Yow for to allye un-to none hasardours.
Sendeth othere wyse embassadours;
For, by my trouthe, me were lever dye,
Than I yow sholde to hasardours allye.
For ye that been so glorious in honours 155
Shul nat allyen yow with hasardours
As by my wil, ne as by my tretee.'
This wyse philosophre thus seyde he.
    Loke eek that, to the king Demetrius
The king of Parthes, as the book seith us, 160
Sente him a paire of dees of gold in scorn,
For he hadde used hasard ther-biforn;
For which he heeld his glorie or his renoun
At no value or reputacioun.
Lordes may finden other maner pley 165
Honeste y-nough to dryve the day awey.
    Now wol I speke of othes false and grete
A word or two, as olde bokes trete.
Gret swering is a thing abhominable,
And false swering is yet more reprevable. 170
The heighe god forbad swering at al,
Witnesse on Mathew; but in special
Of swering seith the holy Ieremye,
'Thou shalt seye sooth thyn othes, and nat lye,
And swere in dome, and eek in rightwisnesse;' 175
But ydel swering is a cursednesse.
Bihold and see, that in the firste table
Of heighe goddes hestes honurable,
How that the seconde heste of him is this—
'Tak nat my name in ydel or amis.' 180
Lo, rather he forbedeth swich swering
Than homicyde or many a cursed thing;

I seye that, as by ordre, thus it stondeth;
This knowen, that his hestes understondeth,
How that the second heste of god is that.   185
And forther over, I wol thee telle al plat,
That vengeance shal nat parten from his hous,
That of his othes is to outrageous.
'By goddes precious herte, and by his nayles,
And by the blode of Crist, that it is in Hayles,   190
Seven is my chaunce, and thyn is cink and treye;
By goddes armes, if thou falsly pleye,
This dagger shal thurgh-out thyn herte go'—
This fruyt cometh of the bicched bones two,
Forswering, ire, falsnesse, homicyde.   195
Now, for the love of Crist that for us dyde,
Leveth your othes, bothe grete and smale;
But, sirs, now wol I telle forth my tale.

    Thise ryotoures three, of whiche I telle,
Longe erst er pryme rong of any belle,   200
Were set hem in a taverne for to drinke;
And as they satte, they herde a belle clinke
Biforn a cors, was caried to his grave;
That oon of hem gan callen to his knave,
'Go bet,' quod he, 'and axe redily,   205
What cors is this that passeth heer forby;
And look that thou reporte his name wel.'
    'Sir,' quod this boy, 'it nedeth never-a-del.
It was me told, er ye cam heer, two houres;
He was, pardee, an old felawe of youres;   210
And sodeynly he was y-slayn to-night,
For-dronke, as he sat on his bench upright;
Ther cam a privee theef, men clepeth Deeth,
That in this contree al the peple sleeth,
And with his spere he smoot his herte a-two,   215
And wente his wey with-outen wordes mo.
He hath a thousand slayn this pestilence:
And, maister, er ye come in his presence,
Me thinketh that it were necessarie
For to be war of swich an adversarie: 220

Beth redy for to mete him evermore.
Thus taughte me my dame, I sey na-more.'
'By seinte Marie,' seyde this taverner,
'The child seith sooth, for he hath slayn this yeer,
Henne over a myle, with-in a greet village,   225
Both man and womman, child and hyne, and page.
I trowe his habitacioun be there;
To been avysed greet wisdom it were,
Er that he dide a man a dishonour.'
'Ye, goddes armes,' quod this ryotour,   230
'Is it swich peril with him for to mete?
I shal him seke by wey and eek by strete,
I make avow to goddes digne bones!
Herkneth, felawes, we three been al ones;
Lat ech of us holde up his hond til other,   235
And ech of us bicomen otheres brother,
And we wol sleen this false traytour Deeth;
He shal be slayn, which that so many sleeth,
By goddes dignitee, er it be night.'

      Togidres han thise three her trouthes plight,   240
To live and dyen ech of hem for other,
As though he were his owene y-boren brother.
And up they sterte al dronken, in this rage,
And forth they goon towardes that village,
Of which the taverner had spoke biforn,   245
And many a grisly ooth than han they sworn,
And Cristes blessed body they to-rente—
'Deeth shal be deed, if that they may him hente.'

      Whan they han goon nat fully half a myle,
Right as they wolde han troden over a style,   250
An old man and a povre with hem mette.
This olde man ful mekely hem grette,
And seyde thus, 'now, lordes, god yow see!'

      The proudest of thise ryotoures three
Answerde agayn, 'what? carl, with sory grace,   255
Why artow al forwrapped save thy face?
Why livestow so longe in so greet age?'

      This olde man gan loke in his visage,
And seyde thus, 'for I ne can nat finde

A man, though that I walked in-to Inde,   260
Neither in citee nor in no village,
That wolde chaunge his youthe for myn age;
And therfore moot I han myn age stille,
As longe time as it is goddes wille.

    Ne deeth, allas! ne wol nat han my lyf;   265
Thus walke I, lyk a restelees caityf,
And on the ground, which is my modres gate,
I knokke with my staf, bothe erly and late,
And seye, "leve moder, leet me in!
Lo, how I vanish, flesh, and blood, and skin!   270
Allas! whan shul my bones been at reste?
Moder, with yow wolde I chaunge my cheste,
That in my chambre longe tyme hath be,
Ye! for an heyre clout to wrappe me!"
But yet to me she wol nat do that grace,   275
For which ful pale and welked is my face.

    But, sirs, to yow it is no curteisye
To speken to an old man vileinye,
But he trespasse in worde, or elles in dede.
In holy writ ye may your-self wel rede,   280
"Agayns an old man, hoor upon his heed,
Ye sholde aryse;" wherfor I yeve yow reed,
Ne dooth un-to an old man noon harm now,
Na-more than ye wolde men dide to yow
In age, if that ye so longe abyde;   285
And god be with yow, wher ye go or ryde.
I moot go thider as I have to go.'

    'Nay, olde cherl, by god, thou shalt nat so,'
Seyde this other hasardour anon;
'Thou partest nat so lightly, by seint Iohn!   290
Thou spak right now of thilke traitour Deeth,
That in this contree alle our frendes sleeth.
Have heer my trouthe, as thou art his aspye,
Tel wher he is, or thou shalt it abye,
By god, and by the holy sacrament!   295
For soothly thou art oon of his assent,
To sleen us yonge folk, thou false theef!'

    Now, sirs,' quod he, 'if that yow be so leef

To finde Deeth, turne up this croked wey,
For in that grove I lafte him, by my fey, 300
Under a tree, and ther he wol abyde;
Nat for your boost he wol him no-thing hyde.
See ye that ook? right ther ye shul him finde.
God save yow, that boghte agayn mankinde,
And yow amende!'—thus seyde this olde man. 305
And everich of thise ryotoures ran,
Til he cam to that tree, and ther they founde
Of florins fyne of golde y-coyned rounde
Wel ny an eighte busshels, as hem thoughte.
No lenger thanne after Deeth they soughte, 310
But ech of hem so glad was of that sighte,
For that the florins been so faire and brighte,
That doun they sette hem by this precious hord.
The worste of hem he spake the firste word.

'Brethren,' quod he, 'tak kepe what I seye; 315
My wit is greet, though that I bourde and pleye.
This tresor hath fortune un-to us yiven,
In mirthe and jolitee our lyf to liven,
And lightly as it comth, so wol we spende.
Ey! goddes precious dignitee! who wende 320
To-day, that we sholde han so fair a grace?
But mighte this gold be caried fro this place
Hoom to myn hous, or elles un-to youres—
For wel ye woot that al this gold is oures—
Than were we in heigh felicitee. 325
But trewely, by daye it may nat be;
Men wolde seyn that we were theves stronge,
And for our owene tresor doon us honge.
This tresor moste y-caried be by nighte
As wysly and as slyly as it mighte. 330
Wherfore I rede that cut among us alle
Be drawe, and lat see wher the cut wol falle;
And he that hath the cut with herte blythe
Shal renne to the toune, and that ful swythe,
And bringe us breed and wyn ful prively. 335
And two of us shul kepen subtilly
This tresor wel; and, if he wol nat tarie,

Whan it is night, we wol this tresor carie
By oon assent, wher-as us thinketh best.'
That oon of hem the cut broughte in his fest,　340
And bad hem drawe, and loke wher it wol falle;
And it fil on the yongeste of hem alle;
And forth toward the toun he wente anon.
And al-so sone as that he was gon,
That oon of hem spak thus un-to that other,　345
'Thou knowest wel thou art my sworne brother,
Thy profit wol I telle thee anon.
Thou woost wel that our felawe is agon;
And heer is gold, and that ful greet plentee,
That shal departed been among us three.　350
But natheles, if I can shape it so
That it departed were among us two,
Hadde I nat doon a freendes torn to thee?'

　That other answerde, 'I noot how that may be;
He woot how that the gold is with us tweye,　355
What shal we doon, what shal we to him seye?'

　'Shal it be conseil?' seyde the firste shrewe,
'And I shal tellen thee, in wordes fewe,
What we shal doon, and bringe it wel aboute.'

　'I graunte,' quod that other, 'out of doute,　360
That, by my trouthe, I wol thee nat biwreye.'

　'Now,' quod the firste, 'thou woost wel we be tweye,
And two of us shal strenger be than oon.
Look whan that he is set, and right anoon
Arys, as though thou woldest with him pleye;　365
And I shal ryve him thurgh the sydes tweye
Whyl that thou strogelest with him as in game,
And with thy dagger look thou do the same;
And than shal al this gold departed be,
My dere freend, bitwixen me and thee;　370
Than may we bothe our lustes al fulfille,
And pleye at dees right at our owene wille.
And thus acorded been thise shrewes tweye
To sleen the thridde, as ye han herd me seye.

　This yongest, which that wente un-to the toun,
Ful ofte in herte he rolleth up and doun　376

The beautee of thise florins newe and brighte.
'O lord!' quod he, 'if so were that I mighte
Have al this tresor to my-self allone,
Ther is no man that liveth under the trone   380
Of god, that sholde live so mery as I!'
And atte laste the feend, our enemy,
Putte in his thought that he shold poyson beye,
With which he mighte sleen his felawes tweye;
For-why the feend fond him in swich lyvinge,   385
That he had leve him to sorwe bringe,
For this was outrely his fulle entente
To sleen hem bothe, and never to repente.
And forth he gooth, no lenger wolde he tarie,
Into the toun, un-to a pothecarie,   390
And preyed him, that he him wolde selle
Som poyson, that he mighte his rattes quelle;
And eek ther was a polcat in his hawe,
That, as he seyde, his capouns hadde y-slawe,
And feyn he wolde wreke him, if he mighte,   395
On vermin, that destroyed him by nighte.

The apothecarie answerde, 'and thou shalt have
A thing that, al-so god my soule save,
In al this world ther nis no creature,
That ete or dronke hath of this confiture   400
Noght but the mountance of a corn of whete,
That he ne shal his lyf anon forlete;
Ye, sterve he shal, and that in lasse whyle
Than thou wolt goon a paas nat but a myle;
This poyson is so strong and violent.'   405

This cursed man hath in his hond y-hent
This poyson in a box, and sith he ran
In-to the nexte strete, un-to a man,
And borwed [of] him large botels three;
And in the two his poyson poured he;   410
The thridde he kepte clene for his drinke.
For al the night he shoop him for to swinke
In caryinge of the gold out of that place.
And whan this ryotour, with sory grace,
Had filled with wyn his grete botels three,   415

To his felawes agayn repaireth he.
What nedeth it to sermone of it more?
For right as they had cast his deeth bifore,
Right so they han him slayn, and that anon.   419
And whan that this was doon, thus spak that oon,
'Now lat us sitte and drinke, and make us merie,
And afterward we wol his body berie.'
And with that word it happed him, par cas,
To take the botel ther the poyson was,
And drank, and yaf his felawe drinke also,   425
For which anon they storven bothe two.

But, certes, I suppose that Avicen
Wroot never in no canon, ne in no fen,
Mo wonder signes of empoisoning
Than hadde thise wrecches two, er hir ending.   430
Thus ended been thise homicydes two,
And eek the false empoysoner also.

O cursed sinne, ful of cursednesse!
O traytours homicyde, o wikkednesse!
O glotonye, luxurie, and hasardrye!   435
Thou blasphemour of Crist with vileinye
And othes grete, of usage and of pryde!
Allas! mankinde, how may it bityde,
That to thy creatour which that thee wroghte,
And with his precious herte-blood thee boghte,
Thou art so fals and so unkinde, allas!   441
Now, goode men, god forgeve yow your trespas,
And ware yow fro the sinne of avaryce.
Myn holy pardoun may yow alle waryce,
So that ye offre nobles or sterlinges,   445
Or elles silver broches, spones, ringes.
Boweth your heed under this holy bulle!
Cometh up, ye wyves, offreth of your wolle!
Your name I entre heer in my rolle anon;
In-to the blisse of hevene shul ye gon;   450
I yow assoile, by myn heigh power,
Yow that wol offre, as clene and eek as cleer
As ye were born; and, lo, sirs, thus I preche.

And Jesu Crist, that is our soules leche,
So graunte yow his pardon to receyve;   455
For that is best; I wol yow nat deceyve.

    But sirs, o word forgat I in my tale,
I have relikes and pardon in my male,
As faire as any man in Engelond,
Whiche were me yeven by the popes hond.   460
If any of yow wol, of devocioun,
Offren, and han myn absolucioun,
Cometh forth anon, and kneleth heer adoun,
And mekely receyveth my pardoun:
Or elles, taketh pardon as ye wende,   465
Al newe and fresh, at every tounes ende,
So that ye offren alwey newe and newe
Nobles and pens, which that be gode and trewe.
It is an honour to everich that is heer,
That ye mowe have a suffisant pardoneer   470
T'assoille yow, in contree as ye ryde,
For aventures which that may bityde.
Peraventure ther may falle oon or two
Doun of his hors, and breke his nekke atwo.
Look which a seuretee is it to yow alle   475
That I am in your felaweship y-falle,
That may assoille yow, bothe more and lasse,
Whan that the soule shal fro the body passe.
I rede that our hoste heer shal biginne,
For he is most envoluped in sinne.   480
Com forth, sir hoste, and offre first anon,
And thou shalte kisse the reliks everichon,
Ye, for a grote! unbokel anon thy purs.'

    'Nay, nay,' quod he, 'than have I Cristes curs!
Lat be,' quod he, 'it shal nat be, so thee'ch!   485
Thou woldest make me kisse thyn old breech,
And swere it were a relik of a seint,
Thogh it were with thy fundement depeint!
But by the croys which that seint Eleyne fond,
I wolde I hadde thy coillons in myn hond   490
In stede of relikes or of seintuarie;
Lat cutte hem of, I wol thee helpe hem carie;

They shul be shryned in an hogges tord.'
   This pardoner answerde nat a word;
So wrooth he was, no word ne wolde he seye.   495
   'Now,' quod our host, 'I wol no lenger pleye
With thee, ne with noon other angry man.'
But right anon the worthy Knight bigan,
Whan that he saugh that al the peple lough,
'Na-more of this, for it is right y-nough;   500
Sir Pardoner, be glad and mery of chere;
And ye, sir host, that been to me so dere,
I prey yow that ye kisse the Pardoner.
And Pardoner, I prey thee, drawe thee neer,
And, as we diden, lat us laughe and pleye.'   505
Anon they kiste, and riden forth hir weye.

OLD BALLADS

King John and the Abbot of Canterbury

I

An ancient story I'll tell you anon
Of a notable prince, that was callèd King John;
And he rulèd England with maine and with might,
For he did great wrong, and maintein'd little right.

II

And I'll tell you a story, a story so merrye,   5
Concerning the Abbot of Canterbùrye;
How, for his house-keeping and high renowne,
They rode poste for him to fair London towne.

III

An hundred men, the King did heare say,
The Abbot kept in his house every day;   10
And fifty golde chaynes, without any doubt,
In velvet coates waited the Abbot about.

IV

'How now, Father Abbot, I heare it of thee
Thou keepest a farre better house than mee,
And for thy house-keeping and high renowne, 15
I feare thou work'st treason against my crown.'—

V

'My liege,' quo' the Abbot, 'I would it were knowne,
I never spend nothing, but what is my owne;
And I trust your Grace will doe me no deere
For spending of my owne true-gotten geere.' 20

VI

'Yes, yes, Father Abbot, thy fault it is highe,
And now for the same thou needest must dye;
For except thou canst answer me questions three,
Thy head shall be smitten from thy bodìe. 24

VII

'And first,' quo' the King, 'when I'm in this stead.
With my crowne of golde so faire on my head,
Among all my liege-men so noble of birthe,
Thou must tell me to one penny what I am worthe.

VIII

'Secondlye, tell me, without any doubt,
How soone I may ride the whole worlde about. 30
And at the third question thou must not shrinke,
But telle me here truly what I do thinke.'—

IX

'O, these are hard questions for my shallow witt,
Nor I cannot answer your Grace as yet:
But if you will give me but three weekes space, 35
I'll do my endeavour to answer your Grace.'

X

'Now three weekes space to thee will I give,
And that is the longest time thou hast to live;
For if thou dost not answer my questions three,
Thy lands and thy livings are forfeit to mee.' 40

XI

Away rode the Abbot all sad at that word,
And he rode to Cambridge, and Oxenford;
But never a doctor there was so wise,
That could with his learning an answer devise.

XII

Then home rode the Abbot of comfort so cold,   45
And he mett with his shepheard a-going to fold:
'How now, my lord Abbot, you are welcome home;
What newes do you bring us from good King
    John?'—

XIII

'Sad newes, sad newes, shepheard, I must give;
That I have but three days more to live: 50
For if I do not answer him questions three,
My head will be smitten from my bodìe.

XIV

'The first is to tell him there in that stead,
With his crowne of golde so fair on his head,
Among all his liege-men so noble of birthe,   55
To within one penny of what he is worthe.

XV

'The seconde, to tell him, without any doubt,
How soone he may ride this whole worlde about:
And at the third question I must not shrinke,
But tell him there truly what he does thinke.'— 60

XVI

'Now cheare up, sire Abbot, did you never hear yet,
That a fool he may learn a wise man witt?
Lend me horse, and serving-men, and your apparel,
And I'll ride to London to answere your quarrel.

XVII

'Nay frowne not, if it hath bin told unto mee,   65
I am like your lordship, as ever may bee:
And if you will but lend me your gowne,
There is none shall knowe us at fair London
    towne.'—

XVIII

'Now horses and serving-men thou shalt have,
With sumptuous array most gallant and brave; 70
With crozier, and miter, and rochet, and cope,
Fit to appeare 'fore our Father the Pope.'—

XIX

'Now welcome, sire Abbot,' the King he did say,
''Tis well thou'rt come back to keepe thy day;
For and if thou canst answer my questions three,
Thy life and thy living both savèd shall bee. 76

XX

'And first, when thou seest me here in this stead
With my crown of golde so fair on my head,
Among all my liege-men so noble of birthe,
Tell me to one penny what I am worthe.'— 80

XXI

'For thirty pence our Saviour was sold
Amonge the false Jewes, as I have bin told;
And twenty-nine is the worthe of thee,
For I thinke thou art one penny worser than hee.'

XXII

The King he laughed, and swore by St. Bittel, 85
'I did not thinke I had been worthe so littel!
—Now secondly tell me, without any doubt,
How soone I may ride this whole world about.'

XXIII

'You must rise with the sun, and ride with the same,
Until the next morning he riseth againe; 90
And then your Grace need not make any doubt,
But in twenty-four hours you'll ride it about.'

XXIV

The King he laughed, and swore by St. Jone,
'I did not think it could be done so soone!
—Now from the third question thou must not
shrinke, 95
But tell me here truly what I do thinke.'—

xxv

'Yea, that shall I do, and make your Grace merry:
You thinke I'm the Abbot of Canterbùrye;
But I'm his poor shepheard, as plain you may see,
That am come to beg pardon for him and for mee.'

xxvi

The King he laughed, and swore by the Masse, 101
'I'll make thee Lord Abbot this day in his place!'—
'Now naye, my liege, be not in such speede,
For alacke I can neither write, ne reade.'—

xxvii

'Four nobles a weeke, then, I will give thee 105
For this merry jest thou hast showne unto mee;
And tell the old Abbot when thou comest home,
Thou hast brought him a pardon from good King
    John.'

Sir Patrick Spens

1. *The Sailing*

I

The king sits in Dunfermline town
    Drinking the blude-red wine;
'O whare will I get a skeely skipper
    To sail this new ship o' mine?'

II

O up and spak an eldern knight, 5
    Sat at the king's right knee:
'Sir Patrick Spens is the best sailor
    That ever sail'd the sea.'

III

Our king has written a braid letter,
    And seal'd it with his hand, 10
And sent it to Sir Patrick Spens,
    Was walking on the strand.

IV

'To Noroway, to Noroway,
  To Noroway o'er the faem;
The king's daughter o' Noroway,   15
  'Tis thou must bring her hame.'

V

The first word that Sir Patrick read
  So loud, loud laugh'd he;
The neist word that Sir Patrick read
  The tear blinded his e'e.   20

VI

'O wha is this has done this deed
  And tauld the king o' me,
To send us out, at this time o' year,
  To sail upon the sea?

VII

'Be it wind, be it weet, be it hail, be it sleet,
  Our ship must sail the faem;   26
The king's daughter o' Noroway,
  'Tis we must fetch her hame.'

VIII

They hoysed their sails on Monenday morn
  Wi' a' the speed they may;   30
They hae landed in Noroway
  Upon a Wodensday.

II. *The Return*

IX

'Mak ready, mak ready, my merry men a'!
  Our gude ship sails the morn.'—
'Now ever alack, my master dear,   35
  I fear a deadly storm.

x

'I saw the new moon late yestreen
 Wi' the auld moon in her arm;
And if we gang to sea, master,
 I fear we'll come to harm.'   40

xi

They hadna sail'd a league, a league,
 A league but barely three,
When the lift grew dark, and the wind blew
  loud,
 And gurly grew the sea.

xii

The ankers brak, and the topmast lap, 45
 It was sic a deadly storm:
And the waves cam owre the broken ship
 Till a' her sides were torn.

xiii

'O where will I get a gude sailor
 To tak' my helm in hand,   50
Till I get up to the tall topmast
 To see if I can spy land?'—

xiv

'O here am I, a sailor gude,
 To tak' the helm in hand,
Till you go up to the tall topmast, 55
 But I fear you'll ne'er spy land.'

xv

He hadna gane a step, a step,
 A step but barely ane,
When a bolt flew out of our goodly ship,
 And the saut sea it came in. 60

xvi

'Go fetch a web o' the silken claith,
 Another o' the twine,
And wap them into our ship's side,
 And let nae the sea come in.'

XVII

They fetch'd a web o' the silken claith, 65
    Another o' the twine,
And they wapp'd them round that gude
    ship's side,
    But still the sea came in.

XVIII

O laith, laith were our gude Scots lords
    To wet their cork-heel'd shoon; 70
But lang or a' the play was play'd
    They wat their hats aboon.

XIX

And mony was the feather bed
    That flatter'd on the faem;
And mony was the gude lord's son 75
    That never mair cam hame.

XX

O lang, lang may the ladies sit,
    Wi' their fans into their hand,
Before they see Sir Patrick Spens
    Come sailing to the strand! 80

XXI

And lang, lang may the maidens sit
    Wi' their gowd kames in their hair,
A-waiting for their ain dear loves!
    For them they'll see nae mair.

XXII

Half-owre, half-owre to Aberdour, 85
    'Tis fifty fathoms deep;
And there lies gude Sir Patrick Spens,
    Wi' the Scots lords at his feet!

Thomas the Rhymer

I

True Thomas lay on Huntlie bank;
    A ferlie he spied wi' his e'e;
And there he saw a ladye bright
    Come riding down by the Eildon Tree.

II

Her skirt was o' the grass-green silk,   5
    Her mantle o' the velvet fyne;
At ilka tett o' her horse's mane
    Hung fifty siller bells and nine.

III

True Thomas he pu'd aff his cap,
    And louted low down on his knee: 10
'Hail to thee, Mary, Queen of Heaven!
    For thy peer on earth could never be.'

IV

'O no, O no, Thomas,' she said,
    That name does not belang to me;
I'm but the Queen o' fair Elfland,   15
    That am hither come to visit thee.

V

'Harp and carp, Thomas,' she said;
    'Harp and carp along wi' me;
And if ye dare to kiss my lips,
    Sure of your bodie I will be.'   20

VI

'Betide me weal, betide me woe,
    That weird shall never daunten me.'
Syne he has kiss'd her rosy lips,
    All underneath the Eildon Tree.

VII

'Now ye maun go wi' me,' she said,   25
    'True Thomas, ye maun go wi' me;
And ye maun serve me seven years,
    Thro' weal or woe as may chance to be.'

VIII

She's mounted on her milk-white steed,
    She's ta'en true Thomas up behind;   30
And aye, whene'er her bridle rang,
    The steed gaed swifter than the wind.

IX

O they rade on, and farther on,
    The steed gaed swifter than the wind;
Until they reach'd a desert wide,   35
    And living land was left behind.

X

'Light down, light down now, true Thomas,
    And lean your head upon my knee;
Abide ye there a little space,
    And I will show you ferlies three.   40

XI

'O see ye not yon narrow road,
    So thick beset wi' thorns and briers?
That is the Path of Righteousness,
    Though after it but few inquires.

XII

'And see ye not yon braid, braid road,   45
    That lies across the lily leven?
That is the Path of Wickedness,
    Though some call it the Road to Heaven.

XIII

'And see ye not yon bonny road
    That winds about the fernie brae?   50
That is the Road to fair Elfland,
    Where thou and I this night maun gae.

XIV

'But, Thomas, ye sall haud your tongue,
    Whatever ye may hear or see;
For speak ye word in Elflyn-land,   55
    Ye'll ne'er win back to your ain countrie.'

XV

O they rade on, and farther on,
    And they waded rivers abune the knee;
And they saw neither sun nor moon,
    But they heard the roaring of the sea.   60

XVI

It was mirk, mirk night, there was nae starlight,
    They waded thro' red blude to the knee;
For a' the blude that's shed on the earth
    Rins through the springs o' that countrie.

XVII

Syne they came to a garden green,   65
    And she pu'd an apple frae a tree:
'Take this for thy wages, true Thomas;
    It will give thee the tongue that can never lee.

XVIII

'My tongue is my ain,' true Thomas he said;
    'A gudely gift ye wad gie to me!   70
I neither dought to buy or sell
    At fair or tryst where I might be.

XIX

'I dought neither speak to prince or peer,
    Nor ask of grace from fair ladye!'—
'Now haud thy peace, Thomas,' she said,   75
    For as I say, so must it be.'

XX

He has gotten a coat of the even cloth,
    And a pair o' shoon of the velvet green;
And till seven years were gane and past,
    True Thomas on earth was never seen.   80

Edom o' Gordon

I

It fell about the Martinmas,
  When the wind blew shrill and cauld,
Said Edom o' Gordon to his men,
  'We maun draw to a hauld.

II

'And what a hauld sall we draw to,   5
  My merry men and me?
We will gae to the house o' the Rodes,
  To see that fair ladye.'

III

The lady stood on her castle wa',
  Beheld baith dale and down;   10
There she was 'ware of a host of men
  Cam' riding towards the town.

IV

'O see ye not, my merry men a',
  O see ye not what I see?
Methinks I see a host of men;   15
  I marvel wha they be.'

V

She ween'd it had been her lovely lord,
  As he cam riding hame;
It was the traitor, Edom o' Gordon,
  Wha reck'd nae sin nor shame.   20

VI

She had nae sooner buskit hersell,
  And putten on her gown,
But Edom o' Gordon an' his men
  Were round about the town.

VII

They had nae sooner supper set,　　　25
　　Nae sooner said the grace,
But Edom o' Gordon an' his men
　　Were lighted about the place.

VIII

The lady ran up to her tower-head,
　　Sae fast as she could hie,　　　30
To see if by her fair speeches
　　She could wi' him agree.

IX

'Come doun to me, ye lady gay,
　　Come doun, come doun to me;
This night sall ye lig within mine arms,　　35
　　To-morrow my bride sall be.'—

X

'I winna come down, ye fals Gordon,
　　I winna come down to thee;
I winna forsake my ain dear lord,
　　That is sae far frae me.'—　　　40

XI

'Gie owre your house, ye lady fair,
　　Gie owre your house to me;
Or I sall brenn yoursel therein,
　　But and your babies three.'—

XII

'I winna gie owre, ye fals Gordon,　　　45
　　To nae sic traitor as yee;
And if ye brenn my ain dear babes,
　　My lord sall make ye dree.

XIII

'Now reach my pistol, Glaud, my man,
　　And charge ye weel my gun;　　　50
For, but an I pierce that bluidy butcher,
　　My babes, we been undone!'

XIV

She stood upon her castle wa',
  And let twa bullets flee:
She miss'd that bluidy butcher's heart,   55
  And only razed his knee.

XV

'Set fire to the house!' quo' fals Gordon,
  All wud wi' dule and ire:
'Fals lady, ye sall rue this deid
  As ye brenn in the fire!'—   60

XVI

'Wae worth, wae worth ye, Jock, my man!
  I paid ye weel your fee;
Why pu' ye out the grund-wa' stane,
  Lets in the reek to me?

XVII

'And e'en wae worth ye, Jock, my man! 65
  I paid ye weel your hire;
Why pu' ye out the grund-wa' stane,
  To me lets in the fire?'—

XVIII

'Ye paid me weel my hire, ladye,
  Ye paid me weel my fee;   70
But now I'm Edom o' Gordon's man,
  Maun either do or dee.'

XIX

O then bespake her little son,
  Sat on the nurse's knee:
Says, 'Mither dear, gie owre this house, 75
  For the reek it smithers me.'—

XX

'I wad gie a' my gowd, my bairn,
  Sae wad I a' my fee,
For ae blast o' the western wind,
  To blaw the reek frae thee.'   80

XXI

O then bespake her dochter dear—
    She was baith jimp and sma':
'O row me in a pair o' sheets,
    And tow me owre the wa'!'

XXII

They row'd her in a pair o' sheets,   85
    And tow'd her owre the wa';
But on the point o' Gordon's spear
    She gat a deadly fa'.

XXIII

O bonnie, bonnie was her mouth,
    And cherry were her cheiks,   90
And clear, clear was her yellow hair,
    Whereon the red blood dreips.

XXIV

Then wi' his spear he turn'd her owre;
    O gin her face was wane!
He said, 'Ye are the first that e'er   95
    I wish'd alive again.'

XXV

He turn'd her owre and owre again;
    O gin her skin was white!
'I might hae spared that bonnie face
    To hae been some man's delight.   100

XXVI

'Busk and boun, my merry men a',
    For ill dooms I do guess;
I canna look in that bonnie face
    As it lies on the grass.'—

XXVII

'Wha looks to freits, my master dear,   105
    It's freits will follow them;
Let it ne'er be said that Edom o' Gordon
    Was daunted by a dame.'

XXVIII

But when the lady saw the fire
  Come flaming owre her head,   110
She wept, and kiss'd her children twain,
  Says, 'Bairns, we been but dead.'

XXIX

The Gordon then his bugle blew,
  And said, 'Awa', awa'!
This house o' the Rodes is a' in a flame;   115
  I hauld it time to ga'.'

XXX

And this way lookit her ain dear lord,
  As he cam owre the lea;
He saw his castle a' in a lowe,
  As far as he could see.   120

XXXI

Then sair, O sair, his mind misgave,
  And all his heart was wae:
'Put on, put on, my wighty men,
  Sae fast as ye can gae.

XXXII

'Put on, put on, my wighty men,   125
  Sae fast as ye can drie!
For he that's hindmost o' the thrang
  Sall ne'er get good o' me.'

XXXIII

Then some they rade, and some they ran,
  Out-owre the grass and bent;   130
But ere the foremost could win up,
  Baith lady and babes were brent.

XXXIV

And after the Gordon he is gane,
  Sae fast as he might drie;
And soon i' the Gordon's foul heart's blude
  He's wroken his dear ladye.   136

Young John

I

A fair maid sat in her bower-door,
　Wringing her lily hands,
And by it came a sprightly youth,
　Fast tripping o'er the strands.

II

'Where gang ye, young John,' she says, 　　　5
　'Sae early in the day?
It gars me think, by your fast trip,
　Your journey's far away.'

III

He turn'd about wi' a surly look,
　And said, 'What's that to thee? 　　　10
I'm gaen to see a lovely maid,
　Mair fairer far than ye.'—

IV

'Now hae ye play'd me this, fause love,
　In simmer, 'mid the flowers?
I shall repay ye back again, 　　　15
　In winter, 'mid the showers.

V

'But again, dear love, and again, dear love,
　Will ye not turn again?
For as ye look to other women,
　Sall I to other men.'— 　　　20

VI

'Go make your choice of whom you please,
　　For I my choice will have;
I've chosen a maid more fair than thee,
　　I never will deceive.'

VII

She's kilted up her claithing fine,　　　25
　　And after him gaed she;
But aye he said, 'Ye'll turn again,
　　Nae farther gang wi' me.'

VIII

'But again, dear love, and again, dear love,
　　Will ye ne'er love me again?　　　30
Alas, for loving you sae well,
　　And you nae me again!'

IX

The firstan town that they cam' till,
　　He bought her brooch and ring;
And aye he bade her turn again,　　　35
　　And nae farther gang wi' him.

X

'But again, dear love, and again, dear love,
　　Will ye ne'er love me again?
Alas, for loving you sae well,
　　And you nae me again!'　　　40

XI

The nextan town that they cam' till,
  He bought her muff and gloves;
But aye he bade her turn again,
  And choose some other loves.

XII

'But again, dear love, and again, dear love,   45
  Will ye ne'er love me again?
Alas, for loving you sae well,
  And you nae me again!'

XIII

The nextan town that they cam' till,
  His heart it grew mair fain,   50
And he was as deep in love wi' her
  As she was ower again.

XIV

The nextan town that they cam' till,
  He bought her wedding gown,
And made her lady of ha's and bowers,   55
  Into sweet Berwick town.

Jock o' the Side

I

Now Liddesdale has ridden a raid,
  But I wat they had better hae staid at hame;
For Michael o' Winfield he is dead,
  And Jock o' the Side is prisoner ta'en.

II

To Sybill o' the Side the tidings came;
  By the waterside there as she ran
She took her kirtle by the hem
  And fast to Mangerton she's gane.

III

Then up and spoke her Lord Mangerton— 9
  'What news, what news, my sister to me?'—
'Bad news, bad news! My Michael is slain;
  And they ha'e taken my son Johnie.'

IV

The lords they wrang their fingers white,
  Ladyes did pull themsells by the hair,
Crying 'Alas and well-a-day! 15
  For Jock o' the Side we'll never see mair!'

V

—'Ne'er fear, sister Sybill,' quo' Mangerton;
  'I have yokes of ousen, eighty and three;
My barns, my byres, and my faulds, a' weil fill'd,
  I'll part wi' them a' ere Johnie shall dee. 20

VI

'Three men I'll send to set him free,
  Well harness'd a' wi' the best o' steel;
The English louns may hear, and drie
  The weight o' their braid-swords to feel.

VII

'The Laird's Jock ane, the Laird's Wat twa, 25
  O Hobbie Noble, thou ane maun be!
Thy coat is blue, thou hast been true,
  Since England banish'd thee, to me.'

VIII

Now Hobbie was an English man,
  In Bewcastle dale was bred and born; 30
But his misdeeds they were sae great,
  They banish'd him ne'er to return.

IX

Lord Mangerton them orders gave,
  'Your horses the wrang way maun be shod,
Like gentlemen ye mauna seem, 35
  But look like corn-caugers ga'en the road.

x

'Your armour gude ye mauna shaw,
　　Nor yet appear like men o' war;
As country lads be a' array'd,
　　Wi' branks and brecham on each mare.'　　40

xi

Their horses are the wrang way shod,
　　And Hobbie has mounted his grey sae fine;
Wat on his auld horse, Jock on his bey,
　　And on they rode for the water of Tyne.

xii

But when they came to Cholerton ford　　45
　　They lighted down by the light o' the moon,
And a tree they cut, wi' nogs on each side,
　　To climb up the wa' of Newcastle toun.

xiii

But when they cam to Newcastle toun,
　　And down were alighted at the wa',　　50
They fand thair tree three ells ower laigh,
　　They fand their stick baith short and sma'.

xiv

Then up spake the Laird's ain Jock:
　　'There's naething for't; the gates we maun
　　　　force.'—
But when they cam the gate until,　　55
　　The porter withstood baith men and horse.

xv

His neck in twa the Armstrangs wrang;
　　Wi' fute or hand he ne'er play'd pa!
His life and his keys at anes they hae ta'en,
　　And cast the body ahint the wa'.　　60

xvi

Now sune they reach Newcastle jail,
　　And to the prisoner thus they call:
'Sleeps thou, wakes thou, Jock o' the Side,
　　Or art thou weary of thy thrall?'

XVII

Jock answers thus, wi' dolefu' tone: 65
  'Aft, aft I wake—I seldom sleep:
But whae's this kens my name sae weel,
  And thus to mese my waes does seek?'—

XVIII

Then out and spak the gude Laird's Jock,
  'Now fear ye na, my billie,' quo' he;   70
'For here are the Laird's Jock, the Laird's Wat,
  And Hobbie Noble to set thee free.'—

XIX

'Now haud thy tongue, my gude Laird's Jock,
  For ever, alas! this canna be;
For if a' Liddesdale were here the night,   75
  The morn's the day that I maun dee.

XX

'Full fifteen stane o' Spanish iron,
  They hae laid a' right sair on me;
Wi' locks and keys I am fast bound
  In this dungeon dark and dreirie.'   80

XXI

'Fear ye na that,' quo' the Laird's Jock;
  'A faint heart ne'er wan a fair ladie;
Work thou within, we'll work without,
  And I'll be sworn we'll set thee free.'

XXII

The first strong door that they cam at,   85
  They loosèd it without a key;
The next chain'd door that they cam at,
  They garr'd it a' to flinders flee.

XXIII

The prisoner now upon his back
  The Laird's Jock has gotten up fu' hie;   90
And, airns and a', down the tolbooth stair,
  Wi' nae sma' speed and joy brings he.

XXIV

'Now, Jock, my man,' quo' Hobbie Noble,
  'Some o' his weight ye may lay on me.'—
'I wat weel no!' quo' the Laird's ain Jock,   95
  'I count him lighter than a flee.'

XXV

Sae out at the gates they a' are gane,
  The prisoner's set on horseback hie;
And now wi' speed they've ta'en the gate,
  While ilk ane jokes fu' wantonlie: 100

XXVI

'O Jock! sae winsomely ye sit,
  Wi' baith your feet upon ae side;
Sae weel ye're harneist, and sae trig,
  In troth ye sit like ony bride!'

XXVII

The night, tho' wat, they did na mind,   105
  But hied them on fu' merrilie,
Until they cam to Cholerton brae,
  Where the water ran like mountains hie.

XXVIII

But when they cam to Cholerton ford,
  There they met with an auld man;   110
Says—'Honest man, will the water ride?
  Tell us in haste, if that ye can.'—

XXIX

'I wat weel no,' quo' the gude auld man;
  'I hae lived here thretty years and three;
Nor man nor horse can go ower Tyne,   115
  Except it were a horse of tree.'—

XXX

Then out and spoke the Laird's saft Wat,
  The greatest coward in the companie:
'Now halt, now halt! we need na try't;
  The day is come we a' maun die!'—   120

XXXI

'Puir faint-hearted thief!' cried the Laird's ain
    Jock,
  'There'll nae man die but him that's fie;
I'll guide ye a' right safely thro';
    Lift ye the pris'ner on ahint me.'

XXXII

Wi' that the water they hae ta'en,   125
  By ane's and twa's they a' swam thro';
'Here are we a' safe,' quo' the Laird's Jock,
    'And, puir faint Wat, what think ye now?'

XXXIII

They scarce the other brae had won,
  When twenty men they saw pursue;   130
Frae Newcastle toun they had been sent,
    A' English lads baith stout and true.

XXXIV

But when the Land-sergeant the water saw,
  'It winna ride, my lads,' says he;
Then cried aloud—'The prisoner take,   135
    But leave the fetters, I pray, to me!'

XXXV

'I wat weel no,' quo' the Laird's ain Jock,
  'I'll keep them, shoon to my mare to be:
My gude bay mare—for I am sure,
    She has bought them a' right dear frae thee.'—

XXXVI

Sae now they are on to Liddesdale,   141
  E'en as fast as they could them hie;
The prisoner is brought to his ain fireside,
    And there o' his airns they mak him free.

XXXVII

Now, Jock, my billie,' quo' a' the three,   145
  'The day is comed thou was to die;
But thou's as weel at thy ain ingle-side,
    Now sitting, I think, 'twixt thee and mee.'

Edward, Edward

I

'Why does your brand sae drop wi' blude,
     Edward, Edward?
Why does your brand sae drop wi' blude,
    And why sae sad gang ye, O?'—
'O I hae kill'd my hawk sae gude,   5
     Mither, mither;
O I hae kill'd my hawk sae gude,
    And I had nae mair but he, O.'

II

'Your hawk's blude was never sae red,
     Edward, Edward;   10
Your hawk's blude was never sae red,
    My dear son, I tell thee, O.'—
'O I hae kill'd my red-roan steed,
     Mither, mither;
O I hae kill'd my red-roan steed,   15
    That erst was sae fair and free, O.'

III

'Your steed was auld, and ye hae got mair,
     Edward, Edward;
Your steed was auld, and ye hae got mair;
    Some other dule ye dree, O.'   20
'O I hae kill'd my father dear,
     Mither, mither;
O I hae kill'd my father dear,
    Alas, and wae is me, O!'

IV

'And whatten penance will ye dree for that,
     Edward, Edward?   26
Whatten penance will ye dree for that?
    My dear son, now tell me, O.'—

'I'll set my feet in yonder boat,
　　Mither, mither;　　　　　　　　30
I'll set my feet in yonder boat,
　　And I'll fare over the sea, O.'

v

'And what will ye do wi' your tow'rs and your ha',
　　Edward, Edward?
And what will ye do wi' your tow'rs and your ha',
　　That were sae fair to see, O?'—　　36
'I'll let them stand till they doun fa',
　　Mither, mither;
I'll let them stand till they doun fa',
　　For here never mair maun I be, O.'　　40

VI

'And what will ye leave to your bairns and your wife,
　　Edward, Edward?
And what will ye leave to your bairns and your wife,
　　When ye gang owre the sea, O?'—
'The warld's room: let them beg through life,　　45
　　Mither, mither;
The warld's room: let them beg through life;
　　For them never mair will I see, O.'

VII

'And what will ye leave to your ain mither dear,
　　Edward, Edward?　　　　　　　　50
And what will ye leave to your ain mither dear,
　　My dear son, now tell me, O?'—
'The curse of hell frae me sall ye bear,
　　Mither, mither;
The curse of hell frae me sall ye bear:　　55
　　Sic counsels ye gave to me, O!'

Mary Ambree

I

When captains couragious, whom death could not
        daunte,
Did march to the siege of the city of Gaunt,
They muster'd their souldiers by two and by three,
And the foremost in battle was Mary Ambree.

II

When brave Sir John Major was slaine in her sight,
Who was her true lover, her joy, and delight,   6
Because he was slaine most treacherouslie,
She vow'd to revenge him, did Mary Ambree.

III

She clothèd herselfe from top to the toe
In buffe of the bravest, most seemelye to showe;   10
A faire shirt of mail then slippèd on she;
Was not this a brave bonny lass, Mary Ambree?

IV

A helmet of proofe she strait did provide,
A strong arminge sword she girt by her side,   14
And on each hand a goodly faire gauntlett put shee;
Was not this a brave bonny lass, Mary Ambree?

V

Then tooke she her sworde and her target in hand,
Bidding all such as wo'ld to be sworn of her band;
To wayte on her person came thousand and three:
Was not this a brave bonny lass, Mary Ambree?   20

VI

'My soldiers,' she saith, 'soe valiant and bold,
Nowe follow your captaine, whom you doe beholde;
Still foremost in battel myself will I be':
Was not this a brave bonny lass, Mary Ambree?   24

VII

Then cry'd out her souldiers, and loude they did say,
'Soe well thou becomest this gallant array,
Thy harte and thy weapons soe well do agree,
There was none that was ever like Mary Ambree.'

VIII

She chearèd her souldiers, that foughten for life, 29
With ancyent and standard, with drum and with fyfe,
With brave clanging trumpetts, that sounded so free;
Was not this a brave bonny lass, Mary Ambree?

IX

'Before I will see the worst of you all
To come into danger of death or of thrall,
This hand and this life I will venture so free': 35
Was not this a brave bonny lass, Mary Ambree?

X

She led up her souldiers in battaile array
Gainst three times theyr number by break of the daye;
Seven howers in skirmish continuèd shee:
Was not this a brave bonny lass, Mary Ambree? 40

XI

She fillèd the skyes with the smoke of her shott,
And her enemyes bodyes with bullets soe hott;
For one of her owne men a score killèd shee:
Was not this a brave bonny lass, Mary Ambree?

XII

And when her false gunner, to spoyle her intent, 45
Away all her pellets and powder had sent,
Straight with her keen weapon she slasht him in three:
Was not this a brave bonny lass, Mary Ambree!

XIII

Being falselye betrayèd for lucre of hyre,
At length she was forcèd to make a retyre; 50
Then her souldiers into a strong castle drew she:
Was not this a brave bonny lass, Mary Ambree?

XIV

Her foes they beset her on everye side,
As thinking close siege shee co'ld never abide;
To beate down the wallès they all did decree: 55
But stoutlye defyed them brave Mary Ambree.

XV

Then tooke she her sword and her target in hand,
And mounting the walls all undaunted did stand,
There daring their captaines to match any three:
O what a brave captaine was Mary Ambree!   60

XVI

'Now saye, English captaine, what woldest thou give
To ransome thy selfe, which else must not live?
Come yield thy selfe quicklye, or slaine thou must
          bee.'—
O then smilèd sweetlye brave Mary Ambree.

XVII

'Ye captaines couragious, of valour so bold,   65
Whom thinke you before you now you doe behold?'—
'A knight, sir, of England, and captaine soe free,
Who shortèleye with us a pris'ner must bee.'—

XVIII

'No captaine of England; behold in your sight   69
Two brests in my bosome, and therfore no knight:
Noe knight, sirs, of England, nor captaine you see,
But a poor simple lass, callèd Mary Ambree.'—

XIX

'But art thou a woman, as thou dost declare,
Whose valor hath prov'd so undaunted in warre?
If England doth yield such brave lasses as thee,   75
Full well may they conquer, faire Mary Ambree!'

XX

Then to her owne country shee backe did returne,
Still holding the foes of faire England in scorne:
Therfore, English captaines of every degree,
Sing forth the brave valours of Mary Ambree!   80

The Battle of Otterburn

I

It fell about the Lammas tide
   When husbands win their hay,
The doughty Douglas bound him to ride
   In England to take a prey.   4

II

He has chosen the Graemes, and the Lindsays light,
   And the gallant Gordons gay;
And the Earl of Fyfe withouten strife,
   He's bound him over Solwày.

III

They come in over Ottercap Hill,
   So down by Rodeley Cragge;   10
Upon Green Leyton they lighted down
   Styrande many a stagge.

IV

And they have brent the dales of Tyne,
   And harryed Bamborowe shire,
And the Otter Dale they have brent it hale   15
   And left it a' on fire.

V

Then spake a berne upon the bent,
   Of comfort that was not cold,
And said, 'We have brent Northumberland,
   We have all wealth in hold.   20

VI

'Now we have harryed all Bamborowe shire,
   All the wealth in the world have we:
I rede we ryde to Newcastell
   So still and stalworthlye.'

VII

Upon the morrow, when it was day,   25
  The standards shone full bright;
To Newcastell they took the way,
  And thither they came full right.

VIII

To Newcastell when that they came,
  The Douglas cry'd on hyght: 30
'Harry Percy, an thou bidest within,
  Come to the field, and fight!—

IX

'For we have brent Northumberland,
  Thy herytage good and right;
And syne my lodging I have ta'en,   35
  With my brand dubb'd many a knight.'

X

Sir Harry Percy came to the walls
  The Scottish host for to see,
Sayd, 'An thou hast brent Northumberland,
  Full sore it rueth me.   40

XI

'If thou hast haryed all Bamborowe shire,
  Thou hast done me great envye;
For this trespasse thou hast me done
  The tone of us shall die.'

XII

'Where shall I bide thee?' sayd the Douglas,
  'Or where wilt thou come to me?'—   46
'But gae ye up to Otterbourne,
  And wait there dayès three.

XIII

'The roe full rekeles there she rins,
  To make the game and glee;   50
The falcon and the phesant both,
  To fend thy men and thee.

XIV

'There may'st thou have thy wealth at will,
    Well lodg'd thou there may'st be:
It shall not be long ere I come thee till,'   55
    Sayd Sir Harry Percy.

XV

'There shall I bide thee,' sayd the Douglas,
    'By the faith of my bodye.'—
'There shall I come,' said Sir Harry Percy,
    'My troth I plight to thee.'   60

XVI

A pipe of wine over the wall,
    He gave them to their pay,
There he made the Douglas drinke,
    And all his host that day.

XVII

The Douglas turn'd him homeward again,   65
    And rode withouten stay;
He pyght his standard at Otterbourne
    Upon a Wedensday.

XVIII

And syne he warned his men to go
    To choose their geldings grass;   70
And he that had no man to send
    His own servant he was.

XIX

A Scottish knight hoved on the bent
    At watch, I dare well say,
So was he ware of the noble Percy   75
    In the dawning of the day.

XX

He pryck'd to his pavilion door
    As fast as he might run:
'Awaken, Douglas!' cried the knight,
    'For his sake that sits in throne!   80

XXI

'Awaken, Douglas!' cried the knight,
  'For thou mayst wake with wynne!
Yonder have I spied the proud Percy,
  And seven standards with him.'

XXII

'Now by my troth,' the Douglas sayd,   85
  'It is but a faynèd tale!
He durst not look on my broad banner
  Were all England in hail!

XXIII

'Was I not yesterday at Newcastell
  That stands so fair on Tyne?   90
For all the men the Percy had
  He could not gar me to dine.'

XXIV

He stepp'd out at his pavilion-door
  To look an it were lease:
'Array you, lordings, one and all!   95
  For here begins no peace.

XXV

'The Earl of Menteith, thou art my eme,
  The vaward I give to thee:
The Earl of Huntley, cante and keen,
  Take him to go with thee.   100

XXVI

'The Lord of Buchan, in armure bright,
  On the other side he shall be;
Lord Johnstone and Lord Maxwell
  They two shall go with me.

XXVII

'Swynton, fair fall upon your pride!   105
  To battle make you bowne.—
Sir Davy Scott, Sir Walter Steward,
  Sir John of Agerstone!'

XXVIII

The Percy came before his host,
  He was ever a gentil knight: 110
Upon the Douglas loud can he cry
  'I will hold that I have hyght.'

XXIX

'For thou hast brent Northumberland,
  And done me great envye,
For this trespasse thou hast me done   115
  The tone of us shall die.'

XXX

The Douglas answer'd him again
  With great words upon hie,
And sayd, 'I have twenty against thy one:
  Behold, and thou mayst see!'   120

XXXI

With that the Percy was grievèd sore,
  Forsooth as I you say:
He lighted down upon his foot
  And schoote his horse away.

XXXII

Every man saw that he did so,   125
  That ryal was ever in rowghte:
Every man schoote his horse him fro
  And lighted him round about.

XXXIII

Sir Harry Percy took the field
  Even thus, as I you say;   130
Jesus Criste in hevyn on height
  Did help him well that day.

XXXIV

But nine thousand, there was no more—
  The chronicle will not layne—
Forty thousand of Scots and four   135
  That day fought them again.

XXXV

But when the battel began to join,
   In haste there came a knight;
And letters fair forth hath he ta'en,
   And thus he sayd full right: 140

XXXVI

'My lord your father greets you well,
   With many a noble knight;
He doth desire you now to bide,
   That he may see this fight.

XXXVII

'The Baron of Graystoke is out of the west
   With a noble companye: 146
All they lodge at your father's this night,
   And the battel fayn would they see.'

XXXVIII

'For Jesus' love,' sayd Sir Harry Percy,
   'That died for you and me,   150
Wend to my lord my father agayn,
   Say thou saw me not with thee.

XXXIX

'My troth is plight to yon Scottish knight,
   —It nede's me not to layne—
That I should bide him upon this bent, 155
   And I have his troth agayn.

XL

'And if that I wend off this growende,
   Forsooth, unfoughten away,
He would call me but a coward knight
   In his land another day.   160

XLI

'Yet had I liefer be rynde and rent,
   —By Mary, that mickle may!—
Than ever my manhood be reproved
   With a Scot another day.

XLII

'Wherefore shoot, archers, for my sake!   165
  And let sharp arrows flee.
Minstrels, play up for your waryson!
  And well quit it shall be.

XLIII

'Every man thynke on his true-love,
  And mark him to the Trinitye: 170
For unto God I make mine avowe
  This day I will not flee.'

XLIV

The blodye herte in the Douglas arms
  His standard stood on hie,
That every man might full wel knowe;   175
  Bysyde stood starrès three.

XLV

The white lyon on the English part,
  Forsooth as I you sayn,
The lucettes and the cressants both
  The Scot fought them again.   180

XLVI

Upon Seynt Andrewe loud can they crye,
  And thrice they showt on hyght,
Syne mark'd them on our English men,
  As I have told you right.

XLVII

Seynt George the bryght, Our Ladye's knyght,
  To name they were full fayne;   186
Our English men they cry'd on hyght,
  And thrice they shot agayne.

XLVIII

With that sharp arrows began to flee,
  I tell you in certayne: 190
Men of arms began to joyne,
  Many a doughty man was slayne.

XLIX

The Percy and the Douglas met
    That either of other was fayne;
They swapp'd together while they swet   195
    With swords of fyne Collayne:

L

Until the blood from their bassonets ran
    As the roke doth in the rayne;
'Yield thou to me,' sayd the Douglas,
    'Or elles thou shalt be slayne.   200

LI

'For I see by thy bryght bassonet
    Thou art some man of myght:
And so I do by thy burnysh'd brand,
    Thou'rt an earl or elles a knyght.'

LII

'By my good faith,' said the noble Percye,   205
    'Now hast thou rede full ryght;
Yet will I never yield me to thee,
    While I may stand and fyght.'

LIII

They swapp'd together, while that they swet,
    With swordès sharp and long;   210
Each on other so fast they bette,
    Their helms came in pieces down.

LIV

The Percy was a man of strength,
    I tell you in this stounde:
He smote the Douglas at the sword's length
    That he fell to the grounde.   216

LV

The Douglas call'd to his little foot-page,
    And sayd, 'Run speedilye,
And fetch my ain dear sister's son,
    Sir Hugh Montgomery.   220

LVI

'My nephew good,' the Douglas sayd,
  'What recks the death of ane?
Last night I dream'd a dreary dream,
  And I ken the day's thy ain.

LVII

'My wound is deep: I am fayn to sleep,   225
  Take thou the vaward of me,
And hide me by the bracken bush
  Grows on yon lilye-lee.'

LVIII

He has lifted up that noble lord
  With the saut tears in his e'e;   230
He has hidden him in the bracken bush
  That his merry men might not see.

LIX

The standards stood still on eke side;
  With many a grievous groan
They fought that day, and all the night;   235
  Many a doughtye man was slone.

LX

The morn was clear, the day drew nie,
  —Yet stiffly in stowre they stood;
Echone hewing another while they might drie,
  Till aye ran down the blood.   240

LXI

The Percy and Montgomery met
  That either of other was fayn:
They swappèd swords, and they two met
  Till the blood ran down between.

LXII

'Now yield thee, yield thee, Percy,' he said,
  'Or I vow I'le lay thee low!'   246
'To whom shall I yield?' said Earl Percy,
  'Now I see it maun be so.'—

LXIII

'Thou shalt not yield to lord nor loun,
  Nor yet shalt thou to me;   250
But yield thee to the bracken bush
  Grows on yon lilye-lee.'—

LXIV

'I winna yield to a bracken bush,
  Nor yet I will to a brere;
But I would yield to Earl Douglas,   255
  Or Montgomery if he was here.'

LXV

As soon as he knew Montgomery,
  He stuck his sword's point in ground;
The Montgomery was a courteous knight,
  And quickly took him by the hand.   260

LXVI

There was slayne upon the Scottès' side,
  For sooth and certaynlye,
Sir James a Douglas there was slayne,
  That day that he cou'd dye.

LXVII

The Earl of Menteith he was slayne,   265
  And gryselye groan'd on the groun';
Sir Davy Scott, Sir Walter Steward,
  Sir John of Agerstone.

LXVIII

Sir Charlès Murray in that place
  That never a foot would flee;   270
Sir Hew Maxwell, a lord he was,
  With the Douglas did he dee.

LXIX

There was slayne upon the Scottès' side
  For sooth as I you say,
Of four and fifty thousand Scottes   275
  Went but eighteen away.

LXX

There was slayne upon the English side
 For sooth and certaynlye,
A gentle Knight, Sir John Fitzhughe,
 It was the more pitye.   280

LXXI

Sir James Hardbotell there was slayne,
 For him their heartes were sore;
The gentle Lovell there was slayne,
 That the Percy's standard bore.

LXXII

There was slayne upon the English part
 For sooth as I you say,   286
Of ninè thousand English men
 Five hundred came away.

LXXIII

The others slayne were in the field;
 Christ keep their souls from woe!   290
Seeing there was so fewè friends
 Against so many a foe.

LXXIV

Then on the morn they made them bieres
 Of birch and hazell gray:
Many a widow with weeping teares   295
 Their makes they fette away.

LXXV

This fray was fought at Otterbourne,
 Between the night and the day;
Earl Douglas was buried at the bracken bush,
 And the Percy led captive away.   300

LXXVI

Now let us all for the Percy pray
 To Jesu most of might,
To bring his soul to the bliss of heaven,
 For he was a gentle knight.

EDMUND SPENSER

1552–1599

The Cave of Despair

(From *The Faerie Queene*)

Thus beene they parted, *Arthur* on his way
 To seeke his love, and th'other for to fight
With *Unaes* foe, that all her realme did pray.
 But she now weighing the decayed plight,
 And shrunken synewes of her chosen knight, 5
 Would not a while her forward course pursew,
 Ne bring him forth in face of dreadfull fight,
 Till he recovered had his former hew:
For him to be yet weake and wearie well she knew.

So as they traveild, lo they gan espy 10
 An armed knight towards them gallop fast,
 That seemed from some feared foe to fly,
 Or other griesly thing, that him agast.
 Still as he fled, his eye was backward cast,
 As if his feare still followed him behind; 15
 Als flew his steed, as he his bands had brast,
 And with his winged heeles did tread the wind,
As he had beene a fole of *Pegasus* his kind.

Nigh as he drew, they might perceive his head
 To be unarmd, and curld uncombed heares 20
 Upstaring stiffe, dismayd with uncouth dread;
 Nor drop of bloud in all his face appeares
 Nor life in limbe: and to increase his feares
 In fowle reproch of knighthoods faire degree,
 About his neck an hempen rope he weares, 25
 That with his glistring armes does ill agree;
But he of rope or armes has now no memoree.

The *Redcrosse* knight toward him crossed fast,
 To weet, what mister wight was so dismayd:

There him he finds all senceless and aghast,   30
  That of him selfe he seemd to be afrayd;
  Whom hardly he from flying forward stayd,
  Till he these wordes to him deliver might;
  Sir knight, aread who hath ye thus arayd,
  And eke from whom make ye this hasty flight: 35
For never knight I saw in such misseeming plight.

He answerd nought at all, but adding new
  Feare to his first amazment, staring wide
  With stony eyes, and hartlesse hollow hew,
  Astonisht stood, as one that had aspide   40
  Infernall furies, with their chaines untide.
  Him yet againe, and yet againe bespake
  The gentle knight; who nought to him replide,
  But trembling every joynt did inly quake,
And foltring tongue at last these words seemd forth
    to shake.   45

For Gods deare love, Sir knight, do me not stay;
  For loe he comes, he comes fast after mee.
  Eft looking backe would faine have runne away;
  But he him forst to stay, and tellen free
  The secret cause of his perplexitie: 50
  Yet nathemore by his bold hartie speach,
  Could his bloud-frosen hart emboldned bee,
  But through his boldnesse rather feare did reach,
Yet forst, at last he made through silence suddein
    breach.

And am I now in safetie sure (quoth he)   55
  From him, that would have forced me to dye?
  And is the point of death now turnd fro mee,
  That I may tell this haplesse history?
  Feare nought: (quoth he) no daunger now is nye,
  Then shall I you recount a ruefull cace,   60
  (Said he) the which with this unlucky eye
  I late beheld, and had not greater grace
Me reft from it, had bene partaker of the place.

I lately chaunst (Would I had never chaunst)
  With a faire knight to keepen companee,   65
  Sir *Terwin* hight, that well himselfe advaunst
  In all affaires, and was both bold and free,
  But not so happie as mote happie bee:
  He lov'd, as was his lot, a Ladie gent,
  That him againe lov'd in the least degree: 70
  For she was proud, and of too high intent,
And joyd to see her lover languish and lament.

From whom returning sad and comfortlesse,
  As on the way together we did fare,
  We met that villen (God from him me blesse)   75
  That cursed wight, from whom I scapt whyleare,
  A man of hell, that cals himselfe *Despaire*:
  Who first us greets, and after faire areedes
  Of tydings strange, and of adventures rare:
  So creeping close, as Snake in hidden weedes,   80
Inquireth of our states, and of our knightly deedes.

Which when he knew, and felt our feeble harts
  Embost with bale, and bitter byting griefe,
  Which love had launched with his deadly darts,
  With wounding words and termes of foule repriefe
  He pluckt from us all hope of due reliefe,   86
  That earst us held in love of lingring life;
  Then hopelesse hartlesse, gan the cunning thiefe
  Perswade us die, to stint all further strife:
To me he lent this rope, to him a rustie knife.   90

With which sad instrument of hastie death,
  That wofull lover, loathing lenger light,
  A wide way made to let forth living breath.
  But I more fearefull, or more luckie wight,
  Dismayd with that deformed dismall sight,   95
  Fled fast away, halfe dead with dying feare:
  Ne yet assur'd of life by you, Sir knight
  Whose like infirmitie like chaunce may beare:
But God you never let his charmed speeches heare.

How may a man (said he) with idle speach   100
   Be wonne, to spoyle the Castle of his health?
   I wote (quoth he) whom triall late did teach,
   That like would not for all this worldes wealth:
   His subtill tongue, like dropping honny, mealt'th
   Into the hart, and searcheth every vaine,   105
   That ere one be aware, by secret stealth
   His powre is reft, and weaknesse doth remaine.
O never Sir desire to try his guilefull traine.

Certes (said he) hence shall I never rest,   109
   Till I that treachours art have heard and tride;
   And you Sir knight, whose name mote I request,
   Of grace do me unto his cabin guide.
   I that hight *Trevisan* (quoth he) will ride
   Against my liking backe, to doe you grace:
   But nor for gold nor glee will I abide   115
   By you, when ye arrive in that same place;
For lever had I die, then see his deadly face.

Ere long they come, where that same wicked wight
   His dwelling has, low in an hollow cave,
   Farre underneath a craggie clift ypight,   120
   Darke, dolefull, drearie, like a greedie grave,
   That still for carrion carcases doth crave:
   On top whereof aye dwelt the ghastly Owle,
   Shrieking his balefull note, which ever drave
   Farre from that haunt all other chearefull fowle;
And all about it wandring ghostes did waile and
      howle.   126

And all about old stockes and stubs of trees,
   Whereon nor fruit, nor leafe was ever seene,
   Did hang upon the ragged rocky knees;
   On which had many wretches hanged beene,   130
   Whose carcases were scattered on the greene,
   And throwne about the cliffs. Arrived there,
   That bare-head knight for dread and dolefull teene,
   Would faine have fled, ne durst approchen neare,
But th'other forst him stay, and comforted in feare.

That darkesome cave they enter, where they find   136
  That cursed man, low sitting on the ground,
  Musing full sadly in his sullein mind;
  His griesie lockes, long growen, and unbound,
  Disordred hong about his shoulders round,   140
  And hid his face; through which his hollow eyne
  Lookt deadly dull, and stared as astound;
  His raw-bone cheekes through penurie and pine,
Were shronke into his jawes, as he did never dine.

His garment nought but many ragged clouts,   145
  With thornes together pind and patched was,
  The which his naked sides he wrapt abouts;
  And him beside there lay upon the gras
  A drearie corse, whose life away did pas,
  All wallowd in his owne yet luke-warme blood,
  That from his wound yet welled fresh alas;   151
  In which a rustie knife fast fixed stood,
And made an open passage for the gushing flood.

Which piteous spectacle, approving trew
  The wofull tale that *Trevisan* had told,   155
  When as the gentle *Redcrosse* knight did vew,
  With firie zeale he burnt in courage bold,
  Him to avenge, before his bloud were cold,
  And to the villein said, Thou damned wight,
  The author of this fact, we here behold,   160
  What justice can but judge against thee right,
With thine owne bloud to price his bloud, here shed
      in sight?

What franticke fit (quoth he) hath thus distraught
  Thee, foolish man, so rash a doome to give?
  What justice ever other judgement taught,   165
  But he should die, who merites not to live?
  None else to death this man despayring drive,
  But his owne guiltie mind deserving death.
  Is then unjust to each his due to give?
  Or let him die, that loatheth living breath?   170
Or let him die at ease, that liveth here uneath?

Who travels by the wearie wandring way,
   To come unto his wished home in haste,
   And meetes a flood, that doth his passage stay,
   Is not great grace to helpe him over past,   175
   Or free his feet, that in the myre sticke fast?
   Most envious man, that grieves at neighbours good,
   And fond, that joyest in the woe thou hast,
   Why wilt not let him passe, that long hath stood
Upon the banke, yet wilt thy selfe not passe the flood?

He there does now enjoy eternall rest   181
   And happie ease, which thou doest want and crave,
   And further from it daily wanderest:
   What if some litle paine the passage have,   184
   That makes fraile flesh to feare the bitter wave?
   Is not short paine well borne, that brings long ease,
   And layes the soule to sleepe in quiet grave?
   Sleepe after toyle, port after stormie seas,
Ease after warre, death after life does greatly please.

The knight much wondred at his suddeine wit,   190
   And said, The terme of life is limited,
   Ne may a man prolong, nor shorten it;
   The souldier may not move from watchfull sted,
   Nor leave his stand, untill his Captaine bed.
   Who life did limit by almightie doome,   195
   (Quoth he) knowes best the termes established;
   And he, that points the Centonell his roome,
Doth license him depart at sound of morning droome.

Is not his deed, what ever thing is donne,
   In heaven and earth? did not he all create   200
   To die againe? all ends that was begonne.
   Their times in his eternall booke of fate
   Are written sure, and have their certain date.
   Who then can strive with strong necessitie,
   That holds the world in his still changing state,
   Or shunne the death ordayned by destinie?   206
When houre of death is come, let none aske whence,
     nor why.

The lenger life, I wote the greater sin,
    The greater sin, the greater punishment: 209
    All those great battels, which thou boasts to win,
    Through strife, and bloud-shed, and avengement,
    Now praysd, hereafter deare thou shalt repent:
    For life must life, and bloud must bloud repay.
    Is not enough thy evill life forespent?
    For he, that once hath missed the right way,   215
The further he doth goe, the further he doth stray.

Then do no further goe, no further stray,
    But here lie downe, and to thy rest betake,
    Th'ill to prevent, that life ensewen may.
    For what hath life, that may it loved make,   220
    And gives not rather cause it to forsake?
    Feare, sicknesse, age, losse, labour, sorrow, strife,
    Paine, hunger, cold, that makes the hart to quake;
    And ever fickle fortune rageth rife,
All which, and thousands mo do make a loathsome
        life.   225

Thou wretched man, of death hast greatest need,
    If in true ballance thou wilt weigh thy state:
    For never knight, that dared warlike deede,
    More lucklesse disaventures did amate:
    Witnesse the dongeon deepe, wherein of late   230
    Thy life shut up, for death so oft did call;
    And though good lucke prolonged hath thy date,
    Yet death then, would the like mishaps forestall,
Into the which hereafter thou maiest happen fall.

Why then doest thou, O man of sin, desire   235
    To draw thy dayes forth to their last degree?
    Is not the measure of thy sinfull hire
    High heaped up with huge iniquitie,
    Against the day of wrath, to burden thee?
    Is not enough, that to this Ladie milde   240
    Thou falsed hast thy faith with perjurie,
    And sold thy selfe to serve *Duessa* vilde,
With whom in all abuse thou hast thy selfe defilde?

Is not he just, that all this doth behold
From highest heaven, and beares an equall eye?
Shall he thy sins up in his knowledge fold,   246
And guiltie be of thy impietie?
Is not his law, Let every sinner die:
Die shall all flesh? what then must needs be donne,
Is it not better to doe willinglie,   250
Then linger, till the glasse be all out ronne?
Death is the end of woes: die soone, O faeries sonne.

The knight was much enmoved with his speach,
That as a swords point through his hart did perse,
And in his conscience made a secret breach,   255
Well knowing true all, that he did reherse,
And to his fresh remembrance did reverse
The ugly vew of his deformed crimes,
That all his manly powres it did disperse,
As he were charmed with inchaunted rimes,   260
That oftentimes he quakt, and fainted oftentimes.

In which amazement, when the Miscreant
Perceived him to waver weake and fraile,
Whiles trembling horror did his conscience dant,
And hellish anguish did his soule assaile,   265
To drive him to despaire, and quite to quaile,
He shew'd him painted in a table plaine,
The damned ghosts, that doe in torments waile,
And thousand feends that doe them endlesse paine
With fire and brimstone, which for ever shall remaine.

The sight whereof so throughly him dismaid,   271
That nought but death before his eyes he saw,
And ever burning wrath before him laid,
By righteous sentence of th'Almighties law:
Then gan the villein him to overcraw,   275
And brought unto him swords, ropes, poison, fire,
And all that might him to perdition draw;
And bad him choose, what death he would desire:
For death was due to him, that had provokt Gods ire.

But when as none of them he saw him take,   280
   He to him raught a dagger sharpe and keene,
   And gave it him in hand: his hand did quake,
   And tremble like a leaf of Aspin greene,
   And troubled bloud through his pale face was seene
   To come, and goe with tydings from the hart,   285
   As it a running messenger had beene.
   At last resolv'd to worke his finall smart,
He lifted up his hand, that backe againe did start.

Which when as *Una* saw, through every vaine
   The crudled cold ran to her well of life,   290
   As in a swowne: but soone reliv'd againe,
   Out of his hand she snatcht the cursed knife,
   And threw it to the ground, enraged rife,
   And to him said, Fie, fie, faint harted knight,
   What meanest thou by this reprochfull strife?
   Is this the battel, which thou vauntst to fight   296
With that fire-mouthed Dragon, horrible and bright?

Come, come away, fraile, feeble, fleshly wight,
   Ne let vaine words bewitch thy manly hart,   299
   Ne divelish thoughts dismay thy constant spright.
   In heavenly mercies hast thou not a part?
   Why shouldst thou then despeire, that chosen art?
   Where justice growes, there grows eke greater grace,
   The which doth quench the brond of hellish smart,
   And that accurst hand-writing doth deface.   305
Arise, Sir knight arise, and leave this cursed place.

So up he rose, and thence amounted streight.
   Which when the carle beheld, and saw his guest
   Would safe depart, for all his subtill sleight,
   He chose an halter from among the rest,   310
   And with it hung himselfe, unbid unblest.
   But death he could not worke himselfe thereby;
   For thousand times he so himselfe had drest,
   Yet nathelesse it could not doe him die,
Till he should die his last, that is eternally.   315

JOHN MILTON
1608–1674

Sin and Death

(From *Paradise Lost*)

Meanwhile the Adversary of God and Man,
Satan with thoughts inflam'd of highest design,
Puts on swift wings, and towards the gates of Hell
Explores his solitary flight; sometimes   4
He scours the right hand coast, sometimes the left,
Now shaves with level wing the deep, then soars
Up to the fiery concave towring high.
As when far off at sea a fleet descri'd
Hangs in the clouds, by equinoctial winds
Close sailing from Bengala, or the iles   10
Of Ternate and Tidore, whence merchants bring
Their spicy drugs; they on the trading flood
Through the wide Ethiopian to the Cape
Ply stemming nightly toward the pole: so seem'd
Far off the flying Fiend: at last appear   15
Hell bounds high reaching to the horrid roof,
And thrice threefold the gates; three folds were brass,
Three iron, three of adamantine rock,
Impenetrable, impal'd with circling fire,
Yet unconsum'd. Before the gates there sat   20
On either side a formidable shape;
The one seem'd woman to the waist, and fair,
But ended foul in many a scaly fold
Voluminous and vast, a serpent arm'd
With mortal sting: about her middle round   25
A cry of Hell-hounds never ceasing bark'd
With wide Cerberean mouths full loud, and rung
A hideous peal: yet, when they list, would creep,
If aught disturb'd their noise, into her womb,   29
And kennel there, yet there still bark'd and howl'd,
Within unseen. Far less abhorr'd than these
Vex'd Scylla bathing in the sea that parts
Calabria from the hoarse Trinacrian shore:

Nor uglier follow the night-hag, when call'd
In secret, riding through the air she comes   35
Lur'd with the smell of infant blood, to dance
With Lapland witches, while the labouring moon
Eclipses at their charms. The other shape,
If shape it might be call'd that shape had none
Distinguishable in member, joint, or limb,   40
Or substance might be call'd that shadow seem'd,
For each seem'd either; black it stood as night,
Fierce as ten furies, terrible as Hell,
And shook a dreadful dart; what seem'd his head
The likeness of a kingly crown had on.   45
Satan was now at hand, and from his seat
The monster moving onward came as fast
With horrid strides, Hell trembled as he strode.
Th' undaunted Fiend what this might be admir'd,
Admir'd, not fear'd; God and his Son except,   50
Created thing naught valu'd he nor shunn'd;
And with disdainful look thus first began.

  'Whence and what art thou, execrable shape,
That dar'st, though grim and terrible, advance
Thy miscreated front athwart my way   55
To yonder gates? Through them I mean to pass,
That be assur'd, without leave askt of thee:
Retire, or taste thy folly, and learn by proof,
Hell-born, not to contend with spirits of Heav'n.'

  To whom the goblin full of wrath repli'd;   60

  'Art thou that traitor Angel, art thou he,
Who first broke peace in Heav'n and faith, till then
Unbrok'n; and in proud rebellious arms,
Drew after him the third part of Heav'ns sons   64
Conjur'd against the Highest; for which both thou
And they outcast from God, are here condemn'd
To waste eternal days in woe and pain?
And reck'n'st thou thyself with spirits of Heav'n,
Hell-doom'd, and breath'st defiance here and scorn
Where I reign king, and to enrage thee more,   70
Thy king and lord? Back to thy punishment,
False fugitive, and to thy speed add wings,

Lest with a whip of scorpions I pursue
Thy ling'ring, or with one stroke of this dart   74
Strange horror seize thee, and pangs unfelt before.'
  So spake the grisly terror, and in shape,
So speaking and so threat'ning, grew tenfold
More dreadful and deform: on th' other side,
Incenst with indignation Satan stood
Unterrifi'd; and like a comet burn'd,   80
That fires the length of Ophiuchus huge
In th' Arctic sky, and from his horrid hair
Shakes pestilence and war. Each at the head
Levell'd his deadly aim; their fatal hands
No second stroke intend, and such a frown   85
Each cast at th' other, as when two black clouds
With Heav'ns artillery fraught, come rattling on
Over the Caspian, then stand front to front
Hov'ring a space, till winds the signal blow
To join their dark encounter in mid air: 90
So frown'd the mighty combatants, that Hell
Grew darker at their frown, so matcht they stood;
For never but once more was either like
To meet so great a foe: and now great deeds
Had been achiev'd, whereof all Hell had rung,   95
Had not the snaky sorceress that sat
Fast by Hell-gate, and kept the fatal key,
Ris'n, and with hideous outcry rush'd between.
'O father, what intends thy hand,' she cri'd,
'Against thy only son? What fury, O son,   100
Possesses thee to bend that mortal dart
Against thy father's head? and know'st for whom?
For him who sits above and laughs the while
At thee ordain'd his drudge, to execute
Whate'er his wrath, which he calls justice, bids;   105
His wrath which one day will destroy ye both.'
  She spake, and at her words the hellish pest
Forbore, then these to her Satan return'd:
'So strange thy outcry, and thy words so strange
Thou interposest, that my sudden hand   110
Prevented spares to tell thee yet by deeds

What it intends; till first I know of thee,
What thing thou art, thus double-form'd, and why
In this infernal vale first met thou call'st
Me father, and that phantasm call'st my son?   115
I know thee not, nor ever saw till now
Sight more detestable than him and thee.'
    T' whom thus the portress of Hell-gate repli'd.
    'Hast thou forgot me then, and do I seem
Now in thine eye so foul? once deem'd so fair   120
In Heav'n, when at th' assembly, and in sight
Of all the seraphim with thee combin'd
In bold conspiracy against Heav'ns King,
All on a sudden miserable pain
Surpris'd thee, dim thine eyes, and dizzy swam   125
In darkness, while thy head flames thick and fast
Threw forth; till on the left side op'ning wide,
Likest to thee in shape and count'nance bright,
Then shining heav'nly fair, a goddess arm'd,
Out of thy head I sprung: amazement seiz'd   130
All th' host of Heav'n; back they recoil'd afraid
At first, and call'd me SIN: and for a sign
Portentous held me; but familiar grown,
I pleas'd, and with attractive graces won
The most averse, thee chiefly, who full oft   135
Thyself in me thy perfect image viewing
Becam'st enamour'd, and such joy thou took'st
With me in secret, that my womb conceiv'd
A growing burden. Meanwhile war arose,   139
And fields were fought in Heav'n; wherein remain'd
(For what could else) to our Almighty Foe
Clear victory, to our part loss and rout
Through all the empyrean: down they fell
Driv'n headlong from the pitch of Heaven, down
Into this deep, and in the general fall   145
I also; at which time this powerful key
Into my hand was giv'n, with charge to keep
These gates for ever shut, which none can pass
Without my op'ning. Pensive here I sat
Alone, but long I sat not, till my womb   150

Pregnant by thee, and now excessive grown,
Prodigious motion felt and rueful throes.
At last this odious offspring whom thou seest
Thine own begotten, breaking violent way   154
Tore through my entrails, that with fear and pain
Distorted, all my nether shape thus grew
Transform'd: but he my inbred enemy
Forth issu'd, brandishing his fatal dart,
Made to destroy: I fled, and cri'd out, DEATH;
Hell trembl'd at the hideous name, and sigh'd   160
From all her caves, and back resounded DEATH.
I fled, but he pursu'd (though more, it seems,
Inflam'd with lust than rage) and swifter far,
Me overtook his mother all dismay'd,
And in embraces forcible and foul   165
Ingendring with me, of that rape begot
These yelling monsters that with ceaseless cry
Surround me, as thou saw'st, hourly conceiv'd
And hourly born, with sorrow infinite
To me; for when they list into the womb   170
That bred them they return, and howl and gnaw
My bowels, their repast; then bursting forth
Afresh, with conscious terrors vex me round,
That rest or intermission none I find.
Before mine eyes in opposition sits   175
Grim Death my son and foe, who sets them on,
And me his parent would full soon devour
For want of other prey, but that he knows
His end with mine involv'd; and knows that I
Should prove a bitter morsel, and his bane,   180
Whenever that shall be; so Fate pronounc'd.
But thou O father, I forewarn thee, shun
His deadly arrow; neither vainly hope
To be invulnerable in those bright arms,
Though temper'd heav'nly; for that mortal dint,
Save he who reigns above, none can resist.'   186
  She finish'd, and the subtle Fiend his lore
Soon learn'd, now milder, and thus answer'd smooth.
  'Dear daughter, since thou claim'st me for thy sire,

And my fair son here show'st me, the dear pledge
Of dalliance had with thee in Heav'n, and joys   191
Then sweet, now sad to mention, through dire change
Befall'n us unforeseen, unthought of, know
I come no enemy, but to set free
From out this dark and dismal house of pain,   195
Both him and thee, and all the heav'nly host
Of spirits that in our just pretences arm'd
Fell with us from on high: from them I go
This uncouth errand sole, and one for all
Myself expose, with lonely steps to tread   200
Th' unfounded deep, and through the void immense
To search with wand'ring quest a place foretold
Should be and by concurring signs, ere now
Created vast and round; a place of bliss
In the purlieus of Heav'n, and therein plac't   205
A race of upstart creatures, to supply
Perhaps our vacant room, though more remov'd,
Lest Heav'n surcharg'd with potent multitude
Might hap to move new broils: be this or aught
Than this more secret now design'd, I haste   210
To know, and this once known, shall soon return,
And bring ye to the place where thou and Death
Shall dwell at ease, and up and down unseen
Wing silently the buxom air, imbalm'd
With odours; there ye shall be fed and fill'd   215
Immeasurably, all things shall be your prey.'
      He ceas'd, for both seem'd highly pleas'd, and
            Death
Grinn'd horrible a gastly smile, to hear
His famine should be fill'd, and blest his maw
Destin'd to that good hour: no less rejoic'd   220
His mother bad, and thus bespake her sire.
   'The key of this infernal pit by due,
And by command of Heav'ns all-powerful King
I keep, by him forbidden to unlock
These adamantine gates; against all force   225
Death ready stands to interpose his dart,
Fearless to be o'ermatcht by living might.

But what owe I to his commands above
Who hates me, and hath hither thrust me down
Into this gloom of Tartarus profound,   230
To sit in hateful office here confin'd,
Inhabitant of Heav'n, and heav'nly-born,
Here in perpetual agony and pain,
With terrors and with clamors compast round
Of mine own brood, that on my bowels feed?   235
Thou art my father, thou my author, thou
My being gav'st me; whom should I obey
But thee, whom follow? thou wilt bring me soon
To that new world of light and bliss, among
The gods who live at ease, where I shall reign   240
At thy right hand voluptuous, as beseems
Thy daughter and thy darling, without end.'
   Thus saying, from her side the fatal key
Sad instrument of all our woe, she took;
And towards the gate rolling her bestial train,   245
Forthwith the huge portcullis high up drew,
Which but herself not all the Stygian powers
Could once have mov'd: then in the keyhole turns
Th' intricate wards, and every bolt and bar,
Of massy iron or solid rock with ease   250
Unfast'ns: on a sudden op'n fly,
With impetuous recoil and jarring sound
Th' infernal doors, and on their hinges grate
Harsh thunder, that the lowest bottom shook
Of Erebus. She op'nd, but to shut   255
Excell'd her power; the gates wide op'n stood,
That with extended wings a banner'd host
Under spread ensigns marching might pass through
With horse and chariots rankt in loose array;
So wide they stood, and like a furnace-mouth   260
Cast forth redounding smoke and ruddy flame.

JOHN DRYDEN
1631–1700

Cymon and Iphigenia
Poeta loquitur,

Old as I am, for ladies' love unfit,
The pow'r of beauty I remember yet,
Which once inflamed my soul, and still inspires my
    wit.
If Love be folly, the severe Divine
Has felt that folly, tho' he censures mine;   5
Pollutes the pleasures of a chaste embrace,
Acts what I write, and propagates in grace
With riotous excess, a priestly race:
Suppose him free, and that I forge th' offence,
He showed the way, perverting first my sense: 10
In malice witty, and with venom fraught,
He makes me speak the things I never thought.
Compute the gains of his ungoverned zeal;
Ill suits his cloth the praise of railing well!
The world will think that what we loosely write   15
Tho' now arraigned, he read, with some delight
Because he seems to chew the cud again,
When his broad comment makes the text too plain,
And teaches more in one explaining page,
Than all the double meanings of the stage.   20
    What needs he paraphrase on what we mean?
We were at worst but wanton; he's obscene.
I, nor my fellows, nor myself excuse;
But Love's the subject of the comick muse:
Nor can we write without it, nor would you   25
A tale of only dry instruction view;
Nor Love is always of a vicious kind,
But oft to virtuous acts inflames the mind,
Awakes the sleepy vigour of the soul,
And, brushing o'er, adds motion to the pool.   30
Love, studious how to please, improves our parts,
With polish'd manners, and adorns with arts.

Love first invented verse, and formed the rhime,
The motion measured, harmonized the chime;
To lib'ral acts, inlarged the narrow-souled,   35
Softened the fierce, and made the coward bold:
The world when wast, he peopled with increase,
And warring nations reconciled in peace.
Ormond, the first, and all the fair may find
In this one legend to their fame designed,   40
When beauty fires the blood, how Love exalts the
    mind.
In that sweet isle where Venus keeps her court,
And every grace, and all the loves resort;
Where either sex is formed of softer earth,
And takes the bent of pleasure from their birth;   45
There lived a Cyprian lord, above the rest
Wise, wealthy, with a numerous issue blest.
  But as no gift of fortune is sincere,
Was only wanting in a worthy heir:
His eldest born, a goodly youth to view,   50
Excelled the rest in shape, and outward show;
Fair, tall, his limbs with due proportion joined,
But of a heavy, dull, degenerate mind.
His soul belied the features of his face;
Beauty was there, but beauty in disgrace.   55
A clownish mien, a voice with rustic sound,
And stupid eyes, that ever loved the ground.
He looked like Nature's error; as the mind
And body were not of a piece designed,
But made for two, and by mistake in one were joined.
  The ruling rod, the father's forming care,   61
Were exercised in vain on wit's despair;
The more informed the less he understood,
And deeper sunk by floundering in the mud.
Now scorned of all, and grown the public shame,
The people from Galesus changed his name,   66
And Cymon called, which signifies a brute;
So well his name did with his nature suit.
  His father, when he found his labour lost,
And care employed that answered not the cost,   70

Chose an ungrateful object to remove,
And loathed to see what Nature made him love;
So to his country farm the fool confined:
Rude work well suited with a rustic mind.
Thus to the wilds the sturdy Cymon went,　　　75
A squire among the swains, and pleased with banishment.
His corn and cattle were his only care,
And his supreme delight a country fair.
　It happened on a summer's holiday,
That to the greenwood shade he took his way;　　80
For Cymon shunned the church, and used not much to pray.
His quarter-staff, which he could ne'er forsake,
Hung half before, and half behind his back.
He trudged along, unknowing what he sought,
And whistled as he went, for want of thought.　　85
　By chance conducted, or by thirst constrained,
The deep recesses of the grove he gained;
Where in a plain, defended by the wood,
Crept through the matted grass a crystal flood,
By which an alabaster fountain stood:　　90
And on the margin of the fount was laid
(Attended by her slaves) a sleeping maid;
Like Dian and her nymphs, when, tired with sport,
To rest by cool Eurotas they resort:
The dame herself the goddess well expressed,　　95
Not more distinguished by her purple vest,
Than by the charming features of her face,
And even in slumber a superior grace:
Her comely limbs composed with decent care,
Her body shaded with a slight cymar;　　100
Her bosom to the view was only bare:
Where two beginning paps were scarcely spied,
For yet their places were but signified:
The fanning wind upon her bosom blows,
To meet the fanning wind the bosom rose;　　105
The fanning wind and purling streams continue her repose.

The fool of Nature stood with stupid eyes
And gaping mouth, that testified surprise,
Fixed on her face, nor could remove his sight,
New as he was to love, and novice in delight: 110
Long mute he stood, and leaning on his staff,
His wonder witnessed with an idiot laugh;
Then would have spoke, but by his glimmering sense
First found his want of words, and feared offence:
Doubted for what he was he should be known, 115
By his clown accent, and his country tone.
    Through the rude chaos thus the running light
Shot the first ray that pierced the native night:
Then day and darkness in the mass were mixed,
Till gathered in a globe, the beams were fixed: 120
Last shone the sun, who radiant in his sphere
Illumined heaven and earth, and rolled around the
        year.
So reason in this brutal soul began:
Love made him first suspect he was a man;
Love made him doubt his broad barbarian sound;
By Love his want of words and wit he found: 126
That sense of want prepared the future way
To knowledge, and disclosed the promise of a day.
    What not his father's care, nor tutor's art
Could plant with pains in his unpolished heart, 130
The best instructor Love at once inspired,
As barren grounds to fruitfulness are fired;
Love taught him shame, and shame with Love at
        strife
Soon taught the sweet civilities of life;
His gross material soul at once could find 135
Somewhat in her excelling all her kind:
Exciting a desire till then unknown,
Somewhat unfound, or found in her alone.
This made the first impression in his mind,
Above, but just above, the brutal kind. 140
For beasts can like, but not distinguish too,
Nor their own liking by reflection know;
Nor why they like or this or t'other face,

Or judge of this or that peculiar grace,
But love in gross, and stupidly admire;   145
As flies allured by light, approach the fire.
Thus our man-beast advancing by degrees
First likes the whole, then separates what he sees;
On several parts a several praise bestows,
The ruby lips, the well-proportioned nose,   150
The snowy skin, in raven-glossy hair,
The dimpled cheek, the forehead rising fair,
And even in sleep itself a smiling air.
From thence his eyes descending viewed the rest,
Her plump round arms, white hands, and heaving
          breast   155
Long on the last he dwelt, though every part
A pointed arrow sped to pierce his heart.
   Thus in a trice a judge of beauty grown,
(A judge erected from a country clown)
He longed to see her eyes, in slumber hid,   160
And wished his own could pierce within the lid:
He would have waked her, but restrained his thought,
And love new-born the first good manners taught.
An awful fear his ardent wish withstood,
Nor durst disturb the goddess of the wood;   165
For such she seemed by her celestial face,
Excelling all the rest of human race:
And things divine, by common sense he knew,
Must be devoutly seen at distant view:
So checking his desire, with trembling heart   170
Gazing he stood, nor would, nor could depart;
Fixed as a pilgrim wildered in his way,
Who dares not stir by night for fear to stray;
But stands with awful eyes to watch the dawn of day.
   At length awaking, Iphigene the fair   175
(So was the beauty called who caused his care)
Unclosed her eyes, and double day revealed,
While those of all her slaves in sleep were sealed.
   The slavering cudden, propped upon his staff,
Stood ready gaping with a grinning laugh,   180
To welcome her awake, nor durst begin

To speak, but wisely kept the fool within.
Then she: What make you Cymon here alone?
(For Cymon's name was round the country known,
Because descended of a noble race,   185
And for a soul ill sorted with his face.)

But still the sot stood silent with surprise,
With fixed regard on her new opened eyes,
And in his breast received the envenomed dart,
A tickling pain that pleased amid the smart.   190
But conscious of her form, with quick distrust
She saw his sparkling eyes, and feared his brutal lust:
This to prevent, she waked her sleepy crew,
And rising hasty took a short adieu.

Then Cymon first his rustic voice essayed,   195
With proffered service to the parting maid
To see her safe; his hand she long denied,
But took at length, ashamed of such a guide.
So Cymon led her home, and leaving there,
No more would to his country clowns repair,   200
But sought his father's house, with better mind,
Refusing in the farm to be confined.

The father wondered at the son's return,
And knew not whether to rejoice or mourn;
But doubtfully received, expecting still   205
To learn the secret causes of his altered will.
Nor was he long delayed; the first request
He made, was like his brothers to be dressed,
And, as his birth required, above the rest.

With ease his suit was granted by his sire,   210
Distinguishing his heir by rich attire:
His body thus adorned, he next designed
With liberal arts to cultivate his mind:
He sought a tutor of his own accord,
And studied lessons he before abhorred.   215

Thus the man-child advanced, and learned so fast,
That in short time his equals he surpassed:
His brutal manners from his breast exiled,
His mien he fashioned, and his tongue he filed;
In every exercise of all admired,   220

He seemed, nor only seemed, but was inspired:
Inspired by Love, whose business is to please;
He rode, he fenced, he moved with graceful ease
More famed for sense, for courtly carriage more,
Than for his brutal folly known before.   225
    What then of altered Cymon shall we say,
But that the fire which choked in ashes lay,
A load too heavy for his soul to move,
Was upward blown below, and brushed away by love?
Love made an active progress through his mind,   230
The dusky parts he cleared, the gross refined;
The drowsy waked; and as he went impressed
The Maker's image on the human beast.
Thus was the man amended by desire,
And, though he loved perhaps with too much fire,
His father all his faults with reason scanned,   236
And liked an error of the better hand;
Excused the excess of passion in his mind,
By flames too fierce, perhaps too much refined:
So Cymon, since his sire indulged his will,   240
Impetuous loved, and would be Cymon still;
Galesus he disowned, and chose to bear
The name of Fool confirmed and bishoped by the
        fair.
    To Cipseus by his friends his suit he moved,
Cipseus the father of the fair he loved: 245
But he was pre-engaged by former ties,
While Cymon was endeavouring to be wise:
And Iphigene, obliged by former vows,
Had given her faith to wed a foreign spouse:
Her sire and she to Rhodian Pasimond,   250
Though both repenting, were by promise bound,
Nor could retract; and thus, as Fate decreed,
Though better loved, he spoke too late to speed.
    The doom was past, the ship already sent
Did all his tardy diligence prevent: 255
Sighed to herself the fair unhappy maid,
While stormy Cymon thus in secret said:
The time is come for Iphigene to find

The miracle she wrought upon my mind;
Her charms have made me man, her ravished love
In rank shall place me with the blessed above.   261
For mine by love, by force she shall be mine,
Or death, if force should fail, shall finish my design.
    Resolved he said: and rigged with speedy care
A vessel strong, and well equipped for war.   265
The secret ship with chosen friends he stored,
And bent to die, or conquer, went aboard.
Ambushed he lay behind the Cyprian shore,
Waiting the sail that all his wishes bore;
Nor long expected, for the following tide   270
Sent out the hostile ship and beauteous bride.
    To Rhodes the rival bark directly steered,
When Cymon sudden at her back appeared,
And stopped her flight: then standing on his prow
In haughty terms he thus defied the foe: 275
Or strike your sails at summons, or prepare
To prove the last extremities of war.
Thus warned, the Rhodians for the fight provide;
Already were the vessels side by side,   279
These obstinate to save, and those to seize the bride.
But Cymon soon his crooked grapples cast,
Which with tenacious hold his foes embraced,
And armed with sword and shield, amid the press he
    passed.
Fierce was the fight, but hastening to his prey,
By force the furious lover freed his way: 285
Himself alone dispersed the Rhodian crew,
The weak disdained, the valiant overthrew;
Cheap conquest for his following friends remained,
He reaped the field, and they but only gleaned.
    His victory confessed, the foes retreat,   290
And cast their weapons at the victor's feet.
Whom thus he cheered: O Rhodian youth, I fought
For love alone, nor other booty sought;
Your lives are safe; your vessel I resign,
Yours be your own, restoring what is mine: 295
In Iphigene I claim my rightful due,

Robbed by my rival, and detained by you:
Your Pasimond a lawless bargain drove,
The parent could not sell the daughter's love;
Or if he could, my love disdains the laws,   300
And like a king by conquest gains his cause:
Where arms take place, all other pleas are vain;
Love taught me force, and force shall love maintain.
You, what by strength you could not keep, release
And at an easy ransom buy your peace.   305

  Fear on the conquered side soon signed the accord,
And Iphigene to Cymon was restored.
While to his arms the blushing bride he took,
To seeming sadness she composed her look;
As if by force subjected to his will,   310
Though pleased, dissembling, and a woman still.
And, for she wept, he wiped her falling tears,
And prayed her to dismiss her empty fears;
For yours I am, he said, and have deserved
Your love much better, whom so long I served,   315
Than he to whom your formal father tied
Your vows; and sold a slave, not sent a bride.
Thus while he spoke he seized the willing prey,
As Paris bore the Spartan spouse away: 319
Faintly she screamed, and even her eyes confessed
She rather would be thought, than was distressed.

  Who now exults but Cymon in his mind?
Vain hopes and empty joys of human kind,
Proud of the present, to the future blind!
Secure of fate, while Cymon ploughs the sea,   325
And steers to Candy with his conquered prey.
Scarce the third glass of measured hours was run,
When like a fiery meteor sunk the sun;
The promise of a storm; the shifting gales
Forsake by fits and fill the flagging sails: 330
Hoarse murmurs of the main from far were heard,
And night came on, not by degrees prepared,
But all at once; at once the winds arise,
The thunders roll, the forky lightning flies:
In vain the master issues out commands,   335

In vain the trembling sailors ply their hands:
The tempest unforeseen prevents their care,
And from the first they labour in despair.
The giddy ship, betwixt the winds and tides,
Forced back, and forwards, in a circle rides,   340
Stunned with the different blows; then shoots amain
Till counterbuffed she stops, and sleeps again.
Not more aghast the proud archangel fell,
Plunged from the height of Heaven to deepest Hell,
Than stood the lover of his love possessed,   345
Now cursed the more, the more he had been blessed;
More anxious for her danger than his own,
Death he defies; but would be lost alone.
　　Sad Iphigene to womanish complaints
Adds pious prayers, and wearies all the saints;   350
Even if she could, her love she would repent,
But since she cannot, dreads the punishment:
Her forfeit faith and Pasimond betrayed
Are ever present, and her crime upbraid.
She blames herself, nor blames her lover less,   355
Augments her anger as her fears increase;
From her own back the burden would remove,
And lays the load on his ungoverned love,
Which interposing durst in Heaven's despite
Invade, and violate another's right: 360
The powers incensed awhile deferred his pain,
And made him master of his vows in vain:
But soon they punished his presumptuous pride,
That for his daring enterprise she died,
Who rather not resisted, than complied.   365
　　Then impotent of mind, with altered sense,
She hugged the offender, and forgave the offence,
Sex to the last: meantime with sails declined,
The wandering vessel drove before the wind:
Tossed, and retossed, aloft, and then alow;   370
Nor port they seek, nor certain course they know,
But every moment wait the coming blow.
Thus blindly driven, by breaking day they viewed
The land before them, and their fears renewed;

The land was welcome, but the tempest bore   375
The threatened ship against a rocky shore.
  A winding bay was near; to this they bent,
And just escaped; their force already spent.
Secure from storms, and panting from the sea,
The land unknown at leisure they survey;   380
And saw (but soon their sickly sight withdrew)
The rising towers of Rhodes at distant view;
And cursed the hostile shore of Pasimond,
Saved from the seas, and shipwrecked on the ground.
  The frightened sailors tried their strength in vain
To turn the stern, and tempt the stormy main;   386
But the stiff wind withstood the labouring oar,
And forced them forward on the fatal shore!
The crooked keel now bites the Rhodian strand,
And the ship moored constrains the crew to land:
Yet still they might be safe, because unknown;   391
But as ill fortune seldom comes alone,
The vessel they dismissed was driven before,
Already sheltered on their native shore;
Known each, they know: but each with change of
     cheer;   395
The vanquished side exults; the victors fear;
Not them but theirs, made prisoners ere they fight,
Despairing conquest, and deprived of flight.
  The country rings around with loud alarms,
And raw in fields the rude militia swarms;   400
Mouths without hands; maintained at vast expense,
In peace a charge, in war a weak defence:
Stout once a month they march, a blustering band,
And ever, but in times of need, at hand:
This was the morn when, issuing on the guard,   405
Drawn up in rank and file they stood prepared
Of seeming arms to make a short essay,
Then hasten to be drunk, the business of the day.
  The cowards would have fled, but that they knew
Themselves so many, and their foes so few;   410
But crowding on, the last the first impel;
Till overborne with weight the Cyprians fell.

Cymon enslaved, who first the war begun,
And Iphigene once more is lost and won.

Deep in a dungeon was the captive cast, 415
Deprived of day, and held in fetters fast;
His life was only spared at their request,
Whom taken he so nobly had released:
But Iphigenia was the ladies care,
Each in their turn addressed to treat the fair; 420
While Pasimond and his the nuptial feast prepare.

Her secret soul to Cymon was inclined,
But she must suffer what her fates assigned;
So passive is the church of womankind.
What worse to Cymon could his fortune deal, 425
Rolled to the lowest spoke of all her wheel?
It rested to dismiss the downward weight,
Or raise him upward to his former height;
The latter pleased; and love (concerned the most)
Prepared the amends, for what by love he lost. 430

The sire of Pasimond had left a son,
Though younger, yet for courage early known,
Ormisda called; to whom, by promise tied,
A Rhodian beauty was the destined bride:
Cassandra was her name, above the rest 435
Renowned for birth, with fortune amply blessed.
Lysymachus, who ruled the Rhodian state,
Was then by choice their annual magistrate:
He loved Cassandra too with equal fire,
But fortune had not favoured his desire; 440
Crossed by her friends, by her not disapproved,
Nor yet preferred, or like Ormisda loved:
So stood the affair: some little hope remained,
That should his rival chance to lose, he gained.

Meantime young Pasimond his marriage pressed,
Ordained the nuptial day, prepared the feast; 446
And frugally resolved (the charge to shun,
Which would be double should he wed alone)
To join his brother's bridal with his own.

Lysymachus oppressed with mortal grief 450
Received the news, and studied quick relief:

The fatal day approached: if force were used,
The magistrate his public trust abused;
To justice liable, as law required;
For when his office ceased, his power expired: 455
While power remained, the means were in his hand
By force to seize, and then forsake the land:
Betwixt extremes he knew not how to move,
A slave to fame, but more a slave to love:
Restraining others, yet himself not free,   460
Made impotent by power, debased by dignity!
Both sides he weighed: but after much debate,
The man prevailed above the magistrate.

   Love never fails to master what he finds,
But works a different way in different minds,   465
The fool enlightens, and the wise he blinds.
This youth proposing to possess, and scape,
Began in murder, to conclude in rape:
Unpraised by me, though Heaven sometime may bless
An impious act with undeserved success: 470
The great, it seems, are privileged alone
To punish all injustice but their own.
But here I stop, not daring to proceed,
Yet blush to flatter an unrighteous deed:
For crimes are but permitted, not decreed.   475

   Resolved on force, his wit the prætor bent
To find the means that might secure the event;
Nor long he laboured, for his lucky thought
In captive Cymon found the friend he sought.
The example pleased: the cause and crime the same;
An injured lover and a ravished dame.   481
How much he durst he knew by what he dared;
The less he had to lose, the less he cared
To menage loathsome life when love was the reward.

   This pondered well, and fixed on his intent,   485
In depth of night he for the prisoner sent;
In secret sent, the public view to shun.
Then with a sober smile he thus begun:
The powers above, who bounteously bestow
Their gifts and graces on mankind below,   490

Yet prove our merit first, nor blindly give
To such as are not worthy to receive:
For valour and for virtue they provide
Their due reward, but first they must be tried:
These fruitful seeds within your mind they sowed;
'Twas yours to improve the talent they bestowed:
They gave you to be born of noble kind, 497
They gave you love to lighten up your mind
And purge the grosser parts; they gave you care
To please, and courage to deserve the fair. 500
   Thus far they tried you, and by proof they found
The grain entrusted in a grateful ground:
But still the great experiment remained,
They suffered you to lose the prize you gained;
That you might learn the gift was theirs alone, 505
And, when restored, to them the blessing own.
Restored it soon will be; the means prepared,
The difficulty smoothed, the danger shared:
Be but yourself, the care to me resign,
Then Iphigene is yours, Cassandra mine. 510
Your rival Pasimond pursues your life,
Impatient to revenge his ravished wife,
But yet not his; to-morrow is behind,
And love our fortunes in one band has joined:
Two brothers are our foes; Ormisda mine, 515
As much declared, as Pasimond is thine:
To-morrow must their common vows be tied;
With love to friend, and fortune for our guide,
Let both resolve to die, or each redeem a bride.
   Right I have none, nor hast thou much to plead;
'Tis force when done must justify the deed: 521
Our task performed, we next prepare for flight;
And let the losers talk in vain of right:
We with the fair will sail before the wind;
If they are grieved, I leave the laws behind. 525
Speak thy resolves; if now thy courage droop,
Despair in prison and abandon hope;
But if thou darest in arms thy love regain,
(For liberty without thy love were vain:)

Then second my design to seize the prey,   530
Or lead to second rape, for well thou knowest the
                    way.
   Said Cymon, overjoyed, Do thou propose
The means to fight, and only show the foes;
For from the first, when love had fired my mind,
Resolved I left the care of life behind.   535
   To this the bold Lysymachus replied,
Let Heaven be neuter, and the sword decide:
The spousals are prepared, already play
The minstrels, and provoke the tardy day:
By this the brides are waked, their grooms are dressed;
All Rhodes is summoned to the nuptial feast,   541
All but myself, the sole unbidden guest.
Unbidden though I am, I will be there,
And, joined by thee, intend to joy the fair.
   Now hear the rest; when day resigns the light, 545
And cheerful torches gild the jolly night,
Be ready at my call; my chosen few
With arms administered shall aid thy crew.
Then entering unexpected will we seize
Our destined prey, from men dissolved in ease,   550
By wine disabled, unprepared for fight;
And hastening to the seas suborn our flight:
The seas are ours, for I command the fort,
A ship well manned expects us in the port:
If they, or if their friends, the prize contest,   555
Death shall attend the man who dares resist.
   It pleased! the prisoner to his hold retired,
His troop with equal emulation fired,
All fixed to fight, and all their wonted work required.
   The sun arose; the streets were thronged around,
The palace opened, and the posts were crowned: 561
The double bridegroom at the door attends
The expected spouse, and entertains the friends:
They meet, they lead to church; the priests invoke
The powers, and feed the flames with fragrant smoke:
This done they feast, and at the close of night   566
By kindled torches vary their delight,

These lead the lively dance, and those the brimming
    bowls invite.
   Now, at the appointed place and hour assigned,
With souls resolved the ravishers were joined: 570
Three bands are formed: the first is sent before
To favour the retreat and guard the shore:
The second at the palace gate is placed,
And up the lofty stairs ascend the last:
A peaceful troop they seem with shining vests,   575
But coats of mail beneath secure their breasts.
   Dauntless they enter, Cymon at their head,
And find the feast renewed, the table spread:
Sweet voices mixed with instrumental sounds   579
Ascend the vaulted roof, the vaulted roof rebounds.
When like the harpies rushing through the hall
The sudden troop appears, the tables fall,
Their smoking load is on the pavement thrown;
Each ravisher prepares to seize his own:
The brides invaded with a rude embrace   585
Shriek out for aid, confusion fills the place:
Quick to redeem the prey their plighted lords
Advance, the palace gleams with shining swords.
   But late is all defence, and succour vain;
The rape is made, the ravishers remain: 590
Two sturdy slaves were only sent before
To bear the purchased prize in safety to the shore.
The troop retires, the lovers close the rear,
With forward faces not confessing fear: 594
Backward they move, but scorn their pace to mend,
Then seek the stairs, and with slow haste descend.
   Fierce Pasimond, their passage to prevent,
Thrust full on Cymon's back in his descent,
The blade returned unbathed, and to the handle bent:
Stout Cymon soon remounts, and cleft in two   600
His rival's head with one descending blow:
And as the next in rank Ormisda stood,
He turned the point; the sword inured to blood
Bored his unguarded breast, which poured a purple
    flood.

With vowed revenge the gathering crowd pursues,
The ravishers turn head, the fight renews;   606
The hall is heaped with corps; the sprinkled gore
Besmears the walls, and floats the marble floor.
Dispersed at length the drunken squadron flies,
The victors to their vessel bear the prize,   610
And hear behind loud groans, and lamentable cries.

The crew with merry shouts their anchors weigh,
Then ply their oars, and brush the buxom sea,
While troops of gathered Rhodians crowd the quay.
What should the people do, when left alone?   615
The governor and government are gone;
The public wealth to foreign parts conveyed;
Some troops disbanded, and the rest unpaid.
Rhodes is the sovereign of the sea no more;
Their ships unrigged, and spent their naval store;
They neither could defend, nor can pursue,   621
But grind their teeth, and cast a helpless view:
In vain with darts a distant war they try,
Short, and more short, the missive weapons fly.
Meanwhile the ravishers their crimes enjoy,   625
And flying sails and sweeping oars employ:
The cliffs of Rhodes in little space are lost;
Jove's Isle they seek; nor Jove denies his coast.

In safety landed on the Candian shore,
With generous wines their spirits they restore;   630
There Cymon with his Rhodian friend resides,
Both court and wed at once the willing brides.
A war ensues, the Cretans own their cause,
Stiff to defend their hospitable laws:
Both parties lose by turns; and neither wins,   635
Till peace propounded by a truce begins.
The kindred of the slain forgive the deed,
But a short exile must for show precede;
The term expired, from Candia they remove;
And happy each at home enjoys his love.   640

THOMAS PARNELL
1679–1718

The Hermit

Far in a wild, unknown to public view,
From youth to age a reverend hermit grew;
The moss his bed, the cave his humble cell,
His food the fruits, his drink the crystal well:
Remote from man, with God he pass'd the days,   5
Prayer all his business, all his pleasure praise.

  A life so sacred, such serene repose,
Seem'd heaven itself, till one suggestion rose;
That vice should triumph, virtue vice obey,
This sprung some doubt of Providence's sway: 10
His hopes no more a certain prospect boast,
And all the tenour of his soul is lost.
So when a smooth expanse receives imprest
Calm nature's image on its watery breast,
Down bend the banks, the trees depending grow,   15
And skies beneath with answering colours glow:
But if a stone the gentle scene divide,
Swift ruffling circles curl on every side,
And glimmering fragments of a broken sun,
Banks, trees, and skies, in thick disorder run.   20

  To clear this doubt, to know the world by sight,
To find if books, or swains, report it right,
(For yet by swains alone the world he knew,
Whose feet came wandering o'er the nightly dew,)
He quits his cell; the pilgrim-staff he bore,   25
And fix'd the scallop in his hat before;
Then with the sun a rising journey went,
Sedate to think, and watching each event.

  The morn was wasted in the pathless grass,
And long and lonesome was the wild to pass;   30
But when the southern sun had warm'd the day,
A youth came posting o'er a crossing way;
His raiment decent, his complexion fair,

And soft in graceful ringlets wav'd his hair.
Then near approaching, 'Father, hail!' he cried;   35
'And hail, my son,' the reverend sire replied;
Words follow'd words, from question answer flow'd,
And talk of various kind deceiv'd the road;
Till each with other pleas'd, and loth to part,
While in their age they differ, join in heart: 40
Thus stands an aged elm in ivy bound,
Thus youthful ivy clasps an elm around.

Now sunk the sun; the closing hour of day
Came onward, mantled o'er with sober gray;
Nature in silence bid the world repose: 45
When near the road a stately palace rose:
There by the moon through ranks of trees they pass,
Whose verdure crown'd their sloping sides of grass.
It chanc'd the noble master of the dome
Still made his house the wandering stranger's home;   50
Yet still the kindness, from a thirst of praise,
Prov'd the vain flourish of expensive ease.
The pair arrive: the liveried servants wait;
Their lord receives them at the pompous gate.
The table groans with costly piles of food,   55
And all is more than hospitably good.
Then led to rest, the day's long toil they drown,
Deep sunk in sleep, and silk, and heaps of down.

At length 'tis morn, and at the dawn of day,
Along the wide canals the zephyrs play;   60
Fresh o'er the gay parterres the breezes creep,
And shake the neighbouring wood to banish sleep.
Up rise the guests, obedient to the call:
An early banquet deck'd the splendid hall;
Rich luscious wine a golden goblet grac'd,   65
Which the kind master forc'd the guests to taste.
Then, pleas'd and thankful, from the porch they go;
And, but the landlord, none had cause of woe;
His cup was vanish'd; for in secret guise
The younger guest purloin'd the glittering prize.   70

As one who spies a serpent in his way,
Glistening and basking in the summer ray,

Disorder'd stops to shun the danger near,
Then walks with faintness on, and looks with fear;
So seem'd the sire; when far upon the road, 75
The shining spoil his wily partner show'd.
He stopp'd with silence, walk'd with trembling heart,
And much he wish'd, but durst not ask to part:
Murmuring he lifts his eyes, and thinks it hard,
That generous actions meet a base reward. 80
    While thus they pass, the sun his glory shrouds,
The changing skies hang out their sable clouds;
A sound in air presag'd approaching rain,
And beasts to covert scud across the plain.
Warn'd by the signs, the wandering pair retreat 85
To seek for shelter at a neighbouring seat.
'Twas built with turrets, on a rising ground,
And strong, and large, and unimprov'd around;
Its owner's temper, timorous and severe,
Unkind and griping, caused a desert there. 90
    As near the miser's heavy doors they drew,
Fierce rising gusts with sudden fury blew;
The nimble lightning mix'd with showers began,
And o'er their heads loud rolling thunders ran.
Here long they knock, but knock or call in vain, 95
Driven by the wind, and batter'd by the rain.
At length some pity warm'd the master's breast,
('Twas then his threshold first receiv'd a guest,)
Slow creaking turns the door with jealous care,
And half he welcomes in the shivering pair; 100
One frugal faggot lights the naked walls,
And nature's fervour through their limbs recalls:
Bread of the coarsest sort, with eager wine,
Each hardly granted, serv'd them both to dine;
And when the tempest first appear'd to cease, 105
A ready warning bid them part in peace.
With still remark the pondering hermit view'd
In one so rich, a life so poor and rude;
And why should such, within himself he cried,
Lock the lost wealth a thousand want beside? 110
But what new marks of wonder soon took place

In every settling feature of his face,
When from his vest the young companion bore
That cup, the generous landlord own'd before,
And paid profusely with the precious bowl,   115
The stinted kindness of this churlish soul!

But now the clouds in airy tumult fly;
The sun emerging opes an azure sky;
A fresher green the smelling leaves display,
And, glittering as they tremble, cheer the day: 120
The weather courts them from their poor retreat,
And the glad master bolts the weary gate.

While hence they walk, the pilgrim's bosom wrought
With all the travel of uncertain thought;
His partner's acts without their cause appear,   125
'Twas there a vice, and seem'd a madness here:
Detesting that, and pitying this, he goes,
Lost and confounded with the various shows.

Now night's dim shades again involve the sky,
Again the wanderers want a place to lie,   130
Again they search, and find a lodging nigh:
The soil improv'd around, the mansion neat,
And neither poorly low, nor idly great:
It seem'd to speak its master's turn of mind,
Content, and not for praise, but virtue kind.   135

Hither the walkers turn with weary feet,
Then bless the mansion, and the master greet:
Their greeting fair bestow'd, with modest guise,
The courteous master hears, and thus replies:
'Without a vain, without a grudging heart,   140
To him who gives us all, I yield a part;
From him you come, for him accept it here,
A frank and sober, more than costly cheer.'
He spoke, and bid the welcome table spread,
Then talk'd of virtue till the time of bed,   145
When the grave household round his hall repair,
Warn'd by a bell, and close the hours with prayer.

At length the world, renew'd by calm repose,
Was strong for toil, the dappled morn arose.

Before the pilgrims part, the younger crept   150
Near the clos'd cradle where an infant slept,
And writh'd his neck: the landlord's little pride,
O strange return! grew black, and gasp'd, and died!
Horror of horrors! what! his only son!
How look'd our hermit when the fact was done?   155
Not hell, though hell's black jaws in sunder part,
And breathe blue fire, could more assault his heart.

   Confus'd, and struck with silence at the deed,
He flies, but, trembling, fails to fly with speed.
His steps the youth pursues: the country lay   160
Perplex'd with roads, a servant show'd the way:
A river cross'd the path; the passage o'er
Was nice to find; the servant trod before:
Long arms of oak an open bridge supplied,
And deep the waves beneath the bending glide.   165
The youth, who seem'd to watch a time to sin,
Approach'd the careless guide, and thrust him in;
Plunging he falls, and rising lifts his head,
Then flashing turns, and sinks among the dead.

   Wild, sparkling rage inflames the father's eyes,
He bursts the bands of fear, and madly cries,   171
'Detested wretch!'—but scarce his speech began,
When the strange partner seem'd no longer man:
His youthful face grew more serenely sweet;
His robe turn'd white, and flow'd upon his feet;   175
Fair rounds of radiant points invest his hair;
Celestial odours breathe through purpled air;
And wings, whose colours glitter'd on the day,
Wide at his back their gradual plumes display.
The form ethereal bursts upon his sight,   180
And moves in all the majesty of light.

   Though loud at first the pilgrim's passion grew,
Sudden he gaz'd, and wist not what to do;
Surprise in secret chains his words suspends,
And in a calm his settling temper ends.   185
But silence here the beauteous angel broke,
The voice of music ravish'd as he spoke.

   'Thy prayer, thy praise, thy life to vice unknown,

In sweet memorial rise before the throne:
These charms, success in our bright region find,   190
And force an angel down, to calm thy mind;
For this, commission'd, I forsook the sky,
Nay, cease to kneel—thy fellow-servant I.

'Then, know the truth of government divine,
And let these scruples be no longer thine.   195

'The Maker justly claims that world he made,
In this the right of Providence is laid;
Its sacred majesty through all depends
On using second means to work his ends:
'Tis thus, withdrawn in state from human eye,   200
The power exerts his attributes on high,
Your actions uses, nor controls your will,
And bids the doubting sons of men be still.

'What strange events can strike with more surprise,
Than those which lately struck thy wondering eyes?
Yet taught by these, confess th' Almighty just,   206
And where you can't unriddle, learn to trust!

'The great vain man, who far'd on costly food,
Whose life was too luxurious to be good;
Who made his ivory stands with goblets shine,   210
And forc'd his guests to morning draughts of wine
Has, with the cup, the graceless custom lost,
And still he welcomes, but with less of cost.

'The mean, suspicious wretch, whose bolted door
Ne'er moved in duty to the wandering poor;   215
With him I left the cup, to teach his mind
That heaven can bless, if mortals will be kind.
Conscious of wanting worth, he views the bowl,
And feels compassion touch his grateful soul.
Thus artists melt the sullen ore of lead,   220
With heaping coals of fire upon its head;
In the kind warmth the metal learns to glow,
And loose from dross, the silver runs below.

'Long had our pious friend in virtue trod,
But now the child half-wean'd his heart from God;
Child of his age, for him he liv'd in pain,   226
And measur'd back his steps to earth again.

To what excesses had this dotage run
But God, to save the father, took the son.
To all but thee, in fits he seem'd to go,   230
And 'twas my ministry to deal the blow.
The poor fond parent, humbled in the dust,
Now owns in tears the punishment was just.
   'But how had all his fortune felt a wrack,
Had that false servant sped in safety back!   235
This night his treasur'd heaps he meant to steal,
And what a fund of charity would fail!
   'Thus Heaven instructs thy mind: this trial o'er,
Depart in peace, resign, and sin no more.'
   On sounding pinions here the youth withdrew,
The sage stood wondering as the seraph flew.   241
Thus look'd Elisha, when, to mount on high,
His master took the chariot of the sky;
The fiery pomp ascending left the view;
The prophet gaz'd, and wish'd to follow too.   245
   The bending hermit here a prayer begun,
'Lord! as in heaven, on earth thy will be done!'
Then gladly turning, sought his ancient place,
And pass'd a life of piety and peace.

ALEXANDER POPE

1688–1744

The Rape of the Lock

CANTO I

What dire offence from amorous causes springs,
What mighty contests rise from trivial things,
I sing—This verse to Caryl, Muse! is due:
This, even Belinda may vouchsafe to view:
Slight is the subject, but not so the praise,   5
If she inspire, and he approve my lays.
   Say what strange motive, Goddess! could compel
A well-bred lord to assault a gentle belle?

O say what stranger cause, yet unexplored,
Could make a gentle belle reject a lord?   10
In tasks so bold, can little men engage,
And in soft bosoms dwells such mighty rage?

    Sol through white curtains shot a timorous ray,
And oped those eyes that must eclipse the day:
Now lap-dogs give themselves the rousing shake,
And sleepless lovers, just at twelve, awake: 16
Thrice rung the bell, the slipper knocked the ground,
And the pressed watch returned a silver sound.
Belinda still her downy pillow pressed,
Her guardian sylph prolonged the balmy rest: 20
'Twas he had summoned to her silent bed
The morning-dream that hovered o'er her head;
A youth more glittering than a birth-night beau,
(That even in slumber caused her cheek to glow)
Seemed to her ear his winning lips to lay,   25
And thus in whispers said, or seemed to say.

    'Fairest of mortals, thou distinguished care
Of thousand bright inhabitants of air!
If e'er one vision touched thy infant thought,
Of all the nurse and all the priest have taught;   30
Of airy elves by moonlight shadows seen,
The silver token, and the circled green,
Or virgins visited by angel-powers,
With golden crowns and wreaths of heavenly flowers;
Hear and believe! thy own importance know,   35
Nor bound thy narrow view to things below.
Some secret truths, from learned pride concealed,
To maids alone and children are revealed:
What though no credit doubting wits may give!
The fair and innocent shall still believe.   40
Know, then, unnumbered spirits round thee fly,
The light militia of the lower sky:
These, though unseen, are ever on the wing,
Hang o'er the box, and hover round the ring.
Think what an equipage thou hast in air,   45
And view with scorn two pages and a chair.
As now your own, our beings were of old,

And once inclosed in woman's beauteous mould;
Thence, by a soft transition, we repair
From earthly vehicles to these of air. 50
Think not, when woman's transient breath is fled,
That all her vanities at once are dead;
Succeeding vanities she still regards,
And though she plays no more, o'erlooks the cards.
Her joy in gilded chariots, when alive, 55
And love of ombre, after death survive.
For when the fair in all their pride expire,
To their first elements their souls retire:
The sprites of fiery termagants in flame
Mount up, and take a salamander's name. 60
Soft yielding minds to water glide away,
And sip, with nymphs, their elemental tea.
The graver prude sinks downward to a gnome,
In search of mischief still on earth to roam.
The light coquettes in sylphs aloft repair, 65
And sport and flutter in the fields of air.
  'Know further yet; whoever fair and chaste
Rejects mankind, is by some sylph embraced:
For spirits, freed from mortal laws, with ease
Assume what sexes and what shapes they please. 70
What guards the purity of melting maids,
In courtly balls, and midnight masquerades,
Safe from the treacherous friend, the daring spark,
The glance by day, the whisper in the dark,
When kind occasion prompts their warm desires, 75
When music softens, and when dancing fires?
'Tis but their sylph, the wise celestials know,
Though honour is the word with men below.
  'Some nymphs there are, too conscious of their face,
For life predestined to the gnomes' embrace. 80
These swell their prospects and exalt their pride,
When offers are disdained, and love denied:
Then gay ideas crowd the vacant brain,
While peers, and dukes, and all their sweeping train,
And garters, stars, and coronets appear, 85
And in soft sounds, "Your Grace" salutes their ear.

'Tis these that early taint the female soul,
Instruct the eyes of young coquettes to roll,
Teach infant-cheeks a bidden blush to know,
And little hearts to flutter at a beau. 90

'Oft, when the world imagine women stray,
The sylphs through mystic mazes guide their way,
Through all the giddy circle they pursue,
And old impertinence expel by new.
What tender maid but must a victim fall 95
To one man's treat, but for another's ball?
When Florio speaks, what virgin could withstand,
If gentle Damon did not squeeze her hand?
With varying vanities, from every part,
They shift the moving toyshop of their heart; 100
Where wigs with wigs, with sword-knots sword-knots
      strive,
Beaux banish beaux, and coaches coaches drive.
This erring mortals levity may call;
Oh blind to truth! the sylphs contrive it all.

'Of these am I, who thy protection claim, 105
A watchful sprite, and Ariel is my name.
Late, as I ranged the crystal wilds of air,
In the clear mirror of thy ruling star
I saw, alas! some dread event impend,
Ere to the main this morning sun descend, 110
But heaven reveals not what, or how, or where:
Warned by the sylph, oh pious maid, beware!
This to disclose is all thy guardian can:
Beware of all, but most beware of man!'

He said; when Shock, who thought she slept too
      long, 115
Leaped up, and waked his mistress with his tongue.
'Twas then, Belinda, if report say true,
Thy eyes first opened on a billet-doux;
Wounds, charms, and ardours were no sooner read,
But all the vision vanished from thy head. 120

And now, unveiled, the toilet stands displayed,
Each silver vase in mystic order laid.
First, robed in white, the nymph intent adores,

With head uncovered, the cosmetic powers.
A heavenly image in the glass appears,　　　125
To that she bends, to that her eyes she rears;
The inferior priestess, at her altar's side,
Trembling begins the sacred rites of pride.
Unnumbered treasures ope at once, and here
The various offerings of the world appear;　　　130
From each she nicely culls with curious toil,
And decks the Goddess with the glittering spoil.
This casket India's glowing gems unlocks,
And all Arabia breathes from yonder box.
The tortoise here and elephant unite,　　　135
Transformed to combs, the speckled, and the white.
Here files of pins extend their shining rows,
Puffs, powders, patches, bibles, billet-doux.
Now awful beauty puts on all its arms;
The fair each moment rises in her charms,　　　140
Repairs her smiles, awakens every grace,
And calls forth all the wonders of her face;
Sees by degrees a purer blush arise,
And keener lightnings quicken in her eyes.
The busy sylphs surround their darling care,　　　145
These set the head, and those divide the hair,
Some fold the sleeve, whilst others plait the gown;
And Betty's praised for labours not her own.

CANTO II

Not with more glories, in the ethereal plain,
The sun first rises o'er the purpled main,
Than, issuing forth, the rival of his beams
Launched on the bosom of the silver Thames.
Fair nymphs, and well-dressed youths around her
　　　shone,　　　5
But every eye was fixed on her alone.
On her white breast a sparkling cross she wore,
Which Jews might kiss, and infidels adore.
Her lively looks a sprightly mind disclose,
Quick as her eyes, and as unfixed as those:　　　10
Favours to none, to all she smiles extends;

Oft she rejects, but never once offends.
Bright as the sun, her eyes the gazers strike,
And, like the sun, they shine on all alike.
Yet graceful ease, and sweetness void of pride,   15
Might hide her faults, if belles had faults to hide:
If to her share some female errors fall,
Look on her face, and you'll forget 'em all.

This nymph, to the destruction of mankind,
Nourished two locks, which graceful hung behind
In equal curls, and well conspired to deck   21
With shining ringlets the smooth iv'ry neck.
Love in these labyrinths his slaves detains,
And mighty hearts are held in slender chains.
With hairy springes we the birds betray,   25
Slight lines of hair surprise the finny prey,
Fair tresses man's imperial race ensnare,
And beauty draws us with a single hair.

The adventurous Baron the bright locks admired;
He saw, he wished, and to the prize aspired.   30
Resolved to win, he meditates the way,
By force to ravish, or by fraud betray;
For when success a lover's toil attends,
Few ask, if fraud or force attained his ends.

For this, ere Phoebus rose, he had implored   35
Propitious heaven, and every power adored,
But chiefly Love—to Love an altar built,
Of twelve vast French romances, neatly gilt.
There lay three garters, half a pair of gloves;
And all the trophies of his former loves;   40
With tender billet-doux he lights the pyre,
And breathes three amorous sighs to raise the fire.
Then prostrate falls, and begs with ardent eyes
Soon to obtain, and long possess the prize:
The powers gave ear, and granted half his prayer,
The rest the winds dispersed in empty air.   46

But now secure the painted vessel glides,
The sun-beams trembling on the floating tides:
While melting music steals upon the sky,
And softened sounds along the waters die;   50

Smooth flow the waves, the zephyrs gently play,
Belinda smiled, and all the world was gay.
All but the sylph—with careful thoughts oppressed,
The impending woe sat heavy on his breast.
He summons straight his denizens of air; 55
The lucid squadrons round the sails repair:
Soft o'er the shrouds aërial whispers breathe,
That seemed but zephyrs to the train beneath.
Some to the sun their insect-wings unfold,
Waft on the breeze, or sink in clouds of gold; 60
Transparent forms, too fine for mortal sight,
Their fluid bodies half dissolved in light,
Loose to the wind their airy garments flew,
Thin glittering textures of the filmy dew,
Dipt in the richest tincture of the skies, 65
Where light disports in ever-mingling dyes,
While every beam new transient colours flings,
Colours that change whene'er they wave their wings.
Amid the circle, on the gilded mast,
Superior by the head, was Ariel placed; 70
His purple pinions opening to the sun,
He raised his azure wand, and thus begun.
 Ye sylphs and sylphids, to your chief give ear!
Fays, fairies, genii, elves, and demons, hear!
Ye know the spheres and various tasks assigned 75
By laws eternal to the aërial kind.
Some in the fields of purest ether play,
And bask and whiten in the blaze of day.
Some guide the course of wandering orbs on high,
Or roll the planets through the boundless sky. 80
Some less refined, beneath the moon's pale light
Pursue the stars that shoot athwart the night,
Or suck the mists in grosser air below,
Or dip their pinions in the painted bow,
Or brew fierce tempests on the wintry main, 85
Or o'er the glebe distil the kindly rain.
Others on earth o'er human race preside,
Watch all their ways, and all their actions guide:
Of these the chief the care of nations own,

And guard with arms divine the British throne.   90
   Our humbler province is to tend the fair,
Not a less pleasing, though less glorious care;
To save the powder from too rude a gale,
Nor let the imprisoned essences exhale;
To draw fresh colours from the vernal flowers;   95
To steal from rainbows ere they drop in showers
A brighter wash; to curl their waving hairs,
Assist their blushes, and inspire their airs;
Nay oft, in dreams, invention we bestow,
To change a flounce, or add a furbelow.   100
   This day, black omens threat the brightest fair,
That e'er deserved a watchful spirit's care;
Some dire disaster, or by force, or slight;
But what, or where, the fates have wrapt in night.
Whether the nymph shall break Diana's law,   105
Or some frail china jar receive a flaw,
Or stain her honour or her new brocade;
Forget her prayers, or miss a masquerade;
Or lose her heart, or necklace, at a ball;
Or whether Heaven has doom'd that Shock must fall.
Haste, then, ye spirits! to your charge repair: 111
The fluttering fan be Zephyretta's care;
The drops to thee, Brillante, we consign;
And, Momentilla, let the watch be thine;
Do thou, Crispissa, tend her favourite lock;   115
Ariel himself shall be the guard of Shock.
   To fifty chosen sylphs, of special note,
We trust th' important charge, the petticoat:
Oft have we known that seven-fold fence to fail,
Though stiff with hoops, and armed with ribs of
    whale: 120
Form a strong line about the silver bound,
And guard the wide circumference around.
   Whatever spirit, careless of his charge,
His post neglects, or leaves the fair at large,
Shall feel sharp vengeance soon o'ertake his sins,   125
Be stopped in vials, or transfixed with pins;
Or plunged in lakes of bitter washes lie,

Or wedged whole ages in a bodkin's eye:
Gums and pomatums shall his flight restrain,
While clogged he beats his silken wings in vain;   130
Or alum styptics with contracting power
Shrink his thin essence like a rivelled flower:
Or, as Ixion fixed, the wretch shall feel
The giddy motion of the whirling mill,
In fumes of burning chocolate shall glow,   135
And tremble at the sea that froths below!

    He spoke; the spirits from the sails descend;
Some, orb in orb, around the nymph extend;
Some thrid the mazy ringlets of her hair;
Some hang upon the pendants of her ear: 140
With beating hearts the dire event they wait,
Anxious, and trembling for the birth of Fate.

CANTO III

Close by those meads, for ever crowned with flowers,
Where Thames with pride surveys his rising towers,
There stands a structure of majestic frame,
Which from the neighb'ring Hampton takes its name.
Here Britain's statesmen oft the fall foredoom   5
Of foreign tyrants and of nymphs at home;
Here thou, great ANNA! whom three realms obey,
Dost sometimes counsel take—and sometimes tea.

    Hither the heroes and the nymphs resort,
To taste awhile the pleasures of a court;   10
In various talk the instructive hours they passed,
Who gave the ball, or paid the visit last;
One speaks the glory of the British queen,
And one describes a charming Indian screen;
A third interprets motions, looks, and eyes;   15
At every word a reputation dies.
Snuff, or the fan, supply each pause of chat,
With singing, laughing, ogling, and all that.

    Meanwhile, declining from the noon of day,
The sun obliquely shoots his burning ray;   20
The hungry judges soon the sentence sign,
And wretches hang that jury-men may dine;

The merchant from the Exchange returns in peace,
And the long labours of the toilet cease.
Belinda now, whom thirst of fame invites,   25
Burns to encounter two adventurous knights,
At ombre singly to decide their doom;
And swells her breast with conquests yet to come.
Straight the three bands prepare in arms to join,
Each band the number of the sacred nine.   30
Soon as she spreads her hand, the aërial guard
Descend, and sit on each important card:
First Ariel perched upon a Matadore,
Then each, according to the rank they bore;
For sylphs, yet mindful of their ancient race,   35
Are, as when women, wondrous fond of place.

   Behold, four kings in majesty revered,
With hoary whiskers and a forky beard;
And four fair queens whose hands sustain a flower,
The expressive emblem of their softer power;   40
Four knaves in garbs succinct, a trusty band,
Caps on their heads, and halberts in their hand;
And parti-coloured troops, a shining train,
Draw forth to combat on the velvet plain.

   The skilful nymph reviews her force with care: 45
Let spades be trumps! she said, and trumps they were.
   Now move to war her sable Matadores,
In show like leaders of the swarthy Moors.
Spadillio first, unconquerable lord!
Led off two captive trumps, and swept the board.   50
As many more Manillio forced to yield,
And marched a victor from the verdant field.
Him Basto followed, but his fate more hard
Gained but one trump and one plebeian card.
With his broad sabre next, a chief in years,   55
The hoary majesty of spades appears,
Puts forth one manly leg, to sight revealed,
The rest, his many-coloured robe concealed.
The rebel knave, who dares his prince engage,
Proves the just victim of his royal rage.   60
Even mighty Pam, that kings and queens o'erthrew,

And mowed down armies in the fights of Lu,
Sad chance of war! now destitute of aid,
Falls undistinguished by the victor spade!

    Thus far both armies to Belinda yield;   65
Now to the Baron fate inclines the field.
His warlike Amazon her host invades,
The imperial consort of the crown of spades.
The club's black tyrant first her victim died,
Spite of his haughty mien, and barbarous pride: 70
What boots the regal circle on his head,
His giant limbs, in state unwieldy spread;
That long behind he trails his pompous robe,
And, of all monarchs, only grasps the globe?

    The Baron now his diamonds pours apace;   75
The embroidered king who shows but half his face,
And his refulgent queen, with powers combined,
Of broken troops an easy conquest find.
Clubs, diamonds, hearts, in wild disorder seen,
With throngs promiscuous strow the level green.   80
Thus when dispersed a routed army runs,
Of Asia's troops, and Afric's sable sons,
With like confusion different nations fly,
Of various habit, and of various dye,
The pierced battalions disunited fall,   85
In heaps on heaps; one fate o'erwhelms them all.

    The knave of diamonds tries his wily arts,
And wins (oh shameful chance!) the queen of hearts.
At this, the blood the virgin's cheek forsook,
A livid paleness spreads o'er all her look;   90
She sees, and trembles at the approaching ill,
Just in the jaws of ruin, and codille.
And now (as oft in some distempered state)
On one nice trick depends the general fate:
An ace of hearts steps forth: the king unseen   95
Lurked in her hand, and mourned his captive queen:
He springs to vengeance with an eager pace,
And falls like thunder on the prostrate ace.
The nymph exulting fills with shouts the sky;
The walls, the woods, and long canals reply.   100

O thoughtless mortals! ever blind to fate,
Too soon dejected, and too soon elate.
Sudden, these honours shall be snatched away,
And cursed for ever this victorious day.

For lo! the board with cups and spoons is crowned,
The berries crackle, and the mill turns round;   106
On shining altars of Japan they raise
The silver lamp; the fiery spirits blaze:
From silver spouts the grateful liquors glide,
While China's earth receives the smoking tide: 110
At once they gratify their scent and taste,
And frequent cups prolong the rich repast.
Straight hover round the fair her airy band;
Some, as she sipped, the fuming liquors fanned,
Some o'er her lap their careful plumes displayed,
Trembling, and conscious of the rich brocade.   116
Coffee, (which makes the politician wise,
And see through all things with his half-shut eyes)
Sent up in vapours to the Baron's brain
New stratagems, the radiant lock to gain.   120
Ah cease, rash youth! desist ere 'tis too late,
Fear the just Gods, and think of Scylla's fate!
Changed to a bird, and sent to flit in air,
She dearly pays for Nisus' injured hair!

But when to mischief mortals bend their will,   125
How soon they find fit instruments of ill!
Just then, Clarissa drew with tempting grace
A two-edged weapon from her shining case:
So ladies in romance assist their knight,
Present the spear, and arm him for the fight.   130
He takes the gift with reverence, and extends
The little engine on his fingers' ends;
This just behind Belinda's neck he spread,
As o'er the fragrant steams she bends her head.
Swift to the lock a thousand sprites repair,   135
A thousand wings, by turns, blow back the hair;
And thrice they twitched the diamond in her ear;
Thrice she looked back, and thrice the foe drew near.
Just in that instant, anxious Ariel sought

The close recesses of the virgin's thought; 140
As on the nosegay in her breast reclined,
He watched the ideas rising in her mind,
Sudden he viewed, in spite of all her art,
An earthly lover lurking at her heart.
Amazed, confused, he found his power expired, 145
Resigned to fate, and with a sigh retired.

The peer now spreads the glittering forfex wide,
To inclose the lock; now joins it, to divide.
Even then, before the fatal engine closed,
A wretched sylph too fondly interposed; 150
Fate urged the shears, and cut the sylph in twain,
(But airy substance soon unites again)
The meeting points the sacred hair dissever
From the fair head, for ever, and for ever! 154

Then flashed the living lightning from her eyes,
And screams of horror rend the affrighted skies.
Not louder shrieks to pitying heaven are cast,
When husbands, or when lap-dogs breathe their last;
Or when rich China vessels fallen from high,
In glittering dust and painted fragments lie! 160

Let wreaths of triumph now my temples twine,
(The victor cried) the glorious prize is mine!
While fish in streams, or birds delight in air,
Or in a coach and six the British fair,
As long as Atalantis shall be read, 165
Or the small pillow grace a lady's bed,
While visits shall be paid on solemn days,
When numerous wax-lights in bright order blaze,
While nymphs take treats, or assignations give,
So long my honour, name, and praise shall live! 170
What time would spare, from steel receives its date,
And monuments, like men, submit to fate!
Steel could the labour of the Gods destroy,
And strike to dust the imperial towers of Troy;
Steel could the works of mortal pride confound, 175
And hew triumphal arches to the ground.
What wonder then, fair nymph! thy hairs should feel
The conquering force of unresisted steel?

CANTO IV

But anxious cares the pensive nymph oppressed,
And secret passions laboured in her breast.
Not youthful kings in battle seized alive,
Not scornful virgins who their charms survive,
Not ardent lovers robbed of all their bliss,   5
Not ancient ladies when refused a kiss,
Not tyrants fierce that unrepenting die,
Not Cynthia when her manteau's pinned awry,
E'er felt such rage, resentment, and despair,
As thou, sad virgin! for thy ravished hair.   10

    For, that sad moment, when the sylphs withdrew
And Ariel weeping from Belinda flew,
Umbriel, a dusky, melancholy sprite,
As ever sullied the fair face of light,
Down to the central earth, his proper scene,   15
Repaired to search the gloomy Cave of Spleen.

    Swift on his sooty pinions flits the gnome,
And in a vapour reached the dismal dome.
No cheerful breeze this sullen region knows,
The dreaded east is all the wind that blows.   20
Here in a grotto, sheltered close from air,
And screened in shades from day's detested glare,
She sighs for ever on her pensive bed,
Pain at her side, and Megrim at her head.

    Two handmaids wait the throne: alike in place,
But differing far in figure and in face.   26
Here stood Ill-nature like an ancient maid,
Her wrinkled form in black and white arrayed;
With store of prayers, for mornings, nights, and noons,
Her hand is filled; her bosom with lampoons.   30

    There Affectation, with a sickly mien,
Shows in her cheek the roses of eighteen,
Practised to lisp, and hang the head aside,
Faints into airs, and languishes with pride,
On the rich quilt sinks with becoming woe,   35
Wrapt in a gown, for sickness, and for show.

The fair ones feel such maladies as these,
When each new night-dress gives a new disease.
  A constant vapour o'er the palace flies;
Strange phantoms rising as the mists arise;   40
Dreadful, as hermit's dreams in haunted shades,
Or bright, as visions of expiring maids.
Now glaring fiends, and snakes on rolling spires,
Pale spectres, gaping tombs, and purple fires:
Now lakes of liquid gold, Elysian scenes,   45
And crystal domes, and angels in machines.
  Unnumbered throngs on every side are seen,
Of bodies changed to various forms by Spleen.
Here living tea-pots stand, one arm held out,
One bent; the handle this, and that the spout: 50
A pipkin there, like Homer's tripod, walks;
Here sighs a jar, and there a goose-pye talks;
Men prove with child, as powerful fancy works,
And maids turned bottles, call aloud for corks.
  Safe passed the gnome through this fantastic band,
A branch of healing spleenwort in his hand.   56
Then thus address'd the power: 'Hail, wayward
      Queen!
Who rule the sex to fifty from fifteen:
Parent of vapours and of female wit,
Who give the hysteric, or poetic fit,   60
On various tempers act by various ways,
Make some take physic, others scribble plays;
Who cause the proud their visits to delay,
And send the godly in a pet to pray.
A nymph there is, that all thy power disdains,   65
And thousands more in equal mirth maintains.
But oh! if e'er thy gnome could spoil a grace,
Or raise a pimple on a beauteous face,
Like citron-waters matrons' cheeks inflame,
Or change complexions at a losing game;   70
If e'er with airy horns I planted heads,
Or rumpled petticoats, or tumbled beds,
Or caused suspicion when no soul was rude,
Or discomposed the head-dress of a prude,

Or e'er to costive lap-dog gave disease,　　75
Which not the tears of brightest eyes could ease:
Hear me, and touch Belinda with chagrin,
That single act gives half the world the spleen.'

The Goddess with a discontented air
Seems to reject him, though she grants his prayer.
A wondrous bag with both her hands she binds,　81
Like that where once Ulysses held the winds;
There she collects the force of female lungs,
Sighs, sobs, and passions, and the war of tongues.
A vial next she fills with fainting fears,　　85
Soft sorrows, melting griefs, and flowing tears.
The gnome rejoicing bears her gifts away,
Spreads his black wings, and slowly mounts to day.

Sunk in Thalestris' arms the nymph he found,
Her eyes dejected and her hair unbound.　　90
Full o'er their heads the swelling bag he rent,
And all the Furies issued at the vent.
Belinda burns with more than mortal ire,
And fierce Thalestris fans the rising fire.　　94
'O wretched maid!' she spread her hands and cried,
(While Hampton's echoes, 'Wretched maid!' replied)
'Was it for this you took such constant care
The bodkin, comb, and essence to prepare?
For this your locks in paper durance bound,
For this with torturing irons wreathed around?　100
For this with fillets strained your tender head,
And bravely bore the double loads of lead?
Gods! shall the ravisher display your hair,
While the fops envy, and the ladies stare!
Honour forbid! at whose unrivalled shrine　105
Ease, pleasure, virtue, all our sex resign.
Methinks already I your tears survey,
Already hear the horrid things they say,
Already see you a degraded toast,
And all your honour in a whisper lost!　　110
How shall I, then, your hapless fame defend?
'Twill then be infamy to seem your friend!
And shall this prize, the inestimable prize,

Exposed through crystal to the gazing eyes,
And heightened by the diamond's circling rays 115
On that rapacious hand for ever blaze?
Sooner shall grass in Hyde-park Circus grow,
And wits take lodgings in the sound of Bow;
Sooner let earth, air, sea, to chaos fall,
Men, monkeys, lap-dogs, parrots, perish all!' 120
    She said; then raging to Sir Plume repairs,
And bids her beau demand the precious hairs:
(Sir Plume of amber snuff-box justly vain,
And the nice conduct of a clouded cane)
With earnest eyes, and round unthinking face, 125
He first the snuff-box opened, then the case,
And thus broke out—'My Lord, why, what the devil?
Zounds! damn the lock! 'fore Gad, you must be civil!
Plague on't! 'tis past a jest—nay prithee, pox!
Give her the hair'—he spoke, and rapp'd his box.
    'It grieves me much' (replied the Peer again) 131
'Who speaks so well should ever speak in vain.
But by this lock, this sacred lock I swear,
(Which never more shall join its parted hair;
Which never more its honours shall renew, 135
Clipped from the lovely head where late it grew)
That while my nostrils draw the vital air,
This hand, which won it, shall for ever wear.'
He spoke, and speaking, in proud triumph spread
The long-contended honours of her head. 140
    But Umbriel, hateful gnome! forbears not so;
He breaks the vial whence the sorrows flow.
Then see! the nymph in beauteous grief appears,
Her eyes half-languishing, half-drowned in tears;
On her heaved bosom hung her drooping head, 145
Which, with a sigh, she raised; and thus she said.
    'For ever cursed be this detested day,
Which snatched my best, my favourite curl away!
Happy! ah ten times happy had I been,
If Hampton-Court these eyes had never seen! 150
Yet am not I the first mistaken maid,
By love of courts to numerous ills betrayed.

Oh had I rather un-admired remained
In some lone isle, or distant northern land;
Where the gilt chariot never marks the way,   155
Where none learn ombre, none e'er taste bohea!
There kept my charms concealed from mortal eye,
Like roses, that in deserts bloom and die.
What moved my mind with youthful lords to roam?
Oh had I stayed, and said my prayers at home!   160
'Twas this, the morning omens seemed to tell,
Thrice from my trembling hand the patch-box fell;
The tottering China shook without a wind,
Nay, Poll sat mute, and Shock was most unkind!
A sylph too warned me of the threats of fate,   165
In mystic visions, now believed too late!
See the poor remnants of these slighted hairs!
My hands shall rend what ev'n thy rapine spares:
These in two sable ringlets taught to break,
Once gave new beauties to the snowy neck;   170
The sister-lock now sits uncouth, alone,
And in its fellow's fate foresees its own;
Uncurled it hangs, the fatal shears demands,
And tempts once more thy sacrilegious hands.
Oh hadst thou, cruel! been content to seize   175
Hairs less in sight, or any hairs but these!'

CANTO V

She said: the pitying audience melt in tears,
But fate and Jove had stopped the Baron's ears.
In vain Thalestris with reproach assails,
For who can move when fair Belinda fails?
Not half so fixed the Trojan could remain,   5
While Anna begged and Dido raged in vain.
Then grave Clarissa graceful waved her fan;
Silence ensued, and thus the nymph began.
   'Say, why are beauties praised and honoured most,
The wise man's passion, and the vain man's toast?   10
Why decked with all that land and sea afford,
Why Angels called, and Angel-like adored?

Why round our coaches crowd the white-gloved
      beaux,
Why bows the side-box from its inmost rows?
How vain are all these glories, all our pains,   15
Unless good sense preserve what beauty gains:
That men may say, when we the front-box grace:
"Behold the first in virtue as in face!"
Oh! if to dance all night, and dress all day,
Charmed the small-pox, or chased old-age away;   20
Who would not scorn what house-wife's cares pro-
      duce,
Or who would learn one earthly thing of use?
To patch, nay ogle, might become a saint,
Nor could it sure be such a sin to paint.
But since, alas! frail beauty must decay,   25
Curled or uncurled, since locks will turn to grey;
Since painted, or not painted, all shall fade,
And she who scorns a man must die a maid;
What then remains but well our power to use,
And keep good-humour still whate'er we lose?   30
And trust me, dear! good-humour can prevail,
When airs, and flights, and screams, and scolding fail.
Beauties in vain their pretty eyes may roll;
Charms strike the sight, but merit wins the soul.'
  So spoke the dame, but no applause ensued;   35
Belinda frowned, Thalestris called her prude.
'To arms, to arms!' the fierce virago cries,
And swift as lightning to the combat flies,
All side in parties, and begin the attack;
Fans clap, silks rustle, and tough whalebones crack;
Heroes' and heroines' shouts confusedly rise,   41
And base and treble voices strike the skies.
No common weapons in their hands are found,
Like gods they fight, nor dread a mortal wound.
  So when bold Homer makes the gods engage,   45
And heavenly breasts with human passions rage;
'Gainst Pallas, Mars; Latona, Hermes arms,
And all Olympus rings with loud alarms:
Jove's thunder roars, heaven trembles all around,

Blue Neptune storms, the bellowing deeps resound:
Earth shakes her nodding towers, the ground gives
    way, 51
And the pale ghosts start at the flash of day!
  Triumphant Umbriel on a sconce's height
Clapped his glad wings, and sate to view the fight:
Propped on their bodkin spears, the sprites survey
The growing combat, or assist the fray. 56
  While through the press enraged Thalestris flies,
And scatters death around from both her eyes,
A beau and witling perished in the throng,
One died in metaphor, and one in song. 60
'O cruel nymph! a living death I bear,'
Cried Dapperwit, and sunk beside his chair.
A mournful glance Sir Fopling upwards cast,
'Those eyes are made so killing'—was his last.
Thus on Maeander's flowery margin lies 65
The expiring swan, and as he sings he dies.
  When bold Sir Plume had drawn Clarissa down,
Chloe stepped in, and killed him with a frown;
She smiled to see the doughty hero slain,
But, at her smile, the beau revived again. 70
  Now Jove suspends his golden scales in air,
Weighs the men's wits against the lady's hair;
The doubtful beam long nods from side to side;
At length the wits mount up, the hairs subside.
  See, fierce Belinda on the Baron flies, 75
With more than usual lightning in her eyes:
Nor feared the chief the unequal fight to try,
Who sought no more than on his foe to die.
But this bold lord with manly strength endued,
She with one finger and a thumb subdued: 80
Just where the breath of life his nostrils drew,
A charge of snuff the wily virgin threw;
The gnomes direct, to every atom just,
The pungent grains of titillating dust.
Sudden, with starting tears each eye o'erflows, 85
And the high dome re-echoes to his nose.
  'Now meet thy fate,' incensed Belinda cried,

And drew a deadly bodkin from her side.
(The same, his ancient personage to deck,
Her great great grandsire wore about his neck, 90
In three seal-rings; which after, melted down,
Formed a vast buckle for his widow's gown:
Her infant grandame's whistle next it grew,
The bells she jingled, and the whistle blew;
Then in a bodkin graced her mother's hairs, 95
Which long she wore, and now Belinda wears.)
  'Boast not my fall' (he cried) 'insulting foe!
Thou by some other shalt be laid as low,
Nor think, to die dejects my lofty mind:
All that I dread is leaving you behind! 100
Rather than so, ah let me still survive,
And burn in Cupid's flames—but burn alive.'
  'Restore the lock!' she cries; and all around
'Restore the lock!' the vaulted roofs rebound.
Not fierce Othello in so loud a strain 105
Roared for the handkerchief that caused his pain,
But see how oft ambitious aims are crossed,
And chiefs contend till all the prize is lost!
The lock, obtained with guilt, and kept with pain,
In every place is sought, but sought in vain: 110
With such a prize no mortal must be blest,
So heaven decrees! with heaven who can contest?
  Some thought it mounted to the lunar sphere,
Since all things lost on earth are treasured there.
There heroes' wits are kept in ponderous vases, 115
And beaux' in snuff-boxes and tweezer-cases.
There broken vows and death-bed alms are found,
And lovers' hearts with ends of ribband bound,
The courtier's promises, and sick men's prayers,
The smiles of harlots, and the tears of heirs, 120
Cages for gnats, and chains to yoke a flea,
Dried butterflies, and tomes of casuistry.
  But trust the Muse—she saw it upward rise,
Though marked by none but quick, poetic eyes:
(So Rome's great founder to the heavens withdrew,
To Proculus alone confessed in view) 126

A sudden star, it shot through liquid air,
And drew behind a radiant trail of hair.
Not Berenice's locks first rose so bright,
The heavens bespangling with dishevelled light.   130
The sylphs behold it kindling as it flies,
And pleased pursue its progress through the skies.
    This the beau monde shall from the Mall survey,
And hail with music its propitious ray.
This the blest lover shall for Venus take,   135
And send up vows from Rosamonda's lake.
This Partridge soon shall view in cloudless skies,
When next he looks through Galileo's eyes;
And hence th' egregious wizard shall foredoom
The fate of Louis, and the fall of Rome.   140
    Then cease, bright nymph! to mourn thy ravished
        hair,
Which adds new glory to the shining sphere!
Not all the tresses that fair head can boast,
Shall draw such envy as the lock you lost.
For, after all the murders of your eye,   145
When, after millions slain, yourself shall die:
When those fair suns shall set, as set they must,
And all those tresses shall be laid in dust,
This lock, the Muse shall consecrate to fame,
And 'midst the stars inscribe Belinda's name.   150

WILLIAM COWPER

1731–1800

John Gilpin

John Gilpin was a citizen
    Of credit and renown,
A train-band captain eke was **he**
    Of famous London Town.

John Gilpin's spouse said to her dear—— 5
  Thou wedded we have been
These twice ten tedious years, yet we
  No holiday have seen.

To-morrow is our wedding-day,
  And we will then repair 10
Unto the Bell at Edmonton
  All in a chaise and pair.

My sister, and my sister's child,
  Myself, and children three,
Will fill the chaise; so you must ride 15
  On horseback after we.

He soon replied—I do admire
  Of womankind but one,
And you are she, my dearest dear,
  Therefore it shall be done. 20

I am a linen-draper bold,
  As all the world doth know,
And my good friend the calender
  Will lend his horse to go.

Quoth Mrs. Gilpin—That's well said; 25
  And, for that wine is dear,
We will be furnish'd with our own,
  Which is both bright and clear.

John Gilpin kissed his loving wife;
  O'erjoyed was he to find 30
That, though on pleasure she was bent,
  She had a frugal mind.

The morning came, the chaise was brought,
  But yet was not allowed
To drive up to the door, lest all 35
  Should say that she was proud.

So three doors off the chaise was stayed,
  Where they did all get in;
Six precious souls, and all agog
  To dash through thick and thin!   40

Smack went the whip, round went the wheels,
  Were never folk so glad;
The stones did rattle underneath,
  As if Cheapside were mad.

John Gilpin, at his horse's side,   45
  Seized fast the flowing mane,
And up he got, in haste to ride,
  But soon came down again;

For saddle-tree scarce reached had he,
  His journey to begin,   50
When, turning round his head, he saw
  Three customers come in.

So down he came; for loss of time,
  Although it grieved him sore,
Yet loss of pence, full well he knew,   55
  Would trouble him much more.

'Twas long before the customers
  Were suited to their mind,
When Betty screaming came downstairs—
  The wine is left behind!   60

Good lack! quoth he—yet bring it me,
  My leathern belt likewise,
In which I bear my trusty sword
  When I do exercise.

Now mistress Gilpin (careful soul!)   65
  Had two stone bottles found,
To hold the liquor that she loved,
  And keep it safe and sound.

Each bottle had a curling ear,
  Through which the belt he drew,   70
And hung a bottle on each side,
  To make his balance true.

Then, over all, that he might be
  Equipped from top to toe,
His long red cloak, well brushed and neat,
  He manfully did throw.   76

Now see him mounted once again
  Upon his nimble steed,
Full slowly pacing o'er the stones,
  With caution and good heed!   80

But finding soon a smoother road
  Beneath his well-shod feet,
The snorting beast began to trot,
  Which galled him in his seat.

So, Fair and softly, John he cried,   85
  But John he cried in vain;
That trot became a gallop soon,
  In spite of curb and rein.

So stooping down, as needs he must
  Who cannot sit upright,   90
He grasped the mane with both his hands,
  And eke with all his might.

His horse, who never in that sort
  Had handled been before,
What thing upon his back had got   95
  Did wonder more and more.

Away went Gilpin, neck or nought;
  Away went hat and wig!—
He little dreamt, when he set out,
  Of running such a rig!   100

The wind did blow, the cloak did fly,
  Like streamer long and gay,
Till, loop and button failing both,
  At last it flew away.

Then might all people well discern   105
  The bottles he had slung;
A bottle swinging at each side,
  As hath been said or sung.

The dogs did bark, the children screamed,
  Up flew the windows all;   110
And every soul cried out—Well done!
  As loud as he could bawl.

Away went Gilpin—who but he?
  His fame soon spread around—
He carries weight! he rides a race!   115
  'Tis for a thousand pound!

And still, as fast as he drew near,
  'Twas wonderful to view
How in a trice the turnpike men
  Their gates wide open threw.   120

And now, as he went bowing down
  His reeking head full low,
The bottles twain behind his back
  Were shattered at a blow.

Down ran the wine into the road,   125
  Most piteous to be seen,
Which made his horse's flanks to smoke
  As they had basted been.

But still he seemed to carry weight,
  With leathern girdle braced;   130
For all might see the bottle-necks
  Still dangling at his waist.

Thus all through merry Islington
   These gambols he did play,
And till he came unto the Wash   135
   Of Edmonton so gay.

And there he threw the wash about
   On both sides of the way,
Just like unto a trundling mop,
   Or a wild goose at play.   140

At Edmonton his loving wife
   From the balcony spied
Her tender husband, wondering much
   To see how he did ride.

Stop, stop, John Gilpin!—Here's the house—
   They all at once did cry;   146
The dinner waits, and we are tired;
   Said Gilpin—So am I!

But yet his horse was not a whit
   Inclined to tarry there;   150
For why? his owner had a house
   Full ten miles off, at Ware.

So like an arrow swift he flew,
   Shot by an archer strong;
So did he fly—which brings me to   155
   The middle of my song.

Away went Gilpin, out of breath,
   And sore against his will,
Till at his friend the calender's
   His horse at last stood still.   160

The calender, amazed to see
   His neighbour in such trim,
Laid down his pipe, flew to the gate,
   And thus accosted him:—

What news? what news? your tidings tell; 165
    Tell me you must and shall—
Say why bare-headed you are come,
    Or why you come at all?

Now Gilpin had a pleasant wit,
    And loved a timely joke; 170
And thus unto the calender
    In merry guise he spoke:—

I came because your horse would come;
    And, if I well forebode,
My hat and wig will soon be here— 175
    They are upon the road.

The calender, right glad to find
    His friend in merry pin,
Returned him not a single word,
    But to the house went in; 180

Whence straight he came with hat and wig;
    A wig that flowed behind,
A hat not much the worse for wear,
    Each comely in its kind.

He held them up, and, in his turn, 185
    Thus showed his ready wit—
My head is twice as big as yours,
    They therefore needs must fit.

But let me scrape the dirt away,
    That hangs upon your face; 190
And stop and eat, for well you may
    Be in a hungry case.

Said John—It is my wedding-day,
    And all the world would stare,
If wife should dine at Edmonton 195
    And I should dine at Ware.

So, turning to his horse, he said—
  I am in haste to dine;
'Twas for your pleasure you came here,
  You shall go back for mine.   200

Ah, luckless speech, and bootless boast!
  For which he paid full dear;
For, while he spake, a braying ass
  Did sing most loud and clear;

Whereat his horse did snort, as he   205
  Had heard a lion roar,
And galloped off with all his might,
  As he had done before.

Away went Gilpin, and away
  Went Gilpin's hat and wig!   210
He lost them sooner than at first—
  For why?—they were too big!

Now, mistress Gilpin, when she saw
  Her husband posting down
Into the country far away,   215
  She pulled out half-a-crown;

And thus unto the youth she said,
  That drove them to the Bell—
This shall be yours when you bring back
  My husband safe and well.   220

The youth did ride, and soon did meet
  John coming back amain;
Whom in a trice he tried to stop,
  By catching at his rein;

But, not performing what he meant,   225
  And gladly would have done,
The frighted steed he frighted more,
  And made him faster run.

Away went Gilpin, and away
    Went post-boy at his heels!—   230
The post-boy's horse right glad to miss
    The lumbering of the wheels.

Six gentlemen upon the road,
    Thus seeing Gilpin fly,
With post-boy scampering in the rear,   235
    They raised the hue and cry:

Stop thief!— stop thief!—a highwayman!
    Not one of them was mute;
And all and each that passed that way
    Did join in the pursuit.   240

And now the turnpike gates again
    Flew open in short space;
The toll-men thinking, as before,
    That Gilpin rode a race.

And so he did—and won it too!—   245
    For he got first to town;
Nor stopped till where he had got up
    He did again get down.

Now let us sing—Long live the king,
    And Gilpin long live he;   250
And, when he next doth ride abroad,
    May I be there to see!

GEORGE CRABBE
1754–1832

Peter Grimes

Old Peter Grimes made fishing his employ,
His wife he cabin'd with him and his boy,
And seem'd that life laborious to enjoy:
To town came quiet Peter with his fish,
And had of all a civil word and wish.   5

He left his trade upon the Sabbath-day,
And took young Peter in his hand to pray:
But soon the stubborn boy from care broke loose,
At first refused, then added his abuse:
His father's love he scorn'd, his power defied,   10
But being drunk, wept sorely when he died.

Yes! then he wept, and to his mind there came
Much of his conduct, and he felt the shame,—
How he had oft the good old man reviled,
And never paid the duty of a child;   15
How, when the father in his Bible read,
He in contempt and anger left the shed:
'It is the word of life,' the parent cried;
—'This is the life itself,' the boy replied;
And while old Peter in amazement stood,   20
Gave the hot spirit to his boiling blood:—
How he, with oath and furious speech, began
To prove his freedom and assert the man;
And when the parent check'd his impious rage,
How he had cursed the tyranny of age,—   25
Nay, once had dealt the sacrilegious blow
On his bare head, and laid his parent low;
The father groan'd—'If thou art old,' said he,
'And hast a son—thou wilt remember me:
Thy mother left me in a happy time,   30
Thou kill'dst not her—Heav'n spares the double
    crime.'

On an inn-settle, in his maudlin grief,
This he revolved, and drank for his relief.

Now lived the youth in freedom, but debarr'd
From constant pleasure, and he thought it hard;   35
Hard that he could not every wish obey,
But must awhile relinquish ale and play;
Hard! that he could not to his cards attend,
But must acquire the money he would spend.

With greedy eye he look'd on all he saw,   40
He knew not justice, and he laugh'd at law.
On all he mark'd, he stretched his ready hand;
He fish'd by water and he filch'd by land:

Oft in the night has Peter dropp'd his oar,
Fled from his boat, and sought for prey on shore;　45
Oft up the hedge-row glided, on his back
Bearing the orchard's produce in a sack,
Or farm-yard load, tugg'd fiercely from the stack;
And as these wrongs to greater numbers rose,
The more he look'd on all men as his foes.　50

He built a mud-wall'd hovel, where he kept
His various wealth, and there he oft-times slept;
But no success could please his cruel soul,
He wished for one to trouble and control;
He wanted some obedient boy to stand　55
And bear the blow of his outrageous hand;
And hoped to find in some propitious hour
A feeling creature subject to his power.

Peter had heard there were in London then,—
Still have they being!—workhouse-clearing men,　60
Who, undisturb'd by feelings just or kind,
Would parish-boys to needy tradesmen bind:
They in their want a trifling sum would take,
And toiling slaves of piteous orphans make.

Such Peter sought, and when a lad was found,　65
The sum was dealt him, and the slave was bound.
Some few in town observed in Peter's trap
A boy, with jacket blue and woollen cap;
But none inquired how Peter used the rope,
Or what the bruise that made the stripling stoop;　70
None could the ridges on his back behold,
None sought him shiv'ring in the winter's cold;
None put the question,—'Peter dost thou give,
The boy his food?—What, man! the lad must live.
Consider, Peter, let the child have bread,　75
He'll serve thee better if he's stroked and fed.'
None reason'd thus—and some, on hearing cries,
Said calmly, 'Grimes is at his exercise.'

Pinn'd, beaten, cold, pinch'd, threaten'd, and
　　　　abused—
His efforts punished and his food refused,—　80
Awake tormented,—soon aroused from sleep,—

Struck if he wept, and yet compell'd to weep,
The trembling boy dropp'd down and strove to pray,
Received a blow, and trembling turn'd away,
Or sobb'd and hid his piteous face;—while he,   85
The savage master, grinn'd in horrid glee:
He'd now the power he ever loved to show,
A feeling being subject to his blow.

Thus lived the lad, in hunger, peril, pain,
His tears despised, his supplications vain: 90
Compell'd by fear to lie, by need to steal,
His bed uneasy and unbless'd his meal,
For three sad years the boy his tortures bore,
And then his pains and trials were no more.

'How died he, Peter?' when the people said,   95
He growl'd—'I found him lifeless in his bed;'
Then tried for softer tone, and sigh'd, 'Poor Sam is
      dead.'
Yet murmurs were there, and some questions ask'd—
How he was fed, how punish'd, and how task'd?
Much they suspected, but they little proved,   100
And Peter pass'd untroubled and unmoved.

Another boy with equal ease was found,
The money granted, and the victim bound;
And what his fate?—One night it chanced he fell
From the boat's mast and perish'd in her well,   105
Where fish were living kept, and where the boy
(So reason'd men) could not himself destroy:—

'Yes! so it was,' said Peter, 'in his play,
(For he was idle both by night and day,)   109
He climb'd the main-mast and then fell below;'—
Then show'd his corpse, and pointed to the blow:
'What said the jury?'—they were long in doubt,
But sturdy Peter faced the matter out:
So they dismissed him, saying at the time,
'Keep fast your hatchway when you've boys who
      climb.'   115
This hit the conscience, and he colour'd more
Than for the closest questions put before.

Thus all his fears the verdict set aside,

And at the slave-shop Peter still applied.

Then came a boy, of manners soft and mild,— 120
Our seamen's wives with grief beheld the child;
All thought (the poor themselves) that he was one
Of gentle blood, some noble sinner's son,
Who had, belike, deceived some humble maid,
Whom he had first seduced and then betray'd:— 125
However this, he seem'd a gracious lad,
In grief submissive, and with patience sad.

Passive he labour'd, till his slender frame
Bent with his loads, and he at length was lame:
Strange that a frame so weak could bear so long 130
The grossest insult and the foulest wrong;
But there were causes—in the town they gave
Fire, food, and comfort, to the gentle slave;
And though stern Peter, with a cruel hand,
And knotted rope, enforced the rude command, 135
Yet he consider'd what he'd lately felt,
And his vile blows with selfish pity dealt.

One day such draughts the cruel fisher made,
He could not vend them in his borough-trade,
But sail'd for London-Mart: the boy was ill, 140
But ever humbled to his master's will;
And on the river, where they smoothly sail'd,
He strove with terror and awhile prevail'd;
But new to danger on the angry sea,
He clung affrighten'd to his master's knee: 145
The boat grew leaky and the wind was strong,
Rough was the passage and the time was long;
His liquor fail'd, and Peter's wrath arose,—
No more is known—the rest we must suppose,
Or learn of Peter:—Peter says, he 'spied 150
The stripling's danger and for harbour tried;
Meantime the fish, and then th' apprentice died.'

The pitying women raised a clamour round,
And weeping said, 'Thou hast thy 'prentice drown'd.'

Now the stern man was summon'd to the hall, 155
To tell his tale before the burghers all:
He gave th' account; profess'd the lad he loved,

And kept his brazen features all unmoved.
    The mayor himself with tone severe replied,—
'Henceforth with thee shall never boy abide;   160
Hire thee a freeman, whom thou durst not beat,
But who, in thy despite, will sleep and eat:
Free thou art now!—again shouldst thou appear,
Thou'lt find thy sentence, like thy soul, severe.'
    Alas! for Peter not a helping hand,   165
So was he hated, could he now command;
Alone he row'd his boat, alone he cast
His nets beside, or made his anchor fast;
To hold a rope or hear a curse was none,—
He toil'd and rail'd; he groan'd and swore alone.   170
    Thus by himself compell'd to live each day,
To wait for certain hours the tide's delay;
At the same times the same dull views to see,
The bounding marsh-bank and the blighted tree;
The water only, when the tides were high,   175
When low, the mud half cover'd and half-dry;
The sun-burnt tar that blisters on the planks,
And bank-side stakes in their uneven ranks;
Heaps of entangled weeds that slowly float,
As the tide rolls by the impeded boat.   180
    When tides were neap, and, in the sultry day,
Through the tall bounding mud-banks made their
         way,
Which on each side rose swelling, and below
The dark warm flood ran silently and slow;
There anchoring, Peter chose from man to hide,   185
There hang his head, and view the lazy tide
In its hot slimy channel slowly glide;
Where the small eels that left the deeper way
For the warm shore, within the shallows play;
Where gaping mussels, left upon the mud,   190
Slope their slow passage to the fallen flood;—
Here dull and hopeless he'd lie down and trace
How sidelong crabs had scrawl'd their crooked race,
Or sadly listen to the tuneless cry
Of fishing gull or clanging golden-eye;   195

What time the sea-birds to the marsh would come,
And the loud bittern, from the bull-rush home,
Gave from the salt ditch side the bellowing boom:
He nursed the feelings these dull scenes produce,
And loved to stop beside the opening sluice;　　200
Where the small stream, confined in narrow bound,
Ran with a dull, unvaried, sadd'ning sound;
Where all, presented to the eye or ear,
Oppress'd the soul with misery, grief, and fear.

Besides these objects, there were places three,　205
Which Peter seem'd with certain dread to see;
When he drew near them he would turn from each,
And loudly whistle till he pass'd the reach.

A change of scene to him brought no relief;
In town, 'twas plain, men took him for a thief:　210
The sailors' wives would stop him in the street,
And say, 'Now, Peter, thou'st no boy to beat:'
Infants at play when they perceived him, ran,
Warning each other—'That's the wicked man:'
He growl'd an oath, and in an angry tone　　215
Cursed the whole place and wish'd to be alone.

Alone he was, the same dull scenes in view,
And still more gloomy in his sight they grew:
Though man he hated, yet employ'd alone
At bootless labour, he would swear and groan,　220
Cursing the shoals that glided by the spot,
And gulls that caught them when his arts could not.

Cold nervous tremblings shook his sturdy frame,
And strange disease—he couldn't say the name;
Wild were his dreams, and oft he rose in fright,　225
Waked by his view of horrors in the night,—
Horrors that would the sternest minds amaze,
Horrors that demons might be proud to raise:
And though he felt forsaken, grieved at heart,
To think he lived from all mankind apart;　　230
Yet, if a man approach'd, in terrors he would start.

A winter pass'd since Peter saw the town,
And summer-lodgers were again come down;
These, idly curious, with their glasses spied

The ships in bay as anchor'd for the tide,—   235
The river's craft,—the bustle of the quay,—
And sea-port views, which landmen love to see.
    One, up the river, had a man and boat
Seen day by day, now anchor'd, now afloat;
Fisher he seem'd, yet used no net nor hook;   240
Of sea-fowl swimming by no heed he took,
But on the gliding waves still fix'd his lazy look:
At certain stations he would view the stream,
As if he stood bewilder'd in a dream,
Or that some power had chain'd him for a time, 245
To feel a curse or meditate on crime.
    This known, some curious, some in pity went,
And others question'd—'Wretch, dost thou repent?'
He heard, he trembled, and in fear resign'd
His boat: new terror fill'd his restless mind;   250
Furious he grew, and up the country ran,
And there they seized him—a distemper'd man:—
Him we received, and to a parish-bed,
Follow'd and cursed, the groaning man was led.
    Here when they saw him, whom they used to shun,
A lost, lone man, so harass'd and undone;   256
Our gentle females, ever prompt to feel,
Perceived compassion on their anger steal;
His crimes they could not from their memories blot,
But they were grieved, and trembled at his lot. 260
    A priest too came, to whom his words are told;
And all the signs they shudder'd to behold.
    'Look! look!' they cried; 'his limbs with horror
        shake,
And as he grinds his teeth, what noise they make!
How glare his angry eyes, and yet he's not awake:
See! what cold drops upon his forehead stand,   266
And how he clenches that broad bony hand.'
    The priest attending, found he spoke at times
As one alluding to his fears and crimes;
'It was the fall,' he mutter'd, 'I can show   270
The manner how,—I never struck a blow:'—
And then aloud,—'Unhand me, free my chain;

On oath, he fell—it struck him to the brain:—
Why ask my father?—that old man will swear
Against my life; besides, he wasn't there:—   275
What, all agreed?—Am I to die to-day?—
My Lord, in mercy give me time to pray.'

    Then, as they watch'd him, calmer he became,
And grew so weak he couldn't move his frame,
But murmuring spake,—while they could see and
    hear   280
The start of terror and the groan of fear;
See the large dew-beads on his forehead rise,
And the cold death-drop glaze his sunken eyes;
Nor yet he died, but with unwonted force
Seem'd with some fancied being to discourse: 285
He knew us not, or with accustom'd art
He hid the knowledge, yet exposed his heart;
'Twas part confession and the rest defence,
A madman's tale, with gleams of waking sense.

    'I'll tell you all,' he said, 'the very day   290
When the old man first placed them in my way:
My father's spirit—he who always tried
To give me trouble, when he lived and died—
When he was gone he could not be content
To see my days in painful labour spent,   295
But would appoint his meetings, and he made
Me watch at these, and so neglect my trade.

    ''Twas one hot noon, all silent, still, serene,
No living being had I lately seen;
I paddled up and down and dipp'd my net,   300
But (such his pleasure) I could nothing get,—
A father's pleasure, when his toil was done,
To plague and torture thus an only son!
And so I sat and look'd upon the stream,
How it ran on, and felt as in a dream: 305
But dream it was not: No!—I fix'd my eyes
On the mid stream and saw the spirits rise:
I saw my father on the water stand,
And hold a thin pale boy in either hand;
And there they glided ghastly on the top   310

Of the salt flood, and never touch'd a drop:
I would have struck them, but they knew th' intent,
And smiled upon the oar, and down they went.
   'Now, from that day, whenever I began
To dip my net, there stood the hard old man—   315
He and those boys: I humbled me and pray'd
They would be gone; they heeded not, but stay'd:
Nor could I turn, nor would the boat go by,
But, gazing on the spirits, there was I: 319
They bade me leap to death, but I was loth to die:
And every day, as sure as day arose,
Would these three spirits meet me ere the close;
To hear and mark them daily was my doom,
And "Come," they said, with weak, sad voices, "come."
To row away, with all my strength I try'd,   325
But there were they, hard by me in the tide,
The three unbodied forms—and "Come," still "come,"
    they cried.
   'Fathers should pity—but this old man shook
His hoary locks, and froze me by a look:
Thrice, when I struck them, through the water came
A hollow groan, that weaken'd all my frame: 331
"Father!" said I, "have mercy:"—he replied,
I know not what—the angry spirit lied,—
"Didst thou not draw thy knife?" said he:—'Twas
    true,
But I had pity and my arm withdrew: 335
He cried for mercy, which I kindly gave,
But he has no compassion in his grave.
   'There were three places, where they ever rose,—
The whole long river has not such as those—
Places accursed, where, if a man remain,   340
He'll see the things which strike him to the brain;
And there they made me on my paddle lean,
And look at them for hours;—accursed scene!
When they would glide to that smooth eddy-space,
Then bid me leap and join them in the place;   345
And at my groans each little villain sprite
Enjoy'd my pains and vanish'd in delight.

'In one fierce summer-day, when my poor brain
Was burning hot, and cruel was my pain,
Then came this father-foe, and there he stood   350
With his two boys again upon the flood:
There was more mischief in their eyes, more glee
In their pale faces when they glared at me:
Still they did force me on the oar to rest,
And when they saw me fainting and oppress'd,   355
He, with his hand, the old man, scoop'd the flood,
And there came flame about him mix'd with blood;
He bade me stoop and look upon the place,
Then flung the hot-red liquor in my face;
Burning it blazed, and then I roar'd for pain,   360
I thought the demons would have turn'd my brain.

'Still there they stood, and forced me to behold
A place of horrors—they can not be told—
Where the flood open'd, there I heard the shriek
Of tortured guilt—no earthly tongue can speak: 365
"All days alike! for ever!" did they say,
"And unremitted torments every day"—
Yes, so they said'—But here he ceased and gazed
On all around, affrighten'd and amazed;
And still he tried to speak, and look'd in dread   370
Of frighten'd females gathering round his bed;
Then dropp'd exhausted and appear'd at rest,
Till the strong foe the vital powers possess'd:
Then with an inward, broken voice he cried,
'Again they come!' and mutter'd as he died.   375

ROBERT BURNS

1759–1796

Tam o' Shanter

When chapman billies leave the street,
And drouthy neibors neibors meet,
As market-days are wearing late,
An' folk begin to tak the gate;

While we sit bousing at the nappy, 5
An' getting fou and unco happy,
We think na on the lang Scots miles,
The mosses, waters, slaps, and styles,
That lie between us and our hame,
Whare sits our sulky sullen dame, 10
Gathering her brows like gathering storm,
Nursing her wrath to keep it warm.

 This truth fand honest Tam o' Shanter,
As he frae Ayr ae night did canter—
(Auld Ayr, wham ne'er a town surpasses 15
For honest men and bonnie lasses).

 O Tam! hadst thou but been sae wise
As ta'en thy ain wife Kate's advice!
She tauld thee weel thou was a skellum,
A bletherin', blusterin', drunken blellum; 20
That frae November till October,
Ae market-day thou was na sober;
That ilka melder wi' the miller
Thou sat as lang as thou had siller;
That every naig was ca'd a shoe on, 25
The smith and thee gat roarin' fou on;
That at the Lord's house, even on Sunday,
Thou drank wi' Kirkton Jean till Monday.
She prophesied that, late or soon,
Thou would be found deep drown'd in Doon;
Or catch'd wi' warlocks in the mirk 31
By Alloway's auld haunted kirk.

 Ah, gentle dames! it gars me greet
To think how mony counsels sweet,
How mony lengthen'd sage advices, 35
The husband frae the wife despises!

 But to our tale: Ae market night,
Tam had got planted unco right,
Fast by an ingle, bleezing finely,
Wi' reaming swats, that drank divinely; 40
And at his elbow, Souter Johnny,
His ancient, trusty, drouthy crony;
Tam lo'ed him like a very brither;

They had been fou for weeks thegither.
The night drave on wi' sangs and clatter,   45
And aye the ale was growing better:
The landlady and Tam grew gracious,
Wi' favours secret, sweet, and precious;
The souter tauld his queerest stories;
The landlord's laugh was ready chorus: 50
The storm without might rair and rustle,
Tam did na mind the storm a whistle.

Care, mad to see a man sae happy,
E'en drown'd himsel amang the nappy.
As bees flee hame wi' lades o' treasure,   55
The minutes wing'd their way wi' pleasure;
Kings may be blest, but Tam was glorious,
O'er a' the ills o' life victorious!

But pleasures are like poppies spread—
You seize the flow'r, its bloom is shed;   60
Or like the snow falls in the river—
A moment white, then melts for ever;
Or like the borealis race,
That flit ere you can point their place;
Or like the rainbow's lovely form   65
Evanishing amid the storm.
Nae man can tether time or tide;
The hour approaches Tam maun ride;
That hour, o' night's black arch the key-stane,
That dreary hour, he mounts his beast in;   70
And sic a night he taks the road in,
As ne'er poor sinner was abroad in.

The wind blew as 'twad blawn its last;
The rattling show'rs rose on the blast;
The speedy gleams the darkness swallow'd;   75
Loud, deep, and lang, the thunder bellow'd:
That night, a child might understand,
The Deil had business on his hand.

Weel mounted on his gray mare, Meg,
A better never lifted leg,   80
Tam skelpit on thro' dub and mire,
Despising wind, and rain, and fire;

Whiles holding fast his gude blue bonnet;
Whiles crooning o'er some auld Scots sonnet;
Whiles glow'ring round wi' prudent cares,   85
Lest bogles catch him unawares.
Kirk-Alloway was drawing nigh,
Whare ghaists and houlets nightly cry.
  By this time he was cross the ford,
Whare in the snaw the chapman smoor'd;   90
And past the birks and meikle stane,
Whare drunken Charlie brak's neck-bane;
And thro' the whins, and by the cairn,
Whare hunters fand the murder'd bairn,
And near the thorn, aboon the well,   95
Whare Mungo's mither hang'd hersel.
Before him Doon pours all his floods;
The doubling storm roars thro' the woods;
The lightnings flash from pole to pole;
Near and more near the thunders roll: 100
When, glimmering thro' the groaning trees,
Kirk-Alloway seem'd in a bleeze;
Thro' ilka bore the beams were glancing;
And loud resounded mirth and dancing.
  Inspiring bold John Barleycorn!   105
What dangers thou canst make us scorn!
Wi' tippenny, we fear nae evil;
Wi' usquebae, we'll face the devil!
The swats sae ream'd in Tammie's noddle,
Fair play, he car'd na deils a boddle!   110
But Maggie stood right sair astonish'd,
Till, by the heel and hand admonish'd,
She ventur'd forward on the light;
And, vow! Tam saw an unco sight!
Warlocks and witches in a dance!   115
Nae cotillon brent new frae France,
But hornpipes, jigs, strathspeys, and reels,
Put life and mettle in their heels.
A winnock-bunker in the east,
There sat auld Nick, in shape o' beast—   120
A touzie tyke, black, grim, and large!

To gie them music was his charge:
He screw'd the pipes and gart them skirl,
Till roof and rafters a' did dirl.
Coffins stood round like open presses,   125
That shaw'd the dead in their last dresses;
And by some devilish cantraip sleight
Each in its cauld hand held a light,
By which heroic Tam was able
To note upon the haly table   130
A murderer's banes in gibbet-airns;
Twa span-lang, wee, unchristen'd bairns;
A thief new-cutted frae a rape—
Wi' his last gasp his gab did gape;
Five tomahawks, wi' blude red-rusted;   135
Five scymitars, wi' murder crusted;
A garter, which a babe had strangled;
A knife, a father's throat had mangled,
Whom his ain son o' life bereft—
The gray hairs yet stack to the heft;   140
Wi' mair of horrible and awefu',
Which even to name wad be unlawfu'.

As Tammie glowr'd, amaz'd, and curious,
The mirth and fun grew fast and furious:
The piper loud and louder blew;   145
The dancers quick and quicker flew;
They reel'd, they set, they cross'd, they cleekit,
Till ilka carlin swat and reekit,
And coost her duddies to the wark,
And linkit at it in her sark!   150

Now Tam, O Tam! had thae been queans,
A' plump and strapping in their teens;
Their sarks, instead o' creeshie flannen,
Been snaw-white seventeen hunder linen!
Thir breeks o' mine, my only pair,   155
That ance were plush, o' gude blue hair,
I wad hae gi'en them off my hurdies,
For ae blink o' the bonnie burdies!

But wither'd beldams, auld and droll,
Rigwoodie hags wad spean a foal,   160

Louping and flinging on a crummock,
I wonder didna turn thy stomach.
　　But Tam kend what was what fu' brawlie
There was ae winsome wench and wawlie
That night enlisted in the core,　　　　　165
Lang after kend on Carrick shore!
(For mony a beast to dead she shot,
And perish'd mony a bonnie boat,
And shook baith meikle corn and bear,
And kept the country-side in fear.)　　　170
Her cutty sark, o' Paisley harn,
That while a lassie she had worn,
In longitude tho' sorely scanty,
It was her best, and she was vauntie.—
Ah! little kend thy reverend grannie　　175
That sark she coft for her wee Nannie
Wi' twa pund Scots ('twas a' her riches)
Wad ever grac'd a dance of witches!
　　But here my Muse her wing maun cour;
Sic flights are far beyond her pow'r—　　180
To sing how Nannie lap and flang,
(A souple jade she was, and strang),
And how Tam stood, like ane bewitch'd,
And thought his very een enrich'd;
Even Satan glowr'd, and fidg'd fu' fain,　185
And hotch'd and blew wi' might and main:
Till first ae caper, syne anither,
Tam tint his reason a' thegither,
And roars out 'Weel done, Cutty-sark!'
And in an instant all was dark!　　　　　190
And scarcely had he Maggie rallied,
When out the hellish legion sallied.
　　As bees bizz out wi' angry fyke
When plundering herds assail their byke,
As open pussie's mortal foes　　　　　　195
When pop! she starts before their nose,
As eager runs the market-crowd,
When 'Catch the thief!' resounds aloud,
So Maggie runs; the witches follow,

Wi' mony an eldritch skriech and hollow.   200
    Ah, Tam! ah, Tam! thou'll get thy fairin'!
In hell they'll roast thee like a herrin'!
In vain thy Kate awaits thy comin'!
Kate soon will be a woefu' woman!
Now do thy speedy utmost, Meg,   205
And win the key-stane of the brig:
There at them thou thy tail may toss,
A running stream they darena cross.
But ere the key-stane she could make,
The fient a tail she had to shake!   210
For Nannie, far before the rest,
Hard upon noble Maggie prest,
And flew at Tam wi' furious ettle;
But little wist she Maggie's mettle!
Ae spring brought off her master hale,   215
But left behind her ain gray tail:
The carlin claught her by the rump,
And left poor Maggie scarce a stump.

    Now, wha this tale o' truth shall read,
Ilk man and mother's son, take heed;   220
Whene'er to drink you are inclin'd,
Or cutty-sarks run in your mind,
Think! ye may buy the joys o'er dear;
Remember Tam o' Shanter's mare.

WILLIAM WORDSWORTH

1770–1850

Michael

A Pastoral Poem

If from the public way you turn your steps
Up the tumultuous brook of Green-head Ghyll,
You will suppose that with an upright path
Your feet must struggle; in such bold ascent
The pastoral mountains front you, face to face.   5
But, courage! for around that boisterous brook

The mountains have all opened out themselves,
And made a hidden valley of their own.
No habitation can be seen; but they
Who journey thither find themselves alone   10
With a few sheep, with rocks and stones, and kites
That overhead are sailing in the sky.
It is in truth an utter solitude;
Nor should I have made mention of this Dell
But for one object which you might pass by,   15
Might see and notice not. Beside the brook
Appears a straggling heap of unhewn stones!
And to that simple object appertains
A story—unenriched with strange events,
Yet not unfit, I deem, for the fireside,   20
Or for the summer shade. It was the first
Of those domestic tales that spake to me
Of Shepherds, dwellers in the valleys, men
Whom I already loved;—not verily
For their own sakes, but for the fields and hills   25
Where was their occupation and abode.
And hence this Tale, while I was yet a Boy
Careless of books, yet having felt the power
Of Nature, by the gentle agency
Of natural objects, led me on to feel   30
For passions that were not my own, and think
(At random and imperfectly indeed)
On man, the heart of man, and human life.
Therefore, although it be a history
Homely and rude, I will relate the same   35
For the delight of a few natural hearts;
And, with yet fonder feeling, for the sake
Of youthful Poets, who among these hills
Will be my second self when I am gone.

Upon the forest-side in Grasmere Vale   40
There dwelt a Shepherd, Michael was his name;
An old man, stout of heart, and strong of limb.
His bodily frame had been from youth to age
Of an unusual strength: his mind was keen,

Intense, and frugal, apt for all affairs, 45
And in his shepherd's calling he was prompt
And watchful more than ordinary men.
Hence had he learned the meaning of all winds,
Of blasts of every tone; and oftentimes,
When others heeded not, He heard the South 50
Make subterranean music, like the noise
Of bagpipers on distant Highland hills.
The Shepherd, at such warning, of his flock
Bethought him, and he to himself would say,
'The winds are now devising work for me!' 55
And, truly, at all times, the storm, that drives
The traveller to a shelter, summoned him
Up to the mountains: he had been alone
Amid the heart of many thousand mists,
That came to him, and left him, on the heights. 60
So lived he till his eightieth year was past.
And grossly that man errs, who should suppose
That the green valleys, and the streams and rocks,
Were things indifferent to the Shepherd's thoughts.
Fields, where with cheerful spirits he had breathed
The common air; hills, which with vigorous step 66
He had so often climbed; which had impressed
So many incidents upon his mind
Of hardship, skill or courage, joy or fear;
Which, like a book, preserved the memory 70
Of the dumb animals, whom he had saved,
Had fed or sheltered, linking to such acts
The certainty of honourable gain;
Those fields, those hills—what could they less? had laid
Strong hold on his affections, were to him 75
A pleasurable feeling of blind love,
The pleasure which there is in life itself.

His days had not been passed in singleness.
His Helpmate was a comely matron, old—
Though younger than himself full twenty years. 80
She was a woman of a stirring life,

Whose heart was in her house: two wheels she had
Of antique form; this large, for spinning wool;
That small, for flax; and, if one wheel had rest,
It was because the other was at work.   85
The Pair had but one inmate in their house,
An only Child, who had been born to them
When Michael, telling o'er his years, began
To deem that he was old,—in shepherd's phrase,
With one foot in the grave. This only Son,   90
With two brave sheep-dogs tried in many a storm,
The one of an inestimable worth,
Made all their household. I may truly say,
That they were as a proverb in the vale
For endless industry. When day was gone,   95
And from their occupations out of doors
The Son and Father were come home, even then,
Their labour did not cease; unless when all
Turned to the cleanly supper-board, and there,
Each with a mess of pottage and skimmed milk,   100
Sat round the basket piled with oaten cakes,
And their plain home-made cheese. Yet when the meal
Was ended, Luke (for so the Son was named)
And his old Father both betook themselves
To such convenient work as might employ   105
Their hands by the fire-side; perhaps to card
Wool for the Housewife's spindle, or repair
Some injury done to sickle, flail, or scythe,
Or other implement of house or field.

Down from the ceiling, by the chimney's edge,
That in our ancient uncouth country style   111
With huge and black projection overbrowed
Large space beneath, as duly as the light
Of day grew dim the Housewife hung a lamp;
An aged utensil, which had performed   115
Service beyond all others of its kind.
Early at evening did it burn—and late,
Surviving comrade of uncounted hours,

Which, going by from year to year, had found,
And left, the couple neither gay perhaps   120
Nor cheerful, yet with objects and with hopes,
Living a life of eager industry.
And now, when Luke had reached his eighteenth year,
There by the light of this old lamp they sate,
Father and Son, while far into the night   125
The Housewife plied her own peculiar work,
Making the cottage through the silent hours
Murmur as with the sound of summer flies.
This light was famous in its neighbourhood,
And was a public symbol of the life   130
That thrifty Pair had lived. For, as it chanced,
Their cottage on a plot of rising ground
Stood single, with large prospect, north and south,
High into Easedale, up to Dunmail-Raise,
And westward to the village near the lake;   135
And from this constant light, so regular,
And so far seen, the House itself, by all
Who dwelt within the limits of the vale,
Both old and young, was named THE EVENING STAR.

Thus living on through such a length of years,
The Shepherd, if he loved himself, must needs   141
Have loved his Helpmate; but to Michael's heart
This son of his old age was yet more dear—
Less from instinctive tenderness, the same   144
Fond spirit that blindly works in the blood of all—
Than that a child, more than all other gifts
That earth can offer to declining man,
Brings hope with it, and forward-looking thoughts,
And stirrings of inquietude, when they
By tendency of nature needs must fail.   150
Exceeding was the love he bare to him,
His heart and his heart's joy! For oftentimes
Old Michael, while he was a babe in arms,
Had done him female service, not alone
For pastime and delight, as is the use   155
Of fathers, but with patient mind enforced

To acts of tenderness; and he had rocked
His cradle, as with a woman's gentle hand.

    And in a later time, ere yet the Boy
Had put on boy's attire, did Michael love,   160
Albeit of a stern unbending mind,
To have the Young-one in his sight, when he
Wrought in the field, or on his shepherd's stool
Sate with a fettered sheep before him stretched
Under the large old oak, that near his door   165
Stood single, and, from matchless depth of shade.
Chosen for the Shearer's covert from the sun,
Thence in our rustic dialect was called
The CLIPPING TREE, a name which yet it bears.
There, while they two were sitting in the shade,   170
With others round them, earnest all and blithe,
Would Michael exercise his heart with looks
Of fond correction and reproof bestowed
Upon the Child, if he disturbed the sheep
By catching at their legs, or with his shouts   175
Scared them, while they lay still beneath the shears.

    And when by Heaven's good grace the boy grew up
A healthy Lad, and carried in his cheek
Two steady roses that were five years old;
Then Michael from a winter coppice cut   180
With his own hand a sapling, which he hooped
With iron, making it throughout in all
Due requisites a perfect shepherd's staff,
And gave it to the Boy; wherewith equipt
He as a watchman oftentimes was placed   185
At gate or gap, to stem or turn the flock;
And, to his office prematurely called,
There stood the urchin, as you will divine,
Something between a hindrance and a help;
And for this cause not always, I believe,   190
Receiving from his Father hire of praise;
Though nought was left undone which staff, or voice,
Or looks, or threatening gestures, could perform.

But soon as Luke, full ten years old, could stand
Against the mountain blasts; and to the heights,
Not fearing toil, or length of weary ways,   196
He with his Father daily went, and they
Were as companions, why should I relate
That objects which the Shepherd loved before
Were dearer now? that from the Boy there came   200
Feelings and emanations—things which were
Light to the sun and music to the wind;
And that the old Man's heart seemed born again?

Thus in his Father's sight the Boy grew up: 204
And now, when he had reached his eighteenth year,
He was his comfort and his daily hope.

While in this sort the simple household lived
From day to day, to Michael's ear there came
Distressful tidings. Long before the time
Of which I speak, the Shepherd had been bound   210
In surety for his brother's son, a man
Of an industrious life, and ample means;
But unforeseen misfortunes suddenly
Had prest upon him; and old Michael now
Was summoned to discharge the forfeiture,   215
A grievous penalty, but little less
Than half his substance. This unlooked-for claim,
At the first hearing, for a moment took
More hope out of his life than he supposed
That any old man ever could have lost.   220
As soon as he had armed himself with strength
To look his trouble in the face, it seemed
The Shepherd's sole resource to sell at once
A portion of his patrimonial fields.
Such was his first resolve; he thought again,   225
And his heart failed him. 'Isabel,' said he,
Two evenings after he had heard the news,
'I have been toiling more than seventy years,
And in the open sunshine of God's love
Have we all lived; yet, if these fields of ours 230

Should pass into a stranger's hand, I think
That I could not lie quiet in my grave.
Our lot is a hard lot; the sun himself
Has scarcely been more diligent than I;
And I have lived to be a fool at last   235
To my own family. An evil man
That was, and made an evil choice, if he
Were false to us; and, if he were not false,
There are ten thousand to whom loss like this
Had been no sorrow. I forgive him;—but   240
'Twere better to be dumb than to talk thus.

When I began, my purpose was to speak
Of remedies and of a cheerful hope.
Our Luke shall leave us, Isabel; the land
Shall not go from us, and it shall be free;   245
He shall possess it, free as is the wind
That passes over it. We have, thou know'st,
Another kinsman—he will be our friend
In this distress. He is a prosperous man,
Thriving in trade—and Luke to him shall go,   250
And with his kinsman's help and his own thrift
He quickly will repair this loss, and then
He may return to us. If here he stay,
What can be done? Where every one is poor,
What can be gained?'
           At this the old Man paused,   255
And Isabel sat silent, for her mind
Was busy, looking back into past times.
There's Richard Bateman, thought she to herself,
He was a parish-boy—at the church-door
They made a gathering for him, shillings, pence,   260
And halfpennies, wherewith the neighbours bought
A basket, which they filled with pedlar's wares;
And, with this basket on his arm, the lad
Went up to London, found a master there,
Who, out of many, chose the trusty boy   265
To go and overlook his merchandise
Beyond the seas; where he grew wondrous rich,

And left estates and monies to the poor,
And, at his birth-place, built a chapel floored
With marble, which he sent from foreign lands. 270
These thoughts, and many others of like sort,
Passed quickly through the mind of Isabel,
And her face brightened. The old Man was glad,
And thus resumed:—'Well, Isabel! this scheme
These two days has been meat and drink to me. 275
Far more than we have lost is left us yet.

We have enough—I wish indeed that I
Were younger;—but this hope is a good hope.
Make ready Luke's best garments, of the best
Buy for him more, and let us send him forth 280
To-morrow, or the next day, or to-night:
—If he *could* go, the Boy should go to-night.'

Here Michael ceased, and to the fields went forth
With a light heart. The Housewife for five days
Was restless morn and night, and all day long 285
Wrought on with her best fingers to prepare
Things needful for the journey of her son.
But Isabel was glad when Sunday came
To stop her in her work: for, when she lay
By Michael's side, she through the last two nights
Heard him, how he was troubled in his sleep: 291
And when they rose at morning she could see
That all his hopes were gone. That day at noon
She said to Luke, while they two by themselves
Were sitting at the door, 'Thou must not go: 295
We have no other Child but thee to lose,
None to remember—do not go away,
For if thou leave thy Father he will die.'
The Youth made answer with a jocund voice;
And Isabel, when she had told her fears, 300
Recovered heart. That evening her best fare
Did she bring forth, and all together sat
Like happy people round a Christmas fire.

With daylight Isabel resumed her work;
And all the ensuing week the house appeared 305

As cheerful as a grove in Spring: at length
The expected letter from their kinsman came,
With kind assurances that he would do
His utmost for the welfare of the Boy;
To which, requests were added, that forthwith   310
He might be sent to him. Ten times or more
The letter was read over; Isabel
Went forth to show it to the neighbours round;
Nor was there at that time on English land
A prouder heart than Luke's. When Isabel   315
Had to her house returned, the old Man said,
'He shall depart to-morrow.' To this word
The Housewife answered, talking much of things
Which, if at such short notice he should go,
Would surely be forgotten. But at length   320
She gave consent, and Michael was at ease.

    Near the tumultuous brook of Green-head Ghyll,
In that deep valley, Michael had designed
To build a Sheep-fold; and, before he heard
The tidings of his melancholy loss,   325
For this same purpose he had gathered up
A heap of stones, which by the streamlet's edge
Lay thrown together, ready for the work.
With Luke that evening thitherward he walked:
And soon as they had reached the place he stopped,
And thus the old Man spake to him:—'My son,   331
To-morrow thou wilt leave me: with full heart
I look upon thee, for thou art the same
That wert a promise to me ere thy birth,
And all thy life hast been my daily joy.   335
I will relate to thee some little part
Of our two histories; 'twill do thee good
When thou art from me, even if I should touch
On things thou canst not know of.——After thou
First cam'st into the world—as oft befalls   340
To new-born infants—thou didst sleep away
Two days, and blessings from thy Father's tongue
Then fell upon thee. Day by day passed on,

And still I loved thee with increasing love.
Never to living ear came sweeter sounds   345
Than when I heard thee by our own fireside
First uttering, without words, a natural tune;
While thou, a feeding babe, didst in thy joy
Sing at thy Mother's breast. Month followed month,
And in the open fields my life was passed   350
And on the mountains; else I think that thou
Hadst been brought up upon thy Father's knees.
But we were playmates, Luke: among these hills,
As well thou knowest, in us the old and young
Have played together, nor with me didst thou   355
Lack any pleasure which a boy can know.'
Luke had a manly heart; but at these words
He sobbed aloud. The old Man grasped his hand,
And said, 'Nay, do not take it so—I see
That these are things of which I need not speak.   360
—Even to the utmost I have been to thee
A kind and a good Father: and herein
I but repay a gift which I myself
Received at others' hands; for, though now old
Beyond the common life of man, I still   365
Remember them who loved me in my youth.
Both of them sleep together: here they lived,
As all their Forefathers had done; and, when
At length their time was come, they were not loth
To give their bodies to the family mould.   370
I wished that thou shouldst live the life they lived,
But 'tis a long time to look back, my Son,
And see so little gain from threescore years.
These fields were burthened when they came to me;
Till I was forty years of age, not more   375
Than half of my inheritance was mine.
I toiled and toiled; God blessed me in my work,
And till these three weeks past the land was free.
—It looks as if it never could endure
Another Master. Heaven forgive me, Luke,   380
If I judge ill for thee, but it seems good
That thou shouldst go.'

                    At this the old Man paused;
Then, pointing to the stones near which they stood,
Thus, after a short silence, he resumed:
'This was a work for us; and now, my Son,   385
It is a work for me. But, lay one stone—
Here, lay it for me, Luke, with thine own hands.
Nay, Boy, be of good hope;—we both may live
To see a better day. At eighty-four
I still am strong and hale;—do thou thy part;   390
I will do mine.—I will begin again
With many tasks that were resigned to thee:
Up to the heights, and in among the storms,
Will I without thee go again, and do
All works which I was wont to do alone,   395
Before I knew thy face.—Heaven bless thee, Boy!
Thy heart these two weeks has been beating fast
With many hopes; it should be so—yes—yes
I knew that thou couldst never have a wish
To leave me, Luke: thou hast been bound to me   400
Only by links of love: when thou art gone,
What will be left to us!—But I forget
My purposes. Lay now the corner-stone,
As I requested; and hereafter, Luke,
When thou art gone away, should evil men   405
Be thy companions, think of me, my Son,
And of this moment; hither turn thy thoughts,
And God will strengthen thee: amid all fear
And all temptation, Luke, I pray that thou
May'st bear in mind the life thy Fathers lived, 410
Who, being innocent, did for that cause
Bestir them in good deeds. Now, fare thee well—
When thou return'st, thou in this place wilt see
A work which is not here: a covenant
'Twill be between us; but, whatever fate   415
Befall thee, I shall love thee to the last,
And bear thy memory with me to the grave.'

    The Shepherd ended here; and Luke stooped down,
And, as his Father had requested, laid

The first stone of the Sheep-fold. At the sight   420
The old Man's grief broke from him; to his heart
He pressed his Son, he kissèd him and wept;
And to the house together they returned.
—Hushed was that House in peace, or seeming peace,
Ere the night fell:—with morrow's dawn the Boy
Began his journey, and, when he had reached   426
The public way, he put on a bold face;
And all the neighbours, as he passed their doors,
Came forth with wishes and with farewell prayers,
That followed him till he was out of sight.   430

A good report did from their Kinsman come,
Of Luke and his well-doing: and the Boy
Wrote loving letters, full of wondrous news,
Which, as the Housewife phrased it, were throughout
'The prettiest letters that were ever seen.'   435
Both parents read them with rejoicing hearts.
So, many months passed on: and once again
The Shepherd went about his daily work
With confident and cheerful thoughts; and now
Sometimes when he could find a leisure hour   440
He to that valley took his way, and there
Wrought at the Sheep-fold. Meantime Luke began
To slacken in his duty; and, at length,
He in the dissolute city gave himself
To evil courses: ignominy and shame   445
Fell on him, so that he was driven at last
To seek a hiding-place beyond the seas.

There is a comfort in the strength of love;
'Twill make a thing endurable, which else
Would overset the brain, or break the heart: 450
I have conversed with more than one who well
Remember the old Man, and what he was
Years after he had heard this heavy news.
His bodily frame had been from youth to age
Of an unusual strength. Among the rocks   455
He went, and still looked up to sun and cloud,

And listened to the wind; and, as before,
Performed all kinds of labour for his sheep,
And for the land, his small inheritance.
And to that hollow dell from time to time   460
Did he repair, to build the Fold of which
His flock had need. 'Tis not forgotten yet
The pity which was then in every heart
For the old Man—and 'tis believed by all,
That many and many a day he thither went,   465
And never lifted up a single stone.

There, by the Sheep-fold, sometimes was he seen
Sitting alone, or with his faithful Dog,
Then old, beside him, lying at his feet.
The length of full seven years, from time to time,
He at the building of this Sheep-fold wrought,   471
And left the work unfinished when he died.
Three years, or little more, did Isabel
Survive her Husband: at her death the estate
Was sold, and went into a stranger's hand.   475
The Cottage which was named the EVENING STAR
Is gone—the ploughshare has been through the
      ground
On which it stood; great changes have been wrought
In all the neighbourhood:—yet the oak is left
That grew beside their door; and the remains   480
Of the unfinished Sheep-fold may be seen
Beside the boisterous brook of Green-head Ghyll.

SIR WALTER SCOTT

1771–1832

Flodden

(From *Marmion*)

And why stands Scotland idly now,
Dark Flodden! on thy airy brow,
Since England gains the pass the while,
And struggles through the deep defile?

What checks the fiery soul of James?   5
Why sits that champion of the dames
   Inactive on his steed,
And sees, between him and his land,
Between him and Tweed's southern strand,
   His host Lord Surrey lead?   10
What 'vails the vain knight-errant's brand?
O, Douglas, for thy leading wand!
   Fierce Randolph, for thy speed!
O for one hour of Wallace wight,
Or well-skill'd Bruce, to rule the fight,   15
And cry 'Saint Andrew and our right!'
Another sight had seen that morn,
From Fate's dark book a leaf been torn,
And Flodden had been Bannockbourne!
The precious hour has pass'd in vain,   20
And England's host has gain'd the plain;
Wheeling their march, and circling still,
Around the base of Flodden hill.
'And see ascending squadrons come
   Between Tweed's river and the hill,   25
Foot, horse, and cannon: hap what hap,
My basnet to a prentice cap,
   Lord Surrey's o'er the Till!
Yet more! yet more!—how far array'd
They file from out the hawthorn shade,   30
   And sweep so gallant by!
With all their banners bravely spread,
   And all their armour flashing high,
Saint George might waken from the dead,
   To see fair England's standards fly.'—   35
'But see! look up—on Flodden bent
The Scottish foe has fired his tent.'
   And sudden, as he spoke,
From the sharp ridges of the hill,
All downward to the banks of Till,   40
   Was wreath'd in sable smoke.
Volum'd and fast, and rolling far,
The cloud envelop'd Scotland's war

As down the hill they broke;
Nor martial shout, nor minstrel tone, 45
Announc'd their march; their tread alone,
At times one warning trumpet blown,
    At times a stifled hum,
Told England, from his mountain throne
    King James did rushing come. 50
Scarce could they hear, or see their foes,
    Until at weapon-point they close.
They close, in clouds of smoke and dust,
With sword-sway, and with lance's thrust;
    And such a yell was there, 55
Of sudden and portentous birth,
As if men fought upon the earth,
    And fiends in upper air.
At length the freshening western blast
Aside the shroud of battle cast; 60
And, first, the ridge of mingled spears
Above the brightening cloud appears;
And in the smoke the pennons flew,
As in the storm the white sea-mew.
Then mark'd they, dashing broad and far, 65
The broken billows of the war,
And plumèd crests of chieftains brave,
Floating like foam upon the wave;
    But nought distinct they see:
Wide rag'd the battle on the plain; 70
Spears shook, and falchions flash'd amain;
Fell England's arrow-flight like rain;
Crests rose, and stoop'd, and rose again,
    Wild and disorderly.
Amid the scene of tumult, high 75
They saw Lord Marmion's falcon fly:
And stainless Tunstall's banner white,
And Edmund Howard's lion bright,
Still bear them bravely in the fight:
    Although against them come, 80
Of gallant Gordons many a one,
And many a stubborn Badenoch-man,

And many a rugged Border clan,
  With Huntly and with Home.
Far on the left, unseen the while, 85
Stanley broke Lennox and Argyle;
Though there the western mountaineer
Rush'd with bare bosom on the spear,
And flung the feeble targe aside,
And with both hands the broadsword plied. 90
'Twas vain:—But Fortune, on the right,
With fickle smile cheer'd Scotland's fight.
Then fell that spotless banner white,
  The Howard's lion fell;
Yet still Lord Marmion's falcon flew 95
With wavering flight, while fiercer grew
  Around the battle-yell.
The Border slogan rent the sky!
A Home! a Gordon! was the cry:
  Loud were the clanging blows; 100
Advanc'd, forc'd back, now low, now high,
  The pennon sunk and rose;
As bends the bark's mast in the gale,
When rent are rigging, shrouds, and sail,
  It waver'd 'mid the foes. 105
But as they left the dark'ning heath,
More desperate grew the strife of death.
The English shafts in volleys hail'd,
In headlong charge their horse assail'd;
Front, flank, and rear, the squadrons sweep
To break the Scottish circle deep, 111
  That fought around their King.
But yet, though thick the shafts as snow,
Though charging knights like whirlwinds go,
Though bill-men ply the ghastly blow, 115
  Unbroken was the ring;
The stubborn spear-men still made good
Their dark impenetrable wood,
Each stepping where his comrade stood,
  The instant that he fell. 120
No thought was there of dastard flight;

Link'd in the serried phalanx tight,
Groom fought like noble, squire like knight,
   As fearlessly and well;
Till utter darkness closed her wing   125
O'er their thin host and wounded King.
Then skilful Surrey's sage commands
Led back from strife his shattered bands;
   And from the charge they drew,
As mountain-waves, from wasted lands,   130
   Sweep back to ocean blue.
Then did their loss his foemen know;
Their King, their Lords, their mightiest low,
They melted from the field as snow,
When streams are swoln and south winds blow,
   Dissolves in silent dew.   136
Tweed's echoes heard the ceaseless plash,
   While many a broken band,
Disorder'd through her currents dash,
   To gain the Scottish land;   140
To town and tower, to down and dale,
To tell red Flodden's dismal tale,
And raise the universal wail.
Tradition, legend, tune, and song,
Shall many an age that wail prolong: 145
Still from the sire the son shall hear
Of the stern strife, and carnage drear,
   Of Flodden's fatal field,
Where shiver'd was fair Scotland's spear,
   And broken was her shield!   150

SAMUEL TAYLOR COLERIDGE

1772–1834

The Rime of the Ancient Mariner

IN SEVEN PARTS

PART THE FIRST

An ancient
Mariner
meeteth
three Gal-
lants bidden
to a wedding-
feast, and
detaineth
one.

It is an ancient Mariner,
And he stoppeth one of three.
'By thy long grey beard and glittering eye,
Now wherefore stopp'st thou me?

The Bridegroom's doors are opened wide,
And I am next of kin;   6
The guests are met, the feast is set:
May'st hear the merry din.'

He holds him with his skinny hand,
'There was a ship,' quoth he.   10
'Hold off! unhand me, greybeard loon!'
Eftsoons his hand dropt he.

The Wed-
ding-Guest
is spell-
bound by
the eye of
the old sea-
faring man,
and con-
strained to
hear his
tale.

He holds him with his glittering eye—
The Wedding-Guest stood still,
And listens like a three years' child: 15
The Mariner hath his will.

The Wedding-Guest sat on a stone:
He cannot choose but hear;
And thus spake on that ancient man,
The bright-eyed Mariner.   20

'The ship was cheered, the harbour cleared,
Merrily did we drop
Below the kirk, below the hill,
Below the lighthouse top.

The Sun came up upon the left,
Out of the sea came he!
And he shone bright, and on the right
Went down into the sea.

25 The Mariner tells how the ship sailed southward with a good wind and fair weather, till it reached the line.

Higher and higher every day,
Till over the mast at noon—'
The Wedding-Guest here beat his breast,
For he heard the loud bassoon.

30 The Wedding-Guest heareth the bridal music; but the Mariner continueth his tale

The bride hath paced into the hall,
Red as a rose is she;
Nodding their heads before her goes
The merry minstrelsy.

The Wedding-Guest he beat his breast,
Yet he cannot choose but hear;
And thus spake on that ancient man,
The bright-eyed Mariner.

'And now the storm-blast came, and he
Was tyrannous and strong:
He struck with his o'ertaking wings,
And chased us south along.

The ship drawn by a storm toward the South Pole.

With sloping masts and dipping prow,
As who pursued with yell and blow
Still treads the shadow of his foe
And forward bends his head,
The ship drove fast, loud roared the blast,
And southward aye we fled.

And now there came both mist and snow
And it grew wondrous cold:
And ice, mast-high, came floating by,
As green as emerald.

The land of ice, and of fearful sounds, where no living thing was to be seen.

And through the drifts the snowy clifts
Did send a dismal sheen:
Nor shapes of men nor beasts we ken—
The ice was all between.

The ice was here, the ice was there,
The ice was all around: 60
It cracked and growled, and roared and
        howled,
Like noises in a swound!

Till a great
sea-bird,
called the
Albatross,
came
through the
snow-fog,
and was
received
with great
joy and
hospitality.
At length did cross an Albatross:
Through the fog it came;
As if it had been a Christian soul,   65
We hailed it in God's name.

It ate the food it ne'er had eat,
And round and round it flew.
The ice did split with a thunder-fit;
The helmsman steered us through!   70

And lo! the
Albatross
proveth a
bird of good
omen, and
followeth
the ship as
it returned
northward
through fog
and floating
ice.
And a good south wind sprung up behind;
The Albatross did follow,
And every day, for food or play,
Came to the mariners' hollo!

In mist or cloud, on mast or shroud,   75
It perched for vespers nine;
Whiles all the night, through fog-smoke
        white,
Glimmered the white moonshine.'

The ancient
Mariner in-
hospitably
killeth the
pious bird
of good
omen.
'God save thee, ancient Mariner!
From fiends that plague thee thus!—   80
Why look'st thou so?'—'With my cross-bow
I shot the Albatross.

PART THE SECOND

'The Sun now rose upon the right:
Out of the sea came he,
Still hid in mist, and on the left   85
Went down into the sea.

And the good south wind still blew behind,
But no sweet bird did follow,
Nor any day for food or play
Came to the mariners' hollo!   90

And I had done an hellish thing,
And it would work 'em woe:
For all averred, I had killed the bird
That made the breeze to blow.
Ah wretch! said they, the bird to slay,   95
That made the breeze to blow!

Nor dim nor red, like God's own head,
The glorious Sun uprist:
Then all averred, I had killed the bird
That brought the fog and mist.   100
'Twas right, said they, such birds to slay,
That bring the fog and mist.

The fair breeze blew, the white foam flew,
The furrow followed free;
We were the first that ever burst   105
Into that silent sea.

Down dropt the breeze, the sails dropt down,
'Twas sad as sad could be;
And we did speak only to break
The silence of the sea!   110

All in a hot and copper sky,
The bloody Sun, at noon,
Right up above the mast did stand,
No bigger than the moon.

Day after day, day after day,   115
We stuck, nor breath nor motion;
As idle as a painted ship
Upon a painted ocean.

His shipmates cry out against the ancient Mariner, for killing the bird of good luck.

But when the fog cleared off, they justify the same, and thus make themselves accomplices in the crime.

The fair breeze continues; the ship enters the Pacific Ocean and sails northward, even till it reaches the Line.

The ship hath been suddenly becalmed.

And the Albatross begins to be avenged.

Water, water, everywhere,
And all the boards did shrink;   120
Water, water, everywhere,
Nor any drop to drink.

The very deep did rot: O Christ!
That ever this should be!
Yea, slimy things did crawl with legs   125
Upon the slimy sea.

About, about, in reel and rout
The death-fires danced at night;
The water, like a witch's oils,
Burnt green, and blue and white.   130

A Spirit had followed them; one of the invisible inhabitants of this planet, neither departed souls nor angels; concerning whom the learned Jew, Josephus, and the Platonic Constantinopolitan, Michael Psellus, may be consulted. They are very numerous, and there is no climate or element without one or more.

And some in dreams assurèd were
Of the spirit that plagued us so;
Nine fathom deep he had followed us
From the land of mist and snow.

And every tongue, through utter drought,
Was withered at the root;   136
We could not speak, no more than if
We had been choked with soot.

The shipmates, in their sore distress, would fain throw the whole guilt on the ancient Mariner: in sign whereof they hang the dead sea-bird round his neck.

Ah! well-a-day! what evil looks
Had I from old and young!   140
Instead of the cross, the Albatross
About my neck was hung.

PART THE THIRD

'There passed a weary time. Each throat
Was parched, and glazed each eye.
A weary time! a weary time!   145
How glazed each weary eye,
When looking westward, I beheld
A something in the sky.

At first it seemed a little speck,
And then it seemed a mist;   150
It moved and moved, and took at last
A certain shape, I wist.

A speck, a mist, a shape, I wist!
And still it neared and neared:
As if it dodged a watersprite,   155
It plunged and tacked and veered.

With throats unslaked, with black lips baked,
We could nor laugh nor wail;
Through utter drought all dumb we stood!
I bit my arm, I sucked the blood,   160
And cried, A sail! a sail!

With throats unslaked, with black lips baked,
Agape they heard me call:
Gramercy! they for joy did grin,
And all at once their breath drew in,   165
As they were drinking all.

See! See! (I cried) she tacks no more!
Hither to work us weal;
Without a breeze, without a tide,
She steadies with upright keel!   170

The western wave was all a-flame.
The day was well-nigh done!
Almost upon the western wave
Rested the broad bright Sun;

The ancient Mariner beholdeth a sign in the element afar off.

At its nearer approach it seemeth him to be a ship; and at a dear ransom he freeth his speech from the bonds of thirst.

A flash of joy;

And horror follows. For can it be a ship that comes onward without wind or tide?

When that strange shape drove suddenly
Betwixt us and the Sun.   176

It seemeth
him but the
skeleton of
a ship.
And straight the Sun was flecked with bars,
(Heaven's Mother send us grace!)
As if through a dungeon-grate he peered
With broad and burning face.   180

Alas! (thought I, and my heart beat loud)
How fast she nears and nears!
Are those *her* sails that glance in the Sun,
Like restless gossameres!

And its ribs
are seen as
bars on the
face of the
setting Sun.
The Spec-
tre-Woman
and her
Death-mate,
Are those *her* ribs through which the Sun
Did peer, as through a grate?   186
And is that Woman all her crew?
Is that a Death? and are there two?
Is Death that woman's mate?
and no other on board the skeleton ship.

Like vessel,
like crew!
Her lips were red, her looks were free,   190
Her locks were yellow as gold:
Her skin was as white as leprosy,
The Night-mare Life-in-Death was she,
Who thicks man's blood with cold.

Death and
Life-in-
Death have
diced for
the ship's
crew, and
she (the
latter) win-
neth the
ancient
Mariner.
The naked hulk alongside came   195
And the twain were casting dice;
"The game is done! I've won, I've won!"
Quoth she, and whistles thrice.

No twi-
light within
the courts of
the Sun.
The Sun's rim dips; the stars rush out:
At one stride comes the dark;   200
With far-heard whisper, o'er the sea,
Off shot the spectre-bark.

We listened and looked sideways up!
Fear at my heart, as at a cup,
My life-blood seemed to sip!   205
The stars were dim, and thick the night,

The steersman's face by his lamp gleamed
    white;
From the sails the dew did drip—
Till clomb above the eastern bar   *At the*
The hornèd moon, with one bright star 210 *rising of the*
Within the nether tip.   *Moon,*

One after one, by the star-dogged Moon,   *One after*
Too quick for groan or sigh,   *another,*
Each turned his face with a ghastly pang,
And cursed me with his eye.   215

Four times fifty living men,   *His ship-*
(And I heard nor sigh nor groan)   *mates drop*
With heavy thump, a lifeless lump,   *down dead;*
They dropped down one by one.

The souls did from their bodies fly,— 220 *But Life-in-*
They fled to bliss or woe!   *Death be-*
And every soul, it passed me by,   *gins her*
Like the whizz of my cross-bow!'   *work on the*
                                 ancient
                                 Mariner.

PART THE FOURTH

'I fear thee, ancient Mariner!   *The Wed-*
I fear thy skinny hand!   225 *ding-Guest*
And thou art long, and lank, and brown,   *feareth that*
As is the ribbed sea-sand.   *a spirit is*
                                 talking to
                                 him;

I fear thee and thy glittering eye,
And thy skinny hand, so brown.'—   *But the*
'Fear not, fear not, thou Wedding-Guest!   *ancient*
This body dropt not down.   231 *Mariner as-*
                                 sureth him
                                 of his
                                 bodily life,
Alone, alone, all, all alone,   *and pro-*
Alone on a wide wide sea!   *ceedeth to*
And never a saint took pity on   *relate his*
My soul in agony.   235 *horrible*
                                 penance.

He despis-
eth the
creatures of
the calm.

The many men, so beautiful!
And they all dead did lie:
And a thousand thousand slimy things
Lived on; and so did I.

And envieth
that they
should live,
and so
many lie
dead.

I looked upon the rotting sea,   240
And drew my eyes away;
I looked upon the rotting deck,
And there the dead men lay.

I looked to Heaven, and tried to pray;
But or ever a prayer had gusht,   245
A wicked whisper came, and made
My heart as dry as dust.

I closed my lids, and kept them close,
And the balls like pulses beat;
For the sky and the sea, and the sea and the
    sky   250
Lay like a load on my weary eye,
And the dead were at my feet.

But the
curse liveth
for him in
the eye of
the dead
men.

The cold sweat melted from their limbs,
Nor rot nor reek did they;
The look with which they looked on me
Had never passed away.   256

An orphan's curse would drag to hell
A spirit from on high;
But oh! more horrible than that
Is a curse in a dead man's eye!   260
Seven days, seven nights, I saw that curse,
And yet I could not die.

In his lone-
liness and
fixedness

The moving Moon went up the sky,
And nowhere did abide:

Softly she was going up,
And a star or two beside—

265 he yearneth towards the journeying Moon, and

the Stars that still sojourn, yet still move onward; and everywhere the
blue sky belongs to them, and is their appointed rest, and their native
country and their own natural homes, which they enter unannounced,
as lords that are certainly expected and yet there is a silent joy at their
arrival.

Her beams bemocked the sultry main,
Like April hoar-frost spread;
But where the ship's huge shadow lay,
The charmèd water burnt alway   270
A still and awful red.

Beyond the shadow of the ship,   By the light
I watched the water-snakes: of the Moon he behold-
They moved in tracks of shining white,   eth God's
And when they reared, the elfish light   275 creatures of
Fell off in hoary flakes.   the great calm.

Within the shadow of the ship
I watched their rich attire:
Blue, glossy green, and velvet black,
They coiled and swam; and every track   280
Was a flash of golden fire.

O happy living things! no tongue   Their
Their beauty might declare: beauty and their hap-
A spring of love gushed from my heart,   piness.
And I blessed them unaware: 285 He blesseth
Sure my kind saint took pity on me,   them in his
And I blessed them unaware.   heart.

The selfsame moment I could pray;   The spell
And from my neck so free   begins to break.
The Albatross fell off, and sank   290
Like lead into the sea.

PART THE FIFTH

'Oh sleep! it is a gentle thing,
Beloved from pole to pole!
To Mary Queen the praise be given!
She sent the gentle sleep from Heaven,   295
That slid into my soul.

By grace of the holy Mother, the ancient Mariner is refreshed with rain.

The silly buckets on the deck,
That had so long remained,
I dreamt that they were filled with dew;
And when I awoke, it rained.   300

My lips were wet, my throat was cold,
My garments all were dank;
Sure I had drunken in my dreams,
And still my body drank.

I moved, and could not feel my limbs: 305
I was so light—almost
I thought that I had died in sleep,
And was a blessèd ghost.

He heareth sounds and seeth strange sights and commotions in the sky and the element.

And soon I heard a roaring wind:
It did not come anear;   310
But with its sound it shook the sails,
That were so thin and sere.

The upper air burst into life!
And a hundred fire-flags sheen,
To and fro they were hurried about!   315
And to and fro, and in and out,
The wan stars danced between.

And the coming wind did roar more loud,
And the sails did sigh like sedge;
And the rain poured down from one black
    cloud;   320
The Moon was at its edge.

The thick black cloud was cleft, and still
The Moon was at its side:
Like waters shot from some high crag,
The lightning fell with never a jag,   325
A river steep and wide.

The loud wind never reached the ship.
Yet now the ship moved on!
Beneath the lightning and the Moon
The dead men gave a groan.   330

The bodies of the ship's crew are inspired, and the ship moves on;

They groaned, they stirred, they all uprose,
Nor spake, nor moved their eyes;
It had been strange, even in a dream,
To have seen those dead men rise.

The helmsman steered, the ship moved on;
Yet never a breeze up blew;   336
The mariners all 'gan work the ropes,
Where they were wont to do;
They raised their limbs like lifeless tools—
We were a ghastly crew.   340

The body of my brother's son
Stood by me, knee to knee:
The body and I pulled at one rope,
But he said nought to me.'

'I fear thee, ancient Mariner!'   345
'Be calm, thou Wedding-Guest!
'Twas not those souls that fled in pain,
Which to their corses came again,
But a troop of spirits blest:

But not by the souls of the men, nor by daemons of earth or middle air, but by a blessed troop of angelic spirits, sent down by the invoca-

For when it dawned—they dropt their arms,
And clustered round the mast;   351
Sweet sounds rose slowly through their
     mouths,
And from their bodies passed.

tion of the guardian saint.

Around, around, flew each sweet sound,
Then darted to the Sun;   355
Slowly the sounds came back again,
Now mixed, now one by one.

Sometimes a-dropping from the sky
I heard the skylark sing;
Sometimes all little birds that are,   360
How they seemed to fill the sea and air
With their sweet jargoning!

And now 'twas like all instruments,
Now like a lonely flute;
And now it is an angel's song,   365
That makes the Heavens be mute.

It ceased; yet still the sails made on
A pleasant noise till noon,
A noise like of a hidden brook
In the leafy month of June,   370
That to the sleeping woods all night
Singeth a quiet tune.

Till noon we quietly sailed on,
Yet never a breeze did breathe:
Slowly and smoothly went the ship,   375
Moved onward from beneath.

Under the keel nine fathom deep,
From the land of mist and snow,
The spirit slid: and it was he
That made the ship to go.   380
The sails at noon left off their tune,
And the ship stood still also.

The Sun, right up above the mast,
Had fixed her to the ocean:
But in a minute she 'gan stir,   385
With a short uneasy motion—
Backwards and forwards half her length
With a short uneasy motion.

The lonesome Spirit from the south-pole carries on the ship as far as the Line, in obedience to the angelic troop, but still requireth vengeance.

Then, like a pawing horse let go,
She made a sudden bound: 390
It flung the blood into my head,
And I fell down in a swound.

How long in that same fit I lay,
I have not to declare;
But ere my living life returned, 395
I heard and in my soul discerned
Two voices in the air.

"Is it he?" quoth one, "Is this the man?
By him who died on cross,
With his cruel bow he laid full low 400
The harmless Albatross.

The Spirit who bideth by himself
In the land of mist and snow,
He loved the bird that loved the man
Who shot him with his bow." 405

The other was a softer voice,
As soft as honeydew:
Quoth he, "The man hath penance done,
And penance more will do."

The Polar Spirit's fellow daemons, the invisible inhabitants of the element, take part in his wrong; and two of them relate, one to the other, that penance long and heavy for the ancient Mariner hath been accorded to the Polar Spirit, who returneth southward.

PART THE SIXTH

First Voice

'"But tell me, tell me! speak again, 410
Thy soft response renewing—
What makes that ship drive on so fast?
What is the ocean doing?"

Second Voice

"Still as a slave before his lord,
The Ocean hath no blast; 415
His great bright eye most silently
Up to the Moon is cast—

If he may know which way to go;
For she guides him smooth or grim.
See, brother, see! how graciously   420
She looketh down on him."

First Voice

The Mariner hath been cast into a trance; for the angelic power causeth the vessel to drive northward faster than human life could endure.

"But why drives on that ship so fast,
Without or wave or wind?"

Second Voice

"The air is cut away before,
And closes from behind.   425

Fly, brother, fly! more high, more high!
Or we shall be belated:
For slow and slow that ship will go,
When the Mariner's trance is abated."

The supernatural motion is retarded; the Mariner awakes, and his penance begins anew.

I woke, and we were sailing on   430
As in a gentle weather:
'Twas night, calm night, the Moon was high;
The dead men stood together.

All stood together on the deck,
For a charnel-dungeon fitter: 435
All fixed on me their stony eyes,
That in the Moon did glitter.

The pang, the curse, with which they died,
Had never passed away:
I could not draw my eyes from theirs,   440
Nor turn them up to pray.

The curse is finally expiated.

And now this spell was snapt: once more
I viewed the ocean green,
And looked far forth, yet little saw
Of what had else been seen—   445

Like one, that on a lonesome road
Doth walk in fear and dread,
And having once turned round walks on,
And turns no more his head;
Because he knows, a frightful fiend   450
Doth close behind him tread.

But soon there breathed a wind on me,
Nor sound nor motion made:
Its path was not upon the sea,
In ripple or in shade.   455

It raised my hair, it fanned my cheek
Like a meadow-gale of spring—
It mingled strangely with my fears,
Yet it felt like a welcoming.

Swiftly, swiftly flew the ship,   460
Yet she sailed softly too:
Sweetly, sweetly blew the breeze—
On me alone it blew.

Oh! dream of joy! is this indeed
The lighthouse top I see?   465
Is this the hill? is this the kirk?
Is this mine own countree?

And the ancient Mariner beholdeth his native country.

We drifted o'er the harbour-bar,
And I with sobs did pray—
O let me be awake, my God!   470
Or let me sleep alway.

The harbour-bay was clear as glass,
So smoothly it was strewn!
And on the bay the moonlight lay,
And the shadow of the Moon.   475

The rock shone bright, the kirk no less,
That stands above the rock:
The moonlight steeped in silentness
The steady weathercock.

And the bay was white with silent light,
Till rising from the same,   481
Full many shapes, that shadows were,
In crimson colours came.

The angelic
spirits leave
the dead
bodies, and
appear in
their own
forms of
light.

A little distance from the prow
Those crimson shadows were: 485
I turned my eyes upon the deck—
Oh, Christ! what saw I there!

Each corse lay flat, lifeless and flat,
And, by the holy rood!
A man all light, a seraph-man,   490
On every corse there stood.

This seraph-band, each waved his hand:
It was a heavenly sight!
They stood as signals to the land,
Each one a lovely light;   495

This seraph-band, each waved his hand,
No voice did they impart—
No voice; but oh! the silence sank
Like music on my heart.

But soon I heard the dash of oars,   500
I heard the Pilot's cheer;
My head was turned perforce away,
And I saw a boat appear.

The Pilot and the Pilot's boy,
I heard them coming fast: 505
Dear Lord in Heaven! it was a joy
The dead men could not blast.

I saw a third—I heard his voice:
It is the Hermit good!
He singeth loud his godly hymns   510
That he makes in the wood.
He'll shrieve my soul, he'll wash away
The Albatross's blood.

PART THE SEVENTH

'This Hermit good lives in that wood   The Hermit
Which slopes down to the sea.   515   of the Wood,
How loudly his sweet voice he rears!
He loves to talk with marineres
That come from a far countree.

He kneels at morn, and noon, and eve—
He hath a cushion plump: 520
It is the moss that wholly hides
The rotted old oak-stump.

The skiff-boat neared: I heard them talk,
"Why this is strange, I trow!
Where are those lights so many and fair,
That signal made but now?"   526

"Strange, by my faith!" the Hermit said—   Approach-
"And they answered not our cheer!   eth the ship
The planks look warped! and see those sails,   with won-
How thin they are and sere!   530   der.
I never saw aught like to them,
Unless perchance it were

Brown skeletons of leaves that lag
My forest-brook along;
When the ivy-tod is heavy with snow,   535
And the owlet whoops to the wolf below,
That eats the she-wolf's young."

"Dear Lord! it hath a fiendish look—"
(The Pilot made reply)
"I am a-feared"—"Push on, push on!"
Said the Hermit cheerily.   541

The boat came closer to the ship,
But I nor spake nor stirred;
The boat came close beneath the ship,
And straight a sound was heard.   545

Under the water it rumbled on,
Still louder and more dread:
It reached the ship, it split the bay;
The ship went down like lead.

The ship suddenly sinketh.

Stunned by that loud and dreadful sound,
Which sky and ocean smote,   551
Like one that hath been seven days drowned
My body lay afloat;
But swift as dreams, myself I found
Within the Pilot's boat.   555

The ancient Mariner is saved in the Pilot's boat.

Upon the whirl, where sank the ship,
The boat spun round and round;
And all was still, save that the hill
Was telling of the sound.

I moved my lips—the Pilot shrieked   560
And fell down in a fit;
The holy Hermit raised his eyes,
And prayed where he did sit.

I took the oars: the Pilot's boy,
Who now doth crazy go,   565
Laughed loud and long, and all the while
His eyes went to and fro.
"Ha! ha!" quoth he, "full plain I see,
The Devil knows how to row."

And now, all in my own countree,   570
I stood on the firm land!
The Hermit stepped forth from the boat,
And scarcely he could stand.

The ancient Mariner earnestly entreateth the Hermit to shrieve him; and the penance of life falls on him.

"O shrieve me, shrieve me, holy man!"
The Hermit crossed his brow.   575
"Say quick," quoth he, "I bid thee say—
What manner of man art thou?"

Forthwith this frame of mine was wrenched
With a woful agony,

Which forced me to begin my tale;   580
And then it left me free.

Since then, at an uncertain hour,
That agony returns:
And till my ghastly tale is told,
This heart within me burns.   585

*And ever
and anon
throughout
his future
life an
agony con-
straineth
him to
travel from
land to
land;*

I pass, like night, from land to land;
I have strange power of speech;
That moment that his face I see,
I know the man that must hear me:
To him my tale I teach.   590

What loud uproar bursts from that door!
The wedding-guests are there:
But in the garden-bower the bride
And bride-maids singing are:
And hark the little vesper bell,   595
Which biddeth me to prayer!

O Wedding-Guest! this soul hath been
Alone on a wide wide sea:
So lonely 'twas, that God himself
Scarce seemèd there to be.   600

O sweeter than the marriage-feast,
'Tis sweeter far to me,
To walk together to the kirk
With a goodly company!—

To walk together to the kirk,   605
And all together pray,
While each to his great Father bends,
Old men, and babes, and loving friends,
And youths and maidens gay!

Farewell, farewell! but this I tell   610 And to
To thee, thou Wedding-Guest!   teach, by
He prayeth well, who loveth well   his own
                                             example,
Both man and bird and beast.   love and
                                             reverence
                                             to all things
He prayeth best, who loveth best   that God
All things both great and small;   615 made and
                                             loveth.
For the dear God who loveth us,
He made and loveth all.'

The Mariner, whose eye is bright,
Whose beard with age is hoar,
Is gone: and now the Wedding-Guest   620
Turned from the bridegroom's door.

He went like one that hath been stunned,
And is of sense forlorn:
A sadder and a wiser man,
He rose the morrow morn.   625

LORD BYRON

1788–1824

The Prisoner of Chillon

I

My hair is grey, but not with years,
    Nor grew it white
    In a single night,
As men's have grown from sudden fears:
My limbs are bow'd, though not with toil,   5
    But rusted with a vile repose,
    For they have been a dungeon's spoil,
    And mine has been the fate of those
To whom the goodly earth and air
Are bann'd, and barr'd—forbidden fare: 10
But this was for my father's faith
I suffer'd chains and courted death;
That father perish'd at the stake

For tenets he would not forsake;
And for the same his lineal race   15
In darkness found a dwelling-place;
We were seven—who now are one,
   Six in youth, and one in age,
Finish'd as they had begun,
   Proud of Persecution's rage;   20
One in fire, and two in field,
Their belief with blood have seal'd,
Dying as their father died,
For the God their foes denied;
Three were in a dungeon cast,   25
Of whom this wreck is left the last.

II

There are seven pillars of Gothic mould,
In Chillon's dungeons deep and old,
There are seven columns, massy and grey,
Dim with a dull imprison'd ray,   30
A sunbeam which hath lost its way,
And through the crevice and the cleft
Of the thick wall is fallen and left;
Creeping o'er the floor so damp,
Like a marsh's meteor lamp: 35
And in each pillar there is a ring,
   And in each ring there is a chain;
That iron is a cankering thing,
   For in these limbs its teeth remain,
With marks that will not wear away,   40
Till I have done with this new day,
Which now is painful to these eyes,
Which have not seen the sun so rise
For years—I cannot count them o'er,
I lost their long and heavy score,   45
When my last brother droop'd and died,
And I lay living by his side.

III

They chain'd us each to a column stone,
And we were three—yet, each alone;
We could not move a single pace,   50
We could not see each other's face,
But with that pale and livid light
That made us strangers in our sight:
And thus together—yet apart,
Fetter'd in hand, but join'd in heart,   55
'Twas still some solace, in the dearth
Of the pure elements of earth,
To hearken to each other's speech,
And each turn comforter to each
With some new hope, or legend old,   60
Or song heroically bold;
But even these at length grew cold.
Our voices took a dreary tone,
An echo of the dungeon stone,
   A grating sound, not full and free,   65
   As they of yore were wont to be:
   It might be fancy, but to me
They never sounded like our own.

IV

I was the eldest of the three,
   And to uphold and cheer the rest   70
   I ought to do—and did my best—
And each did well in his degree.
   The youngest, whom my father loved,
Because our mother's brow was given
To him, with eyes as blue as heaven—   75
   For him my soul was sorely moved;
And truly might it be distress'd
To see such bird in such a nest;
For he was beautiful as day—
   (When day was beautiful to me   80
   As to young eagles, being free)—
   A polar day, which will not see

A sunset till its summer's gone,
  Its sleepless summer of long light,
The snow-clad offspring of the sun: 85
  And thus he was as pure and bright,
And in his natural spirit gay,
With tears for nought but others' ills,
And then they flow'd like mountain rills,
Unless he could assuage the woe 90
Which he abhorred to view below.

v

The other was as pure of mind,
But form'd to combat with his kind;
Strong in his frame, and of a mood
Which 'gainst the world in war had stood, 95
And perish'd in the foremost rank
  With joy:—but not in chains to pine:
His spirit wither'd with their clank,
  I saw it silently decline—
  And so perchance in sooth did mine: 100
But yet I forced it on to cheer
Those relics of a home so dear.
He was a hunter of the hills,
  Had follow'd there the deer and wolf;
  To him his dungeon was a gulf, 105
And fetter'd feet the worst of ills.

vi

  Lake Leman lies by Chillon's walls:
A thousand feet in depth below
Its massy waters meet and flow;
Thus much the fathom-line was sent 110
From Chillon's snow-white battlement,
  Which round about the wave inthrals:
A double dungeon wall and wave
Have made—and like a living grave
Below the surface of the lake 115
The dark vault lies wherein we lay,

We heard it ripple night and day;
   Sounding o'er our heads it knock'd;
And I have felt the winter's spray
Wash through the bars when winds were high
And wanton in the happy sky;   121
   And then the very rock hath rock'd,
   And I have felt it shake, unshock'd,
Because I could have smiled to see
The death that would have set me free.   125

VII

I said my nearer brother pined,
I said his mighty heart declined,
He loathed and put away his food;
It was not that 'twas coarse and rude,
For we were used to hunter's fare,   130
And for the like had little care:
The milk drawn from the mountain goat
Was changed for water from the moat,
Our bread was such as captives' tears
Have moisten'd many a thousand years   135
Since man first pent his fellow men
Like brutes within an iron den;
But what were these to us or him?
These wasted not his heart or limb;
My brother's soul was of that mould   140
Which in a palace had grown cold,
Had his free breathing been denied
The range of the steep mountain's side;
But why delay the truth?—he died.
I saw, and could not hold his head,   145
Nor reach his dying hand—nor dead,—
Through hard I strove, but strove in vain,
To rend and gnash my bonds in twain.
He died, and they unlock'd his chain,
And scoop'd for him a shallow grave   150
Even from the cold earth of our cave,
I begg'd them as a boon to lay

His corse in dust whereon the day
Might shine—it was a foolish thought,
But then within my brain it wrought,   155
That even in death his freeborn breast
In such a dungeon could not rest.
I might have spared my idle prayer—
They coldly laugh'd and laid him there;
The flat and turfless earth above   160
The being we so much did love;
His empty chain above it leant,
Such murder's fitting monument!

VIII

But he, the favourite and the flower,
Most cherish'd since his natal hour,   165
His mother's image in fair face,
The infant love of all his race,
His martyr'd father's dearest thought,
My latest care, for whom I sought
To hoard my life, that his might be   170
Less wretched now, and one day free;
He, too, who yet had held untired
A spirit natural or inspired—
He, too, was struck, and day by day
Was wither'd on the stalk away.   175
Oh, God! it is a fearful thing
To see the human soul take wing
In any shape, in any mood:
I've seen it rushing forth in blood,
I've seen it on the breaking ocean   180
Strive with a swoln convulsive motion,
I've seen the sick and ghastly bed
Of Sin delirious with its dread;
But these were horrors—this was woe
Unmix'd with such—but sure and slow: 185
He faded, and so calm and meek,
So softly worn, so sweetly weak,
So tearless, yet so tender, kind,

And grieved for those he left behind;
With all the while a cheek whose bloom   190
Was as a mockery of the tomb,
Whose tints as gently sunk away
As a departing rainbow's ray;
An eye of most transparent light,
That almost made the dungeon bright,   195
And not a word of murmur, not
A groan o'er his untimely lot,—
A little talk of better days,
A little hope my own to raise,
For I was sunk in silence—lost   200
In this last loss, of all the most;
And then the sighs he would suppress
Of fainting nature's feebleness,
More slowly drawn, grew less and less:
I listen'd, but I could not hear;   205
I call'd, for I was wild with fear;
I knew 'twas hopeless, but my dread
Would not be thus admonished;
I call'd, and thought I heard a sound—
I burst my chain with one strong bound,   210
And rush'd to him:—I found him not,
I only stirr'd in this black spot,
I only lived, *I* only drew
The accursed breath of dungeon-dew;
The last, the sole, the dearest link   215
Between me and the eternal brink,
Which bound me to my failing race,
Was broken in this fatal place.
One on the earth, and one beneath—
My brothers—both had ceased to breathe:
I took that hand which lay so still,   221
Alas! my own was full as chill;
I had not strength to stir, or strive,
But felt that I was still alive—
A frantic feeling, when we know   225
That what we love shall ne'er be so.
        I know not why

I could not die,
I had no earthly hope but faith,
And that forbade a selfish death.   230

IX

What next befell me then and there
    I know not well—I never knew—
First came the loss of light, and air,
    And then of darkness too:
I had no thought, no feeling—none—   235
Among the stones I stood a stone,
And was, scarce conscious what I wist,
As shrubless crags within the mist;
For all was blank, and bleak, and grey;
It was not night, it was not day;   240
It was not even the dungeon-light,
So hateful to my heavy sight,
But vacancy absorbing space,
And fixedness without a place;
There were no stars, no earth, no time,   245
No check, no change, no good, no crime,
But silence, and a stirless breath
Which neither was of life nor death;
A sea of stagnant idleness,
Blind, boundless, mute, and motionless!   250

X

A light broke in upon my brain,—
    It was the carol of a bird;
It ceased, and then it came again,
    The sweetest song ear ever heard.
And mine was thankful till my eyes   255
Ran over with the glad surprise,
And they that moment could not see
I was the mate of misery;
But then by dull degrees came back
My senses to their wonted track;   260
I saw the dungeon walls and floor

Close slowly round me as before,
I saw the glimmer of the sun
Creeping as it before had done,
But through the crevice where it came   265
That bird was perch'd, as fond and tame,
    And tamer than upon the tree;
A lovely bird, with azure wings,
And song that said a thousand things,
    And seem'd to say them all for me.   270
I never saw its like before,
I ne'er shall see its likeness more:
It seem'd like me to want a mate,
But was not half so desolate,
And it was come to love me when   275
None lived to love me so again,
And cheering from my dungeon's brink,
Had brought me back to feel and think.
I know not if it late were free,
    Or broke its cage to perch on mine,   280
But knowing well captivity,
    Sweet bird! I could not wish for thine!
Or if it were, in winged guise,
A visitant from Paradise;   284
For—Heaven forgive that thought! the while
Which made me both to weep and smile—
I sometimes deem'd that it might be
My brother's soul come down to me;
But then at last away it flew,
And then 'twas mortal well I knew,   290
For he would never thus have flown,
And left me twice so doubly lone,
Lone as the corse within its shroud,
Lone as a solitary cloud,—
    A single cloud on a sunny day,   295
While all the rest of heaven is clear,
A frown upon the atmosphere,
That hath no business to appear
    When skies are blue, and earth is gay.

XI

A kind of change came in my fate,   300
My keepers grew compassionate;
I know not what had made them so,
They were inured to sights of woe,
But so it was:—my broken chain
With links unfasten'd did remain,   305
And it was liberty to stride
Along my cell from side to side,
And up and down and then athwart,
And tread it over every part;
And round the pillars one by one,   310
Returning where my walk begun,
Avoiding only, as I trod,
My brothers' graves without a sod;
For if I thought with heedless tread
My step profaned their lowly bed,   315
My breath came gaspingly and thick,
And my crush'd heart felt blind and sick.

XII

I made a footing in the wall,
    It was not therefrom to escape,
For I had buried one and all   320
    Who loved me in a human shape;
And the whole earth would henceforth be
A wider prison unto me:
No child, no sire, no kin had I,
No partner in my misery;   325
I thought of this, and I was glad,
For thought of them had made me mad;
But I was curious to ascend
To my barr'd windows, and to bend
Once more, upon the mountains high,   330
The quiet of a loving eye.

XIII

I saw them, and they were the same,
They were not changed like me in frame;

I saw their thousand years of snow
On high—their wide long lake below, 335
And the blue Rhone in fullest flow;
I heard the torrents leap and gush
O'er channell'd rock and broken bush;
I saw the white-wall'd distant town,
And whiter sails go skimming down; 340
And then there was a little isle,
Which in my very face did smile,
    The only one in view:
A small green isle, it seem'd no more,
Scarce broader than my dungeon floor, 345
But in it there were three tall trees,
And o'er it blew the mountain breeze,
And by it there were waters flowing,
And on it there were young flowers growing,
    Of gentle breath and hue. 350
The fish swam by the castle wall,
And they seem'd joyous each and all;
The eagle rode the rising blast,
Methought he never flew so fast
As then to me he seem'd to fly; 355
And then new tears came in my eye,
And I felt troubled—and would fain
I had not left my recent chain;
And when I did descend again,
The darkness of my dim abode 360
Fell on me as a heavy load;
It was as is a new-dug grave,
Closing o'er one we sought to save,—
And yet my glance, too much opprest,
Had almost need of such a rest. 365

XIV

It might be months, or years, or days,
    I kept no count, I took no note,
I had no hope my eyes to raise,
    And clear them of their dreary mote;
At last men came to set me free; 370

I ask'd not why, and reck'd not where;
It was at length the same to me,
Fetter'd or fetterless to be,
　I learned to love despair.
And thus when they appear'd at last,　375
And all my bonds aside were cast,
These heavy walls to me had grown
A heritage—and all my own!
And half I felt as they were come
To tear me from a second home:　380
With spiders I had friendship made,
And watch'd them in their sullen trade,
Had seen the mice by moonlight play,
And why should I feel less than they?
We were all inmates of one place,　385
And I, the monarch of each race,
Had power to kill—yet, strange to tell!
In quiet we had learned to dwell;
My very chains and I grew friends,
So much a long communion tends　390
To make us what we are:—even I
Regain'd my freedom with a sigh.

JOHN KEATS

1795–1821

The Eve of St. Agnes

I

St. Agnes' Eve—Ah, bitter chill it was!
The owl, for all his feathers, was a-cold;
The hare limped trembling through the frozen
　grass,
And silent was the flock in woolly fold:　4
Numb were the Beadsman's fingers, while he told
His rosary, and while his frosted breath,

Like pious incense from a censer old,
  Seemed taking flight for Heaven, without a death,
Past the sweet Virgin's picture, while his prayer he
    saith.

II

His prayer he saith, this patient, holy man; 10
Then takes his lamp, and riseth from his knees,
And back returneth, meagre, barefoot, wan,
Along the chapel aisle by slow degrees:
The sculptured dead on each side, seem to freeze,
Imprisoned in black, purgatorial rails: 15
Knights, ladies, praying in dumb orat'ries,
He passeth by; and his weak spirit fails
To think how they may ache in icy hoods and mails.

III

Northward he turneth through a little door, 19
And scarce three steps, ere Music's golden tongue
Flattered to tears this aged man and poor;
But no—already had his deathbell rung:
The joys of all his life were said and sung:
His was harsh penance on St. Agnes' Eve:
Another way he went, and soon among 25
Rough ashes sat he for his soul's reprieve,
And all night kept awake, for sinners' sake to grieve.

IV

That ancient Beadsman heard the prelude soft;
And so it chanced, for many a door was wide,
From hurry to and fro. Soon, up aloft, 30
The silver, snarling trumpets 'gan to chide:
The level chambers, ready with their pride,
Were glowing to receive a thousand guests:
The carved angels, ever eager-eyed, 34
Stared, where upon their heads the cornice rests,
With hair blown back, and wings put crosswise on
    their breasts.

V

At length burst in the argent revelry,
With plume, tiara, and all rich array,
Numerous as shadows haunting faerily
The brain, new stuffed, in youth, with triumphs gay
Of old romance. These let us wish away,   41
And turn, sole-thoughted, to one Lady there,
Whose heart had brooded, all that wintry day,
On love, and winged St. Agnes' saintly care,   44
As she had heard old dames full many times declare.

VI

They told her how, upon St. Agnes' Eve,
Young virgins might have visions of delight,
And soft adorings from their loves receive
Upon the honeyed middle of the night,
If ceremonies due they did aright;   50
As, supperless to bed they must retire,
And couch supine their beauties, lily white;
Nor look behind, nor sideways, but require
Of Heaven with upward eyes for all that they desire.

VII

Full of this whim was thoughtful Madeline: 55
The music, yearning like a God in pain,
She scarcely heard: her maiden eyes divine,
Fixed on the floor, saw many a sweeping train
Pass by—she heeded not at all: in vain
Came many a tiptoe, amorous cavalier,   60
And back retired; not cooled by high disdain,
But she saw not: her heart was otherwhere:
She sighed for Agnes' dreams, the sweetest of the
year.

VIII

She danced along with vague, regardless eyes,   64
Anxious her lips, her breathing quick and short:
The hallowed hour was near at hand: she sighs

Amid the timbrels, and the thronged resort
Of whisperers in anger, or in sport;
'Mid looks of love, defiance, hate, and scorn,
Hoodwinked with faery fancy; all amort,   70
Save to St. Agnes and her lambs unshorn,
And all the bliss to be before to-morrow morn.

IX

So, purposing each moment to retire,
She lingered still. Meantime, across the moors,
Had come young Porphyro, with heart on fire   75
For Madeline. Beside the portal doors,
Buttressed from moonlight, stands he, and implores
All saints to give him sight of Madeline,
But for one moment in the tedious hours,
That he might gaze and worship all unseen;   80
Perchance speak, kneel, touch, kiss—in sooth such
            things have been.

X

He ventures in: let no buzzed whisper tell:
All eyes be muffled, or a hundred swords
Will storm his heart, Love's fev'rous citadel:
For him, those chambers held barbarian hordes,
Hyena foemen, and hot-blooded lords,   86
Whose very dogs would execrations howl
Against his lineage: not one breast affords
Him any mercy, in that mansion foul,
Save one old beldame, weak in body and in soul.   90

XI

Ah, happy chance! the aged creature came,
Shuffling along with ivory-headed wand,
To where he stood, hid from the torch's flame,
Behind a broad hall-pillar, far beyond
The sound of merriment and chorus bland: 95
He startled her; but soon she knew his face,
And grasped his fingers in her palsied hand,

Saying, 'Mercy, Porphyro! hie thee from this place:
They are all here to-night, the whole blood-thirsty
    race!

XII

'Get hence! get hence! there's dwarfish Hilde-
    brand; 100
He had a fever late, and in the fit
He cursed thee and thine, both house and land:
Then there's that old Lord Maurice, not a whit
More tame for his gray hairs—Alas me! flit!
Flit like a ghost away.'—'Ah, Gossip dear, 105
We're safe enough; here in this arm chair sit,
And tell me how'—'Good saints! not here, not here;
Follow me, child, or else these stones will be thy bier.'

XIII

He followed through a lowly archèd way,
Brushing the cobwebs with his lofty plume, 110
And as she muttered 'Well-a—well-a-day!'
He found him in a little moonlight room,
Pale, latticed, chill, and silent as a tomb.
'Now tell me where is Madeline', said he,
'O tell me Angela, by the holy loom 115
Which none but secret sisterhood may see,
When they St. Agnes' wool are weaving piously.'

XIV

'St. Agnes! Ah! it is St. Agnes' Eve—
Yet men will murder upon holy days:
Thou must hold water in a witch's sieve, 120
And be liege-lord of all the Elves and Fays,
To venture so: it fills me with amaze
To see thee, Porphyro!—St. Agnes' Eve!
God's help! my lady fair the conjuror plays
This very night: good angels her deceive! 125
But let me laugh awhile, I've mickle time to grieve.'

XV

Feebly she laugheth in the languid moon,
While Porphyro upon her face doth look,
Like puzzled urchin on an aged crone
Who keepeth closed a wond'rous riddle-book,   130
As spectacle she sits in chimney nook.
But soon his eyes grew brilliant, when she told
His lady's purpose; and he scarce could brook
Tears, at the thought of those enchantments cold,
And Madeline asleep in lap of legends old.   135

XVI

Sudden a thought came like a full-blown rose,
Flushing his brow, and in his painèd heart
Made purple riot: then doth he propose
A stratagem, that makes the beldame start:
'A cruel man and impious thou art: 140
Sweet lady, let her pray, and sleep, and dream
Alone with her good angels, far apart
From wicked men like thee. Go, go!—I deem
Thou canst not surely be the same that thou didst
            seem.'

XVII

'I will not harm her, by all saints I swear,'   145
Quoth Porphyro: 'O may I ne'er find grace
When my weak voice shall whisper its last prayer,
If one of her soft ringlets I displace,
Or look with ruffian passion in her face:
Good Angela, believe me by these tears;   150
Or I will, even in a moment's space,
Awake, with horrid shout, my foemen's ears,
And beard them, though they be more fanged than
            wolves and bears.'

XVIII

'Ah! why wilt thou affright a feeble soul?   154
A poor, weak, palsy-stricken, churchyard thing,

Whose passing-bell may ere the midnight toll;
Whose prayers for thee, each morn and evening,
Were never missed.'—Thus plaining, doth she bring
A gentler speech from burning Porphyro;
So woful, and of such deep sorrowing,   160
That Angela gives promise she will do
Whatever he shall wish, betide her weal or woe.

XIX

Which was, to lead him, in close secrecy,
Even to Madeline's chamber, and there hide
Him in a closet, of such privacy   165
That he might see her beauty unespied,
And win perhaps that night a peerless bride,
While legioned faeries paced the coverlet,
And pale enchantment held her sleepy-eyed.
Never on such a night have lovers met,   170
Since Merlin paid his Demon all the monstrous debt.

XX

'It shall be as thou wishest,' said the Dame:
'All cates and dainties shall be storèd there
Quickly on this feast-night: by the tambour frame
Her own lute thou wilt see: no time to spare,   175
For I am slow and feeble, and scarce dare
On such a catering trust my dizzy head.
Wait here, my child, with patience; kneel in prayer
The while: Ah! thou must needs the lady wed,
Or may I never leave my grave among the dead.'

XXI

So saying she hobbled off with busy fear.   181
The lover's endless minutes slowly passed;
The dame returned, and whispered in his ear
To follow her; with aged eyes aghast
From fright of dim espial. Safe at last,   185
Through many a dusky gallery, they gain
The maiden's chamber, silken, hushed, and chaste;
Where Porphyro took covert, pleased amain.
His poor guide hurried back with agues in her brain.

XXII

Her faltering hand upon the balustrade,   190
Old Angela was feeling for the stair,
When Madeline, St. Agnes' charmèd maid,
Rose, like a missioned spirit, unaware:
With silver taper's light, and pious care,
She turned, and down the aged gossip led   195
To a safe level matting. Now prepare,
Young Porphyro, for gazing on that bed;
She comes, she comes again, like ring-dove frayed and
    fled.

XXIII

Out went the taper as she hurried in;
Its little smoke, in pallid moonshine, died: 200
She closed the door, she panted, all akin
To spirits of the air, and visions wide:
No uttered syllable, or, woe betide!
But to her heart, her heart was voluble,
Paining with eloquence her balmy side;   205
As though a tongueless nightingale should swell
Her throat in vain, and die, heart-stifled, in her dell.

XXIV

A casement high and triple-arched there was,
All garlanded with carven imag'ries   209
Of fruits, and flowers, and bunches of knot-grass,
And diamonded with panes of quaint device,
Innumerable of stains and splendid dyes,
As are the tiger-moth's deep-damasked wings;
And in the midst, 'mong thousand heraldries,
And twilight saints, and dim emblazonings,   215
A shielded scutcheon blushed with blood of queens
    and kings.

XXV

Full on this casement shone the wintry moon,
And threw warm gules on Madeline's fair breast,
As down she knelt for heaven's grace and boon;

Rose-bloom fell on her hands, together prest,   220
  And on her silver cross soft amethyst,
  And on her hair a glory, like a saint:
She seemed a splendid angel, newly drest,
  Save wings, for heaven:—Porphyro grew faint:
She knelt, so pure a thing, so free from mortal taint.

XXVI

Anon his heart revives: her vespers done,   226
  Of all its wreathèd pearls her hair she frees;
  Unclasps her warmèd jewels one by one;
Loosens her fragrant bodice; by degrees
  Her rich attire creeps rustling to her knees: 230
Half-hidden like a mermaid in sea-weed,
  Pensive awhile she dreams awake, and sees,
In fancy, fair St. Agnes in her bed,
But dares not look behind, or all the charm is fled.

XXVII

Soon, trembling in her soft and chilly nest,   235
  In sort of wakeful swoon, perplexed she lay,
Until the poppied warmth of sleep oppressed
  Her soothèd limbs, and soul fatigued away;
Flown, like a thought, until the morrow-day;
  Blissfully havened both from joy and pain;   240
Clasped like a missal where swart Paynims pray;
  Blinded alike from sunshine and from rain,
As though a rose should shut, and be a bud again.

XXVIII

Stolen to this paradise, and so entranced,
  Porphyro gazed upon her empty dress,   245
And listened to her breathing, if it chanced
  To wake into a slumberous tenderness;
Which when he heard, that minute did he bless,
  And breathed himself: then from the closet crept,
Noiseless as fear in a wide wilderness,   250
  And over the hushed carpet, silent stept,
And 'tween the curtains peeped, where, lo!—how fast
    she slept.

XXIX

Then by the bed-side where the faded moon,
Made a dim, silver twilight, soft he set
A table, and, half anguished, threw thereon   255
A cloth of woven crimson, gold, and jet:—
O for some drowsy Morphean amulet!
The boisterous, midnight, festive clarion,
The kettle-drum, and far-heard clarinet,
Affray his ears, though but in dying tone:—   260
The hall door shuts again, and all the noise is gone.

XXX

And still she slept an azure-lidded sleep,
In blanchèd linen, smooth, and lavendered,
While he from forth the closet brought a heap
Of candied apple, quince, and plum, and gourd;
With jellies soother than the creamy curd,   266
And lucent syrups, tinct with cinnamon;
Manna and dates, in argosy transferred
From Fez; and spiced dainties, every one,
From silken Samarcand to cedared Lebanon.   270

XXXI

These delicates he heaped with glowing hand
On golden dishes and in baskets bright
Of wreathèd silver: sumptuous they stand
In the retirèd quiet of the night,
Filling the chilly room with perfume light.—   275
'And now, my love, my seraph fair, awake!
Thou art my heaven, and I thine eremite:
Open thine eyes for meek St. Agnes' sake,
Or I shall drowse beside thee, so my soul doth ache.'

XXXII

Thus whispering, his warm, unnervèd arm   280
Sank in her pillow. Shaded was her dream
By the dusk curtains:—'twas a midnight charm
Impossible to melt as icèd stream:

The lustrous salvers in the moonlight gleam;
Broad golden fringe upon the carpet lies: 285
It seemed he never, never could redeem
From such a stedfast spell his lady's eyes;
So mused awhile, entoiled in woofèd phantasies.

XXXIII

Awakening up, he took her hollow lute,—
Tumultuous,—and, in chords that tenderest be,
He played an ancient ditty, long since mute,   291
In Provence called, 'La belle dame sans mercy':
Close to her ear touching the melody;—
Wherewith disturbed, she uttered a soft moan:
He ceased—she panted quick—and suddenly   295
Her blue affrayèd eyes wide open shone:
Upon his knees he sank, pale as smooth-sculptured
    stone.

XXXIV

Her eyes were open, but she still beheld,
Now wide awake, the vision of her sleep:
There was a painful change, that nigh expelled
The blisses of her dream so pure and deep;   301
At which fair Madeline began to weep,
And moan forth witless words with many a sigh;
While still her gaze on Porphyro would keep;
Who knelt, with joined hands and piteous eye,
Fearing to move or speak, she looked so dreamingly.

XXXV

'Ah, Porphyro!' said she, 'but even now
Thy voice was at sweet tremble in mine ear,
Made tuneable with every sweetest vow,
And those sad eyes were spiritual and clear: 310
How changed thou art! how pallid, chill, and drear!
Give me that voice again, my Porphyro,
Those looks immortal, those complainings dear!
Oh leave me not in this eternal woe,   314
For if thou diest, my Love, I know not where to go.'

XXXVI

Beyond a mortal man impassioned far
At these voluptuous accents, he arose,
Ethereal, flushed, and like a throbbing star
Seen mid the sapphire heaven's deep repose;
Into her dream he melted, as the rose   320
Blendeth its odour with the violet,—
Solution sweet: meantime the frost-wind blows
Like Love's alarum pattering the sharp sleet
Against the window-panes; St. Agnes' moon hath set.

XXXVII

'Tis dark: quick pattereth the flaw-blown sleet:
'This is no dream, my bride, my Madeline!'   326
'Tis dark: the icèd gusts still rave and beat:
'No dream, alas! alas! and woe is mine!
Porphyro will leave me here to fade and pine.—
Cruel! what traitor could thee hither bring?   330
I curse not, for my heart is lost in thine,
Though thou forsakest a deceivèd thing;—
A dove forlorn and lost with sick unprunèd wing.'

XXXVIII

'My Madeline! sweet dreamer! lovely bride!
Say, may I be for aye thy vassal blest?   335
Thy beauty's shield, heart-shaped and vermeil
    dyed?
Ah, silver shrine, here will I take my rest
After so many hours of toil and quest,
A famished pilgrim,—saved by miracle.
Though I have found, I will not rob thy nest   340
Saving of thy sweet self; if thou think'st well
To trust, fair Madeline, to no rude infidel.

XXXIX

'Hark! 'tis an elfin-storm from faery land,
Of haggard seeming, but a boon indeed:
Arise—arise! the morning is at hand;—   345

The bloated wassaillers will never heed:—
Let us away, my love, with happy speed;
There are no ears to hear, or eyes to see,—
Drowned all in Rhenish and the sleepy mead:
Awake! arise! my love, and fearless be, 350
For o'er the southern moors I have a home for thee.'

XL

She hurried at his words, beset with fears,
For there were sleeping dragons all around,
At glaring watch, perhaps, with ready spears—
Down the wide stairs a darkling way they found.—
In all the house was heard no human sound. 356
A chain-drooped lamp was flickering by each door;
The arras, rich with horseman, hawk, and hound,
Fluttered in the besieging wind's uproar;
And the long carpets rose along the gusty floor. 360

XLI·

They glide, like phantoms, into the wide hall;
Like phantoms, to the iron porch they glide;
Where lay the Porter, in uneasy sprawl,
With a huge empty flagon by his side:
The wakeful bloodhound rose, and shook his hide,
But his sagacious eye an inmate owns: 366
By one, and one, the bolts full easy slide:—
The chains lie silent on the footworn stones;—
The key turns, and the door upon its hinges groans.

XLII

And they are gone: ay, ages long ago 370
These lovers fled away into the storm.
That night the Baron dreamt of many a woe,
And all his warrior-guests, with shade and form
Of witch, and demon, and large coffin-worm,
Were long be-nightmared. Angela the old 375
Died palsy-twitched, with meagre face deform;
The Beadsman, after thousand aves told,
For aye unsought for slept among his ashes cold.

LORD MACAULAY
1800–1859

The Keeping of the Bridge

(From *Horatius*)

Lars Porsena of Clusium
  By the Nine Gods he swore
That the great house of Tarquin
  Should suffer wrong no more.
By the Nine Gods he swore it,   5
  And named a trysting day,
And bade his messengers ride forth,
East and west and south and north,
  To summon his array.

East and west and south and north   10
  The messengers ride fast,
And tower and town and cottage
  Have heard the trumpet's blast.
Shame on the false Etruscan
  Who lingers in his home,   15
When Porsena of Clusium
  Is on the march for Rome.

And now hath every city
  Sent up her tale of men;
The foot are fourscore thousand,   20
  The horse are thousands ten:
Before the gates of Sutrium
  Is met the great array.
A proud man was Lars Porsena
  Upon the trysting day.   25

But by the yellow Tiber
  Was tumult and affright:
From all the spacious champaign
  To Rome men took their flight.

A mile around the city,   30
  The throng stopped up the ways;
A fearful sight it was to see
  Through two long nights and days.

Now, from the rock Tarpeian,
  Could the wan burghers spy   35
The line of blazing villages
  Red in the midnight sky.
The Fathers of the city,
  They sat all night and day,
For every hour some horseman came   40
  With tidings of dismay.

I wis, in all the Senate,
  There was no heart so bold,
But sore it ached and fast it beat,
  When that ill news was told.   45
Forthwith up rose the Consul,
  Up rose the Fathers all;
In haste they girded up their gowns,
  And hied them to the wall.

They held a council standing   50
  Before the River-Gate;
Short time was there, ye well may guess,
  For musing or debate.
Out spake the Consul roundly:
  'The bridge must straight go down;   55
For, since Janiculum is lost,
  Naught else can save the town.'

Just then a scout came flying,
  All wild with haste and fear;
'To arms! to arms! Sir Consul: 60
  Lars Porsena is here.'
On the low hills to westward
  The Consul fixed his eye,
And saw the swarthy storm of dust
  Rise fast along the sky.   65

And nearer fast and nearer
  Doth the red whirlwind come;
And louder still and still more loud,
From underneath that rolling cloud,
Is heard the trumpet's war-note proud,   70
  The trampling, and the hum.
And plainly and more plainly
  Now through the gloom appears,
Far to left and far to right,
In broken gleams of dark-blue light,   75
The long array of helmets bright,
  The long array of spears.

But the Consul's brow was sad,
  And the Consul's speech was low,
And darkly looked he at the wall,   80
  And darkly at the foe.
'Their van will be upon us
  Before the bridge goes down;
And if they once may win the bridge,
  What hope to save the town?'   85

Then out spake brave Horatius,
  The Captain of the Gate:
'To every man upon this earth
  Death cometh soon or late.
And how can man die better   90
  Than facing fearful odds,
For the ashes of his fathers,
  And the temples of his Gods?

'Hew down the bridge, Sir Consul,
  With all the speed ye may;   95
I, with two more to help me,
  Will hold the foe in play.
In yon strait path a thousand
  May well be stopped by three.
Now who will stand on either hand,   100
  And keep the bridge with me?'

Then out spake Spurius Lartius;
  A Ramnian proud was he:
'Lo, I will stand at thy right hand,
  And keep the bridge with thee.'   105
And out spake strong Herminius;
  Of Titian blood was he:
'I will abide on thy left side,
  And keep the bridge with thee.'

'Horatius,' quoth the Consul,   110
  'As thou sayest, so let it be.'
And straight against that great array
  Forth went the dauntless Three.
For Romans in Rome's quarrel
  Spared neither land nor gold,   115
Nor son nor wife, nor limb nor life,
  In the brave days of old.

Now while the Three were tightening
  Their harness on their backs,
The Consul was the foremost man   120
  To take in hand an axe:
And Fathers mixed with Commons
  Seized hatchet, bar, and crow,
And smote upon the planks above,
  And loosed the props below.   125

Meanwhile the Tuscan army,
  Right glorious to behold,
Came flashing back the noonday light,
Rank behind rank, like surges bright
  Of a broad sea of gold.   130
Four hundred trumpets sounded
  A peal of warlike glee,
As that great host, with measured tread,
And spears advanced, and ensigns spread,
Rolled slowly towards the bridge's head,
  Where stood the dauntless Three.   136

The Three stood calm and silent,
    And looked upon the foes,
And a great shout of laughter
    From all the vanguard rose: 140
And forth three chiefs came spurring
    Before that deep array;
To earth they sprang, their swords they drew,
And lifted high their shields, and flew
    To win the narrow way;   145

Aunus from green Tifernum,
    Lord of the Hill of Vines;
And Seius, whose eight hundred slaves
    Sicken in Ilva's mines;
And Picus, long to Clusium   150
    Vassal in peace and war,
Who led to fight his Umbrian powers
From that grey crag where, girt with towers,
The fortress of Nequinum lowers
    O'er the pale waves of Nar.   155

Stout Lartius hurled down Aunus
    Into the stream beneath.
Herminius struck at Seius,
    And clove him to the teeth:
At Picus brave Horatius   160
    Darted one fiery thrust;
And the proud Umbrian's gilded arms
    Clashed in the bloody dust.

Then Ocnus of Falerii
    Rushed on the Roman three;   165
And Lausulus of Urgo,
    The rover of the sea;
And Aruns of Volsinium,
    Who slew the great wild boar,
The great wild boar that had his den   170
Amidst the reeds of Cosa's fen,
And wasted fields, and slaughtered men,
    Along Albinia's shore.

Herminius smote down Aruns:
   Lartius laid Ocnus low;   175
Right to the heart of Lausulus
   Horatius sent a blow.
'Lie there,' he cried, 'fell pirate!
   No more, aghast and pale,
From Ostia's walls the crowd shall mark
The track of thy destroying bark.   181
No more Campania's hinds shall fly
To woods and caverns when they spy
   Thy thrice accursed sail.'

But now no sound of laughter   185
   Was heard among the foes.
A wild and wrathful clamour
   From all the vanguard rose.
Six spears' lengths from the entrance
   Halted that deep array,   190
And for a space no man came forth
   To win the narrow way.

But hark! the cry is Astur:
   And lo! the ranks divide;
And the great Lord of Luna   195
   Comes with his stately stride.
Upon his ample shoulders
   Clangs loud the fourfold shield,
And in his hand he shakes the brand
   Which none but he can wield.   200

He smiled on those bold Romans
   A smile serene and high;
He eyed the flinching Tuscans,
   And scorn was in his eye.
Quoth he, 'The she-wolf's litter   205
   Stand savagely at bay;
But will ye dare to follow,
   If Astur clears the way?'

Then, whirling up his broadsword
   With both hands to the height,   210

He rushed against Horatius,
   And smote with all his might.
With shield and blade Horatius
   Right deftly turned the blow.   214
The blow, though turned, came yet too nigh;
   It missed his helm, but gashed his thigh:
The Tuscans raised a joyful cry
   To see the red blood flow.

He reeled, and on Herminius
   He leaned one breathing-space;   220
Then, like a wild cat mad with wounds,
   Sprang right at Astur's face:
Through teeth, and skull, and helmet
   So fierce a thrust he sped,
The good sword stood a hand-breadth out
   Behind the Tuscan's head.   226

And the great Lord of Luna
   Fell at that deadly stroke,
As falls on Mount Alvernus
   A thunder-smitten oak.   230
Far o'er the crashing forest
   The giant arms lie spread;
And the pale augurs, muttering low,
   Gaze on the blasted head.

On Astur's throat Horatius   235
   Right firmly pressed his heel,
And thrice and four times tugged amain,
   Ere he wrenched out the steel.
'And see', he cried, 'the welcome,
   Fair guests, that waits you here!   240
What noble Lucumo comes next
   To taste our Roman cheer?'

But at his haughty challenge
   A sullen murmur ran,
Mingled of wrath, and shame, and dread,
   Along that glittering van.   246

There lacked not men of prowess,
  Nor men of lordly race;
For all Etruria's noblest
  Were round the fatal place.   250

But all Etruria's noblest
  Felt their hearts sink to see
On the earth the bloody corpses,
  In the path the dauntless Three:
And, from the ghastly entrance   255
  Where those bold Romans stood,
All shrank, like boys who unaware,
Ranging the woods to start a hare,
Come to the mouth of the dark lair
Where, growling low, a fierce old bear   260
  Lies amidst bones and blood.

Was none who would be foremost
  To lead such dire attack:
But those behind cried 'Forward!'
  And those before cried 'Back'.   265
And backward now and forward
  Wavers the deep array;
And on the tossing sea of steel
To and fro the standards reel;
And the victorious trumpet-peal   270
  Dies fitfully away.

But meanwhile axe and lever
  Have manfully been plied;
And now the bridge hangs tottering
  Above the boiling tide.   275
'Come back, come back, Horatius!'
  Loud cried the Fathers all.
'Back, Lartius! back, Herminius!
  Back, ere the ruin fall!'

Back darted Spurius Lartius;   280
  Herminius darted back:
And, as they passed, beneath their feet
  They felt the timbers crack.

But when they turned their faces,
　　And on the farther shore   285
Saw brave Horatius stand alone,
　　They would have crossed once more.

But with a crash like thunder
　　Fell every loosened beam,
And, like a dam, the mighty wreck   290
　　Lay right athwart the stream.
And a long shout of triumph
　　Rose from the walls of Rome,
As to the highest turret-tops
　　Was splashed the yellow foam.   295

And, like a horse unbroken
　　When first he feels the rein,
The furious river struggled hard,
　　And tossed his tawny mane,
And burst the curb, and bounded,   300
　　Rejoicing to be free,
And whirling down, in fierce career,
Battlement, and plank, and pier,
　　Rushed headlong to the sea.

Alone stood brave Horatius,   305
　　But constant still in mind;
Thrice thirty thousand foes before,
　　And the broad flood behind.
'Down with him!' cried false Sextus,
　　With a smile on his pale face.   310
'Now yield thee,' cried Lars Porsena,
　　'Now yield thee to our grace.'

Round turned he, as not deigning
　　Those craven ranks to see;
Naught spake he to Lars Porsena,   315
　　To Sextus naught spake he;
But he saw on Palatinus
　　The white porch of his home;
And he spake to the noble river
　　That rolls by the towers of Rome.   320

'Oh, Tiber! father Tiber!
  To whom the Romans pray,
A Roman's life, a Roman's arms,
  Take thou in charge this day!'
So he spake, and speaking sheathed   325
  The good sword by his side,
And with his harness on his back
  Plunged headlong in the tide.

No sound of joy or sorrow
  Was heard from either bank;   330
But friends and foes in dumb surprise,
With parted lips and straining eyes,
  Stood gazing where he sank;
And when above the surges
  They saw his crest appear,   335
All Rome sent forth a rapturous cry,
And even the ranks of Tuscany
  Could scarce forbear to cheer.

But fiercely ran the current,
  Swollen high by months of rain: 340
And fast his blood was flowing;
  And he was sore in pain,
And heavy with his armour,
  And spent with changing blows:
And oft they thought him sinking,   345
  But still again he rose.

Never, I ween, did swimmer,
  In such an evil case,
Struggle through such a raging flood
  Safe to the landing place: 350
But his limbs were borne up bravely
  By the brave heart within,
And our good father Tiber
  Bore bravely up his chin.

And now he feels the bottom;   355
  Now on dry earth he stands;

Now round him throng the Fathers
  To press his gory hands;
And now, with shouts and clapping,
  And noise of weeping loud,   360
He enters through the River-Gate,
  Borne by the joyous crowd.

They gave him of the corn-land,
  That was of public right,
As much as two strong oxen   365
  Could plough from morn till night;
And they made a molten image,
  And set it up on high,
And there it stands unto this day
  To witness if I lie.   370

It stands in the Comitium,
  Plain for all folks to see;
Horatius in his harness,
  Halting upon one knee:
And underneath is written,   375
  In letters all of gold,
How valiantly he kept the bridge
  In the brave days of old.

And still his name sounds stirring
  Unto the men of Rome,   380
As the trumpet-blast that cries to them
  To charge the Volscian home;
And wives still pray to Juno
  For boys with hearts as bold
As his who kept the bridge so well   385
  In the brave days of old.

And in the nights of winter,
  When the cold north winds blow,
And the long howling of the wolves
  Is heard amidst the snow;   390
When round the lonely cottage
  Roars loud the tempest's din,

And the good logs of Algidus
   Roar louder yet within;

When the oldest cask is opened,   395
   And the largest lamp is lit;
When the chestnuts glow in the embers,
   And the kid turns on the spit;
When young and old in circle
   Around the firebrands close;   400
When the girls are weaving baskets,
   And the lads are shaping bows;

When the goodman mends his armour,
   And trims his helmet's plume;
When the goodwife's shuttle merrily   405
   Goes flashing through the loom;
With weeping and with laughter
   Still is the story told,
How well Horatius kept the bridge
   In the brave days of old.   410

LORD TENNYSON

1809–1892

Maud

PART I

I

I

I hate the dreadful hollow behind the little wood,
Its lips in the field above are dabbled with blood-red
   heath,
The red-ribb'd ledges drip with a silent horror of
   blood,
And Echo there, whatever is ask'd her, answers
   'Death.'

II

For there in the ghastly pit long since a body was
found,   5
His who had given me life—O father! O God! was it
well?—
Mangled, and flatten'd, and crush'd, and dinted into
the ground:
There yet lies the rock that fell with him when he fell.

III

Did he fling himself down? who knows? for a vast
speculation had fail'd,
And ever he mutter'd and madden'd, and ever wann'd
with despair,   10
And out he walk'd when the wind like a broken
worldling wail'd,
And the flying gold of the ruin'd woodlands drove
thro' the air.

IV

I remember the time, for the roots of my hair were
stirr'd
By a shuffled step, by a dead weight trail'd, by a
whispered fright,
And my pulses closed their gates with a shock on my
heart as I heard   15
The shrill-edged shriek of a mother divide the shuddering night.

V

Villainy somewhere! whose? One says, we are villains
all.
Not he: his honest fame should at least by me be
maintain'd:
But that old man, now lord of the broad estate and
the Hall,
Dropt off gorged from a scheme that had left us
flaccid and drain'd.   20

VI

Why do they prate of the blessings of Peace? we have
made them a curse,
Pickpockets, each hand lusting for all that is not its
own;
And the lust of gain, in the spirit of Cain, is it better
or worse
Than the heart of the citizen hissing in war on his
own hearthstone?

VII

But these are the days of advance, the works of the
men of mind,   25
When who but a fool would have faith in a trades-
man's ware or his word?
Is it peace or war? Civil war, as I think, and that of a
kind
The viler, as underhand, not openly bearing the
sword.

VIII

Sooner or later I too may passively take the print
Of the golden age—why not? I have neither hope nor
trust;   30
May make my heart as a millstone, set my face as a
flint,
Cheat and be cheated, and die: who knows? we are
ashes and dust.

IX

Peace sitting under her olive, and slurring the days
gone by,
When the poor are hovell'd and hustled together,
each sex, like swine,
When only the ledger lives, and when only not all
men lie;   35
Peace in her vineyard—yes!—but a company forges
the wine.

X

And the vitriol madness flushes up in the ruffian's
    head,
Till the filthy by-lane rings to the yell of the trampled
    wife,
While chalk and alum and plaster are sold to the poor
    for bread,
And the spirit of murder works in the very means of
    life,   40

XI

And Sleep must lie down arm'd, for the villainous
    centre-bits
Grind on the wakeful ear in the hush of the moonless
    nights,
While another is cheating the sick of a few last gasps,
    as he sits
To pestle a poison'd poison behind his crimson lights.

XII

When a Mammonite mother kills her babe for a
    burial fee,   45
And Timour-Mammon grins on a pile of children's
    bones,
Is it peace or war? better, war! loud war by land and
    by sea,
War with a thousand battles, and shaking a hundred
    thrones.

XIII

For I trust if an enemy's fleet came yonder round by
    the hill,
And the rushing battle-bolt sang from the three-
    decker out of the foam,   50
That the smooth-faced snubnosed rogue would leap
    from his counter and till,
And strike, if he could, were it but with his cheating
    yardwand, home.——

XIV

What! am I raging alone as my father raged in his
    mood?
Must *I* too creep to the hollow and dash myself down
    and die
Rather than hold by the law that I made, nevermore
    to brood   55
On a horror of shatter'd limbs and a wretched
    swindler's lie?

XV

Would there be sorrow for *me*? there was *love* in the
    passionate shriek,
Love for the silent thing that had made false haste to
    the grave—
Wrapt in a cloak, as I saw him, and thought he would
    rise and speak
And rave at the lie and the liar, ah God, as he used to
    rave.   60

XVI

I am sick of the Hall and the hill, I am sick of the
    moor and the main.
Why should I stay? can a sweeter chance ever come
    to me here?
O, having the nerves of motion as well as the nerves
    of pain,
Were it not wise if I fled from the place and the pit
    and the fear?

XVII

Workmen up at the Hall!—they are coming back
    from abroad;   65
The dark old place will be gilt by the touch of a
    millionaire:
I have heard, I know not whence, of the singular
    beauty of Maud;
I play'd with the girl when a child; she promised then
    to be fair.

XVIII

Maud with her venturous climbings and tumbles and
　　childish escapes,
Maud the delight of the village, the ringing joy of the
　　Hall,　　　　　　　　　　　　　　　　　　　70
Maud with her sweet purse-mouth when my father
　　dangled the grapes,
Maud the beloved of my mother, the moon-faced
　　darling of all,—

XIX

What is she now? My dreams are bad. She may bring
　　me a curse.
No, there is fatter game on the moor; she will let me
　　alone.
Thanks, for the fiend best knows whether woman or
　　man be the worse.　　　　　　　　　　　　　75
I will bury myself in myself, and the Devil may pipe
　　to his own.

II

Long have I sigh'd for a calm: God grant I may find
　　it at last!
It will never be broken by Maud, she has neither
　　savour nor salt,
But a cold and clear-cut face, as I found when her
　　carriage past,
Perfectly beautiful: let it be granted her: where is the
　　fault?　　　　　　　　　　　　　　　　80
All that I saw (for her eyes were downcast, not to be
　　seen)
Faultily faultless, icily regular, splendidly null,
Dead perfection, no more; nothing more, if it had not
　　been
For a chance of travel, a paleness, an hour's defect of
　　the rose,

Or an underlip, you may call it a little too ripe, too
full, 85
Or the least little delicate aquiline curve in a sensitive
nose,
From which I escaped heart-free, with the least little
touch of spleen.

III

Cold and clear-cut face, why come you so cruelly
meek,
Breaking a slumber in which all spleenful folly was
drown'd,
Pale with the golden beam of an eyelash dead on the
cheek, 90
Passionless, pale, cold face, star-sweet on a gloom
profound;
Womanlike, taking revenge too deep for a transient
wrong
Done but in thought to your beauty, and ever as pale
as before
Growing and fading and growing upon me without a
sound,
Luminous, gemlike, ghostlike, deathlike, half the
night long 95
Growing and fading and growing, till I could bear it
no more,
But arose, and all by myself in my own dark garden
ground,
Listening now to the tide in its broad-flung ship-
wrecking roar,
Now to the scream of a madden'd beach dragg'd
down by the wave,
Walk'd in a wintry wind by a ghastly glimmer, and
found 100
The shining daffodil dead, and Orion low in his grave.

IV

I

A million emeralds break from the ruby-budded lime
In the little grove where I sit—ah, wherefore cannot
  I be
Like things of the season gay, like the bountiful
  season bland,
When the far-off sail is blown by the breeze of a
  softer clime,   105
Half-lost in the liquid azure bloom of a crescent of
  sea,
The silent sapphire-spangled marriage ring of the
  land?

II

Below me, there, is the village, and looks how quiet
  and small!
And yet bubbles o'er like a city, with gossip, scandal,
  and spite;
And Jack on his ale-house bench has as many lies as
  a Czar;   110
And here on the landward side, by a red rock,
  glimmers the Hall;
And up in the high Hall-garden I see her pass like a
  light;
But sorrow seize me if ever that light be my leading
  star!

III

When have I bow'd to her father, the wrinkled head
  of the race?
I met her to-day with her brother, but not to her
  brother I bow'd;   115
I bow'd to his lady-sister as she rode by on the moor;
But the fire of a foolish pride flash'd over the beautiful face.

O child, you wrong your beauty, believe it, in being
    so proud;
Your father has wealth well-gotten, and I am name-
    less and poor.

IV

I keep but a man and a maid, ever ready to slander
    and steal; 120
I know it, and smile a hard-set smile, like a stoic, or
    like
A wiser epicurean, and let the world have its way:
For nature is one with rapine, a harm no preacher
    can heal;
The Mayfly is torn by the swallow, the sparrow
    spear'd by the shrike,
And the whole little wood where I sit is a world of
    plunder and prey. 125

V

We are puppets, Man in his pride, and Beauty fair in
    her flower;
Do we move ourselves, or are moved by an unseen
    hand at a game
That pushes us off from the board, and others ever
    succeed?
Ah yet, we cannot be kind to each other here for an
    hour;
We whisper, and hint, and chuckle, and grin at a
    brother's shame; 130
However we brave it out, we men are a little breed.

VI

A monstrous eft was of old the Lord and Master of
    Earth,
For him did this high sun flame, and his river billow-
    ing ran,
And he felt himself in his force to be Nature's crown-
    ing race.

As nine months go to the shaping an infant ripe for
 his birth,   135
So many a million ages have gone to the making of
 man:
He now is first, but is he the last? is he not too base?

VII

The man of science himself is fonder of glory, and
 vain,
An eye well-practised in nature, a spirit bounded and
 poor;
The passionate heart of the poet is whirl'd into folly
 and vice.   140
I would not marvel at either, but keep a temperate
 brain;
For not to desire or admire, if a man could learn it,
 were more
Than to walk all day like the sultan of old in a garden
 of spice.

VIII

For the drift of the Maker is dark, an Isis hid by the
 veil.
Who knows the ways of the world, how God will bring
 them about?   145
Our planet is one, the suns are many, the world is
 wide.
Shall I weep if a Poland fall? shall I shriek if a
 Hungary fail?
Or an infant civilization be ruled with rod or with
 knout?
I have not made the world, and He that made it will
 guide.

IX

Be mine a philosopher's life in the quiet woodland
 ways,   150
Where if I cannot be gay let a passionless peace be
 my lot,

Far-off from the clamour of liars belied in the hubbub
  of lies;
From the long-neck'd geese of the world that are ever
  hissing dispraise
Because their natures are little, and, whether he heed
  it or not,
Where each man walks with his head in a cloud of
  poisonous flies.   155

x

And most of all would I flee from the cruel madness
  of love,
The honey of poison-flowers and all the measureless
  ill.
Ah Maud, you milkwhite fawn, you are all unmeet
  for a wife.
Your mother is mute in her grave as her image in
  marble above;
Your father is ever in London, you wander about at
  your will;   160
You have but fed on the roses, and lain in the lilies of
  life.

V

i

A voice by the cedar tree,
In the meadow under the Hall!
She is singing an air that is known to me,
A passionate ballad gallant and gay,   165
A martial song like a trumpet's call!
Singing alone in the morning of life,
In the happy morning of life and of May,
Singing of men in that battle array,
Ready in heart and ready in hand,   170
March with banner and bugle and fife
To the death, for their native land.

II

Maud with her exquisite face,
And wild voice pealing up to the sunny sky,
And feet like sunny gems on an English green,   175
Maud in the light of her youth and her grace,
Singing of Death, and of Honour that cannot die,
Till I well could weep for a time so sordid and mean,
And myself so languid and base.

III

Silence, beautiful voice!   180
Be still, for you only trouble the mind
With a joy in which I cannot rejoice,
A glory I shall not find.
Still! I will hear you no more,
For your sweetness hardly leaves me a choice   185
But to move to the meadow and fall before
Her feet on the meadow grass, and adore,
Not her, who is neither courtly nor kind,
Not her, not her, but a voice.

VI

I

Morning arises stormy and pale,   190
No sun, but a wannish glare
In fold upon fold of hueless cloud,
And the budded peaks of the wood are bow'd
Caught and cuff'd by the gale:
I had fancied it would be fair.   195

II

Whom but Maud should I meet
Last night, when the sunset burn'd
On the blossom'd gable-ends
At the head of the village street,
Whom but Maud should I meet?   200
And she touch'd my hand with a smile so sweet,

She made me divine amends
For a courtesy not return'd.

III

And thus a delicate spark
Of glowing and growing light   205
Thro' the livelong hours of the dark
Kept itself warm in the heart of my dreams,
Ready to burst in a colour'd flame;
Till at last when the morning came
In a cloud, it faded, and seems   210
But an ashen-grey delight.

IV

What if with her sunny hair,
And smile as sunny as cold,
She meant to weave me a snare
Of some coquettish deceit,   215
Cleopatra-like as of old
To entangle me when we met,
To have her lion roll in a silken net
And fawn at a victor's feet.

V

Ah, what shall I be at fifty   220
Should Nature keep me alive,
If I find the world so bitter
When I am but twenty-five?
Yet, if she were not a cheat,
If Maud were all that she seem'd,   225
And her smile were all that I dream'd,
Then the world were not so bitter
But a smile could make it sweet.

VI

What if tho' her eye seem'd full
Of a kind intent to me,   230
What if that dandy-despot, he,
That jewell'd mass of millinery,

That oil'd and curl'd Assyrian Bull
Smelling of musk and insolence,
Her brother, from whom I keep aloof,   235
Who wants the finer politic sense
To mask, tho' but in his own behoof,
With a glassy smile his brutal scorn—
What if he had told her yestermorn
How prettily for his own sweet sake   240
A face of tenderness might be feign'd,
And a moist mirage in desert eyes,
That so, when the rotten hustings shake
In another month to his brazen lies,
A wretched vote may be gain'd.   245

VII

For a raven ever croaks, at my side,
Keep watch and ward, keep watch and ward,
Or thou wilt prove their tool.
Yea, too, myself from myself I guard,
For often a man's own angry pride   250
Is cap and bells for a fool.

VIII

Perhaps the smile and tender tone
Came out of her pitying womanhood,
For am I not, am I not, here alone
So many a summer since she died,   255
My mother, who was so gentle and good?
Living alone in an empty house,
Here half-hid in the gleaming wood,
Where I hear the dead at midday moan,
And the shrieking rush of the wainscot mouse,
And my own sad name in corners cried,   261
When the shiver of dancing leaves is thrown
About its echoing chambers wide,
Till a morbid hate and horror have grown
Of a world in which I have hardly mixt,   265
And a morbid eating lichen fixt
On a heart half-turn'd to stone.

IX

O heart of stone, are you flesh, and caught
By that you swore to withstand?
For what was it else within me wrought   270
But, I fear, the new strong wine of love,
That made my tongue so stammer and trip
When I saw the treasured splendour, her hand,
Come sliding out of her sacred glove,
And the sunlight broke from her lip?   275

X

I have play'd with her when a child;
She remembers it now we meet.
Ah well, well, well, I *may* be beguiled
By some coquettish deceit.
Yet, if she were not a cheat,   280
If Maud were all that she seem'd,
And her smile had all that I dream'd,
Then the world were not so bitter
But a smile could make it sweet.

VII

I

Did I hear it half in a doze   285
   Long since, I know not where?
Did I dream it an hour ago,
   When asleep in this arm-chair?

II

Men were drinking together,
   Drinking and talking of me: 290
'Well, if it prove a girl, the boy
   Will have plenty: so let it be.'

III

Is it an echo of something
   Read with a boy's delight,

Viziers nodding together   295
In some Arabian night?

IV

Strange, that I hear two men,
Somewhere, talking of me;
'Well, if it prove a girl, my boy
Will have plenty: so let it be.'   300

VIII

She came to the village church,
And sat by a pillar alone;
An angel watching an urn
Wept over her, carved in stone;
And once, but once, she lifted her eyes,   305
And suddenly, sweetly, strangely blush'd
To find they were met by my own;
And suddenly, sweetly, my heart beat stronger
And thicker, until I heard no longer
The snowy-banded, dilettante,   310
Delicate-handed priest intone;
And thought, is it pride, and mused and sigh'd
'No surely, now it cannot be pride.'

IX

I was walking a mile,
More than a mile from the shore,   315
The sun look'd out with a smile
Betwixt the cloud and the moor,
And riding at set of day
Over the dark moor land,
Rapidly riding far away,   320
She waved to me with her hand.
There were two at her side,
Something flash'd in the sun,
Down by the hill I saw them ride,

In a moment they were gone: 325
Like a sudden spark
Struck vainly in the night,
And back returns the dark
With no more hope of light.

X

I

Sick, am I sick of a jealous dread?   330
Was not one of the two at her side
This new-made lord, whose splendour plucks
The slavish hat from the villager's head?
Whose old grandfather has lately died,
Gone to a blacker pit, for whom   335
Grimy nakedness dragging his trucks
And laying his trams in a poison'd gloom
Wrought, till he crept from a gutted mine
Master of half a servile shire,
And left his coal all turn'd into gold   340
To a grandson, first of his noble line,
Rich in the grace all women desire,
Strong in the power that all men adore,
And simper and set their voices lower,
And soften as if to a girl, and hold   345
Awe-stricken breaths at a work divine,
Seeing his gewgaw castle shine,
New as his title, built last year,
There amid perky larches and pine,
And over the sullen-purple moor   350
(Look at it) pricking a cockney ear.

II

What, has he found my jewel out?
For one of the two that rode at her side
Bound for the Hall, I am sure was he:
Bound for the Hall, and I think for a bride.   355
Blithe would her brother's acceptance be.

Maud could be gracious too, no doubt,
To a lord, a captain, a padded shape,
A bought commission, a waxen face,
A rabbit mouth that is ever agape—   360
Bought? what is it he cannot buy?
And therefore splenetic, personal, base,
A wounded thing with a rancorous cry,
At war with myself and a wretched race,
Sick, sick to the heart of life, am I.   365

III

Last week came one to the county town,
To preach our poor little army down,
And play the game of the despot kings,
Tho' the state has done it and thrice as well:
This broad-brimm'd hawker of holy things,
Whose ear is cramm'd with his cotton, and rings   372
Even in dreams to the chink of his pence,
This huckster put down war! can he tell
Whether war be a cause or a consequence?
Put down the passions that make earth Hell!
Down with ambition, avarice, pride,   376
Jealousy, down! cut off from the mind
The bitter springs of anger and fear;
Down too, down at your own fireside,
With the evil tongue and the evil ear,   380
For each is at war with mankind.

IV

I wish I could hear again
The chivalrous battle-song
That she warbled alone in her joy!
I might persuade myself then   385
She would not do herself this great wrong,
To take a wanton dissolute boy
For a man and leader of men.

V

Ah God, for a man with heart, head, hand,
Like some of the simple great ones gone   390

For ever and ever by,
One still strong man in a blatant land,
Whatever they call him, what care I,
Aristocrat, democrat, autocrat—one
Who can rule and dare not lie. 395

VI

And ah for a man to arise in me,
That the man I am may cease to be!

XI

I

O let the solid ground
    Not fail beneath my feet
Before my life has found 400
    What some have found so sweet;
Then let come what come may,
What matter if I go mad,
I shall have had my day.

II

Let the sweet heavens endure, 405
    Not close and darken above me
Before I am quite quite sure
    That there is one to love me;
Then let come what come may
To a life that has been so sad, 410
I shall have had my day.

XII

I

Birds in the high Hall-garden
    When twilight was falling,
Maud, Maud, Maud, Maud,
    They were crying and calling. 415

II

Where was Maud? in our wood;
    And I, who else, was with her,
Gathering woodland lilies,
    Myriads blow together.

III

Birds in our wood sang   420
    Ringing thro' the valleys,
Maud is here, here, here
    In among the lilies.

IV

I kiss'd her slender hand,
    She took the kiss sedately;   425
Maud is not seventeen,
    But she is tall and stately.

V

I to cry out on pride
    Who have won her favour!
O Maud were sure of Heaven   430
    If lowliness could save her.

VI

I know the way she went
    Home with her maiden posy,
For her feet have touch'd the meadows
    And left the daisies rosy.   435

VII

Birds in the high Hall-garden
    Were crying and calling to her,
Where is Maud, Maud, Maud?
    One is come to woo her.

VIII

Look, a horse at the door,   440
    And little King Charley snarling,

Go back, my lord, across the moor,
  You are not her darling.

XIII

I

Scorn'd, to be scorn'd by one that I scorn,
Is that a matter to make me fret? 445
That a calamity hard to be borne?
Well, he may live to hate me yet.
Fool that I am to be vext with his pride!
I past him, I was crossing his lands;
He stood on the path a little aside; 450
His face, as I grant, in spite of spite,
Has a broad-blown comeliness, red and white,
And six feet two, as I think, he stands;
But his essences turn'd the live air sick,
And barbarous opulence jewel-thick 455
Sunn'd itself on his breast and his hands.

II

Who shall call me ungentle, unfair,
I long'd so heartily then and there
To give him the grasp of fellowship;
But while I past he was humming an air, 460
Stopt, and then with a riding whip
Leisurely tapping a glossy boot,
And curving a contumelious lip,
Gorgonized me from head to foot
With a stony British stare. 465

III

Why sits he here in his father's chair?
That old man never comes to his place:
Shall I believe him ashamed to be seen?
For only once, in the village street,
Last year, I caught a glimpse of his face, 470
A grey old wolf and a lean.

Scarcely, now, would I call him a cheat;
For then, perhaps, as a child of deceit,
She might by a true descent be untrue;
And Maud is as true as Maud is sweet: 475
Tho' I fancy her sweetness only due
To the sweeter blood by the other side;
Her mother has been a thing complete,
However she came to be so allied.
And fair without, faithful within,   480
Maud to him is nothing akin:
Some peculiar mystic grace
Made her the only child of her mother,
And heap'd the whole inherited sin
On that huge scapegoat of the race,   485
All, all upon the brother.

IV

Peace, angry spirit, and let him be!
Has not his sister smiled on me?

XIV

I

Maud has a garden of roses
And lilies fair on a lawn;   490
There she walks in her state
And tends upon bed and bower,
And thither I climb'd at dawn
And stood by her garden-gate;
A lion ramps at the top,   495
He is claspt by a passion-flower.

II

Maud's own little oak-room
(Which Maud, like a precious stone
Set in the heart of the carven gloom,
Lights with herself, when alone   500

She sits by her music and books,
And her brother lingers late
With a roystering company) looks
Upon Maud's own garden-gate:
And I thought as I stood, if a hand, as white   505
As ocean-foam in the moon, were laid
On the hasp of the window, and my Delight
Had a sudden desire, like a glorious ghost, to glide,
Like a beam of the seventh heaven, down to my side,
There were but a step to be made.   510

III

The fancy flatter'd my mind,
And again seem'd over bold;
Now I thought that she cared for me,
Now I thought she was kind
Only because she was cold.   515

IV

I heard no sound where I stood
But the rivulet on from the lawn
Running down to my own dark wood;
Or the voice of a long sea-wave as it swell'd
Now and then in the dim-grey dawn;   520
But I look'd, and round, all round the house I beheld
The death-white curtain drawn;
Felt a horror over me creep,
Prickle my skin and catch my breath,
Knew that the death-white curtain meant but sleep,
Yet I shudder'd and thought like a fool of the sleep
    of death.   526

XV

So dark a mind within me dwells,
    And I make myself such evil cheer,
That if *I* be dear to some one else,
    Then some one else may have much to fear;   530
But if *I* be dear to some one else,

Then I should be to myself more dear.
Shall I not take care of all that I think,
Yea ev'n of wretched meat and drink,
If I be dear,   535
If I be dear to some one else.

XVI

I

This lump of earth has left his estate
The lighter by the loss of his weight;
And so that he find what he went to seek,
And fulsome Pleasure clog him, and drown   540
His heart in the gross mud-honey of town,
He may stay for a year who has gone for a week:
But this is the day when I must speak,
And I see my Oread coming down,
O this is the day!   545
O beautiful creature, what am I
That I dare look her way;
Think I may hold dominion sweet,
Lord of the pulse that is lord of her breast,
And dream of her beauty with tender dread,
From the delicate Arab arch of her feet   551
To the grace that, bright and light as the crest
Of a peacock, sits on her shining head,
And she knows it not: O, if she knew it,
To know her beauty might half undo it.   555
I know it the one bright thing to save
My yet young life in the wilds of Time,
Perhaps from madness, perhaps from crime,
Perhaps from a selfish grave.

II

What, if she be fasten'd to this fool lord,   560
Dare I bid her abide by her word?
Should I love her so well if she
Had given her word to a thing so low?
Shall I love her so well if she

Can break her word were it even for me?. 565
I trust that it is not so.

III

Catch not my breath, O clamorous heart,
Let not my tongue be a thrall to my eye,
For I must tell her before we part,
I must tell her, or die. 570

XVII

Go not, happy day,
    From the shining fields,
Go not, happy day,
    Till the maiden yields.
Rosy is the West, 575
    Rosy is the South,
Roses are her cheeks,
    And a rose her mouth.
When the happy Yes
    Falters from her lips, 580
Pass and blush the news
    O'er the blowing ships.
Over blowing seas,
    Over seas at rest,
Pass the happy news, 585
    Blush it thro' the West;
Till the red man dance
    By his red cedar tree,
And the red man's babe
    Leap, beyond the sea. 590
Blush from West to East,
    Blush from East to West,
Till the West is East,
    Blush it thro' the West.
Rosy is the West, 595
    Rosy is the South,
Roses are her cheeks,
    And a rose her mouth.

XVIII

I

I have led her home, my love, my only friend.
There is none like her, none.   600
And never yet so warmly ran my blood
And sweetly, on and on
Calming itself to the long-wish'd-for end,
Full to the banks, close on the promised good.

II

None like her, none.   605
Just now the dry-tongued laurels' pattering talk
Seem'd her light foot along the garden walk,
And shook my heart to think she comes once more;
But even then I heard her close the door,
The gates of Heaven are closed, and she is gone.

III

There is none like her, none.   611
Nor will be when our summers have deceased.
O, art thou sighing for Lebanon
In the long breeze that streams to thy delicious East,
Sighing for Lebanon,   615
Dark cedar, tho' thy limbs have here increased,
Upon a pastoral slope as fair,
And looking to the South, and fed
With honey'd rain and delicate air,
And haunted by the starry head   620
Of her whose gentle will has changed my fate,
And made my life a perfumed altar-flame;
And over whom thy darkness must have spread
With such delight as theirs of old, thy great
Forefathers of the thornless garden, there   625
Shadowing the snow-limb'd Eve from whom she
        came.

IV

Here will I lie, while these long branches sway,
And you fair stars that crown a happy day

Go in and out as if at merry play,
Who am no more so all forlorn,   630
As when it seem'd far better to be born
To labour and the mattock-harden'd hand,
Than nursed at ease and brought to understand
A sad astrology, the boundless plan
That makes you tyrants in your iron skies,   635
Innumerable, pitiless, passionless eyes,
Cold fires, yet with power to burn and brand
His nothingness into man.

v

But now shine on, and what care I,
Who in this stormy gulf have found a pearl   640
The countercharm of space and hollow sky,
And do accept my madness, and would die
To save from some slight shame one simple girl.

vi

Would die; for sullen-seeming Death may give
More life to Love than is or ever was   645
In our low world, where yet 'tis sweet to live.
Let no one ask me how it came to pass;
It seems that I am happy, that to me
A livelier emerald twinkles in the grass,
A purer sapphire melts into the sea.   650

vii

Not die, but live a life of truest breath,
And teach true life to fight with mortal wrongs.
O, why should Love, like men in drinking songs,
Spice his fair banquet with the dust of death?
Make answer, Maud my bliss,   655
Maud made my Maud by that long lover's kiss,
Life of my life, wilt thou not answer this?
'The dusky strand of Death inwoven here
With dear Love's tie, makes Love himself more dear.'

VIII

Is that enchanted moan only the swell   660
Of the long waves that roll in yonder bay?
And hark the clock within, the silver knell
Of twelve sweet hours that past in bridal white,
And died to live, long as my pulses play;
But now by this my love has closed her sight   665
And given false death her hand, and stol'n away
To dreamful wastes where footless fancies dwell
Among the fragments of the golden day.
May nothing there her maiden grace affright!
Dear heart, I feel with thee the drowsy spell.   670
My bride to be, my evermore delight,
My own heart's heart and ownest own farewell;
It is but for a little space I go:
And ye meanwhile far over moor and fell
Beat to the noiseless music of the night!   675
Has our whole earth gone nearer to the glow
Of your soft splendours that you look so bright?
I have climb'd nearer out of lonely Hell.
Beat, happy stars, timing with things below,
Beat with my heart more blest than heart can tell,
Blest, but for some dark undercurrent woe   681
That seems to draw—but it shall not be so:
Let all be well, be well.

XIX

I

Her brother is coming back to-night,
Breaking up my dream of delight.   685

II

My dream? do I dream of bliss?
I have walk'd awake with Truth.
O when did a morning shine
So rich in atonement as this

For my dark-dawning youth,   690
Darken'd watching a mother decline
And that dead man at her heart and mine:
For who was left to watch her but I?
Yet so did I let my freshness die.

III

I trust that I did not talk   695
To gentle Maud in our walk
(For often in lonely wanderings
I have cursed him even to lifeless things)
But I trust that I did not talk,
Not touch on her father's sin: 700
I am sure I did but speak
Of my mother's faded cheek
When it slowly grew so thin,
That I felt she was slowly dying   704
Vext with lawyers and harass'd with debt:
For how often I caught her with eyes all wet,
Shaking her head at her son and sighing
A world of trouble within!

IV

And Maud too, Maud was moved
To speak of the mother she loved   710
As one scarce less forlorn,
Dying abroad and it seems apart
From him who had ceased to share her heart,
And ever mourning over the feud,
The household Fury sprinkled with blood
By which our houses are torn: 716
How strange was what she said,
When only Maud and the brother
Hung over her dying bed—
That Maud's dark father and mine   720
Had bound us one to the other,
Betrothed us over their wine,
On the day when Maud was born;
Seal'd her mine from her first sweet breath.

Mine, mine by a right, from birth till death,
Mine, mine—our fathers have sworn.   726

v

But the true blood spilt had in it a heat
To dissolve the precious seal on a bond,
That, if left uncancell'd, had been so sweet:
And none of us thought of a something beyond,
A desire that awoke in the heart of the child,
As it were a duty done to the tomb,
To be friends for her sake, to be reconciled;
And I was cursing them and my doom,   734
And letting a dangerous thought run wild
While often abroad in the fragrant gloom
Of foreign churches—I see her there,
Bright English lily, breathing a prayer
To be friends, to be reconciled!

vi

But then what a flint is he!   740
Abroad, at Florence, at Rome,
I find whenever she touch'd on me
This brother had laugh'd her down,
And at last, when each came home,
He had darken'd into a frown,   745
Chid her, and forbid her to speak
To me, her friend of the years before;
And this was what had redden'd her cheek
When I bow'd to her on the moor.

vii

Yet Maud, altho' not blind   750
To the faults of his heart and mind,
I see she cannot but love him,
And says he is rough but kind,
And wishes me to approve him,
And tells me, when she lay   755

Sick once, with a fear of worse,
That he left his wine and horses and play,
Sat with her, read to her, night and day,
And tended her like a nurse.

VIII

Kind? but the deathbed desire   760
Spurn'd by this heir of the liar—
Rough but kind? yet I know
He has plotted against me in this,
That he plots against me still.
Kind to Maud? that were not amiss.   765
Well, rough but kind; why let it be so:
For shall not Maud have her will?

IX

For, Maud, so tender and true,
As long as my life endures
I feel I shall owe you a debt,   770
That I never can hope to pay;
And if ever I should forget
That I owe this debt to you
And for your sweet sake to yours;
O then, what then shall I say?—   775
If ever I *should* forget,
May God make me more wretched
Than ever I have been yet!

X

So now I have sworn to bury
All this dead body of hate,   780
I feel so free and so clear
By the loss of that dead weight,
That I should grow light-headed, I fear,
Fantastically merry;
But that her brother comes, like a blight   785
On my fresh hope, to the Hall to-night.

XX

I

Strange, that I felt so gay,
Strange, that *I* tried to-day
To beguile her melancholy;
The Sultan, as we name him,— 790
She did not wish to blame him—
But he vext and perplext her
With his worldly talk and folly:
Was it gentle to reprove her
For stealing out of view 795
From a little lazy lover
Who but claims her as his due?
Or for chilling his caresses
By the coldness of her manners,
Nay, the plainness of her dresses? 800
Now I know her but in two,
Nor can pronounce upon it
If one should ask me whether
The habit, hat, and feather,
Or the frock and gipsy bonnet 805
Be the neater and completer;
For nothing can be sweeter
Than maiden Maud in either.

II

But to-morrow, if we live,
Our ponderous squire will give 810
A grand political dinner
To half the squirelings near;
And Maud will wear her jewels,
And the bird of prey will hover,
And the titmouse hope to win her 815
With his chirrup at her ear.

III

A grand political dinner
To the men of many acres,

A gathering of the Tory,
A dinner and then a dance 820
For the maids and marriage-makers,
And every eye but mine will glance
At Maud in all her glory.

IV

For I am not invited,
But, with the Sultan's pardon, 825
I am all as well delighted,
For I know her own rose-garden,
And mean to linger in it
Till the dancing will be over;
And then, oh then, come out to me 830
For a minute, but for a minute,
Come out to your own true lover,
That your true lover may see
Your glory also, and render
All homage to his own darling, 835
Queen Maud in all her splendour.

XXI

Rivulet crossing my ground,
And bringing me down from the Hall
This garden-rose that I found,
Forgetful of Maud and me, 840
And lost in trouble and moving round
Here at the head of a tinkling fall,
And trying to pass to the sea;
O Rivulet, born at the Hall,
My Maud has sent it by thee 845
(If I read her sweet will right)
On a blushing mission to me,
Saying in odour and colour, 'Ah, be
Among the roses to-night.'

XXII

I

Come into the garden, Maud,   850
  For the black bat, night, has flown,
Come into the garden, Maud,
  I am here at the gate alone;
And the woodbine spices are wafted abroad,
  And the musk of the rose is blown.   855

II

For a breeze of morning moves,
  And the planet of Love is on high,
Beginning to faint in the light that she loves
  On a bed of daffodil sky,
To faint in the light of the sun she loves,   860
  To faint in his light, and to die.

III

All night have the roses heard
  The flute, violin, bassoon;
All night has the casement jessamine stirr'd
  To the dancers dancing in tune;   865
Till a silence fell with the waking bird,
  And a hush with the setting moon.

IV

I said to the lily, 'There is but one
  With whom she has heart to be gay.
When will the dancers leave her alone?   870
  She is weary of dance and play.'
Now half to the setting moon are gone,
  And half to the rising day;
Low on the sand and loud on the stone
  The last wheel echoes away.   875

V

I said to the rose, 'The brief night goes
  In babble and revel and wine.

O young lord-lover, what sighs are those,
    For one that will never be thine?
But mine, but mine,' so I sware to the rose,   880
    'For ever and ever, mine.'

VI

And the soul of the rose went into my blood,
    As the music clash'd in the hall;
And long by the garden lake I stood,
    For I heard your rivulet fall   885
From the lake to the meadow and on to the wood,
    Our wood, that is dearer than all;

VII

From the meadow your walks have left so sweet
    That whenever a March-wind sighs
He sets the jewel-print of your feet   890
    In violets blue as your eyes,
To the woody hollows in which we meet
    And the valleys of Paradise.

VIII

The slender acacia would not shake
    One long milk-bloom on the tree;   895
The white lake-blossom fell into the lake
    As the pimpernel dozed on the lea;
But the rose was awake all night for your sake,
    Knowing your promise to me;
The lilies and roses were all awake,   900
    They sigh'd for the dawn and thee.

IX

Queen rose of the rosebud garden of girls,
    Come hither, the dances are done,
In gloss of satin and glimmer of pearls,
    Queen lily and rose in one;   905
Shine out, little head, sunning over with curls,
    To the flowers, and be their sun.

X

There has fallen a splendid tear
   From the passion-flower at the gate.
She is coming, my dove, my dear;   910
   She is coming, my life, my fate;
The red rose cries, 'She is near, she is near;'
   And the white rose weeps, 'She is late;'
The larkspur listens, 'I hear, I hear;'
   And the lily whispers, 'I wait.'   915

XI

She is coming, my own, my sweet;
   Were it ever so airy a tread,
My heart would hear her and beat,
   Were it earth in an earthy bed;
My dust would hear her and beat,   920
   Had I lain for a century dead;
Would start and tremble under her feet,
   And blossom in purple and red.

PART II

I

I

'The fault was mine, the fault was mine'—
Why am I sitting here so stunn'd and still,
Plucking the harmless wild-flower on the hill?—
It is this guilty hand!—
And there rises ever a passionate cry   5
From underneath in the darkening land—
What is it, that has been done?
O dawn of Eden bright over earth and sky,
The fires of Hell brake out of thy rising sun,
The fires of Hell and of Hate;   10
For she, sweet soul, had hardly spoken a word,
When her brother ran in his rage to the gate,
He came with the babe-faced lord;

Heap'd on her terms of disgrace,
And while she wept, and I strove to be cool, 15
He fiercely gave me the lie,
Till I with as fierce an anger spoke,
And he struck, madman, over the face,
Struck me before the languid fool,
Who was gaping and grinning by: 20
Struck for himself an evil stroke;
Wrought for his house an irredeemable woe;
For front to front in an hour we stood,
And a million horrible bellowing echoes broke
From the red-ribb'd hollow behind the wood, 25
And thunder'd up into Heaven the Christless code,
That must have life for a blow.
Ever and ever afresh they seem'd to grow.
Was it he lay there with a fading eye?
'The fault was mine,' he whisper'd, 'fly!' 30
Then glided out of the joyous wood
The ghastly Wraith of one that I know;
And there rang on a sudden a passionate cry,
A cry for a brother's blood:
It will ring in my heart and my ears, till I die, till I
        die. 35

II

Is it gone? my pulses beat—
What was it? a lying trick of the brain?
Yet I thought I saw her stand,
A shadow there at my feet,
High over the shadowy land. 40
It is gone; and the heavens fall in a gentle rain,
When they should burst and drown with deluging
        storms
The feeble vassals of wine and anger and lust,
The little hearts that know not how to forgive: 44
Arise, my God, and strike, for we hold Thee just,
Strike dead the whole weak race of venomous worms,
That sting each other here in the dust;
We are not worthy to live.

II

I

See what a lovely shell,
Small and pure as a pearl,   50
Lying close to my foot,
Frail, but a work divine,
Made so fairly well
With delicate spire and whorl,
How exquisitely minute,   55
A miracle of design!

II

What is it? a learned man
Could give it a clumsy name.
Let him name it who can,
The beauty would be the same.   60

III

The tiny cell is forlorn,
Void of the little living will
That made it stir on the shore.
Did he stand at the diamond door
Of his house in a rainbow frill?   65
Did he push, when he was uncurl'd,
A golden foot or a fairy horn
Thro' his dim water-world?

IV

Slight, to be crush'd with a tap
Of my finger-nail on the sand,   70
Small, but a work divine,
Frail, but of force to withstand,
Year upon year, the shock
Of cataract seas that snap
The three-decker's oaken spine   75
Athwart the ledges of rock,
Here on the Breton strand!

v

Breton, not Briton; here
Like a shipwreck'd man on a coast
Of ancient fable and fear—   80
Plagued with a flitting to and fro,
A disease, a hard mechanic ghost
That never came from on high
Nor ever arose from below,
But only moves with the moving eye,   85
Flying along the land and the main—
Why should it look like Maud?
Am I to be overawed
By what I cannot but know
Is a juggle born of the brain?   90

VI

Back from the Breton coast,
Sick of a nameless fear,
Back to the dark sea-line
Looking, thinking of all I have lost;
An old song vexes my ear;   95
But that of Lamech is mine.

VII

For years, a measureless ill,
For years, for ever, to part—
But she, who would love me still;
And as long, O God, as she   100
Have a grain of love for me,
So long, no doubt, no doubt,
Shall I nurse in my dark heart,
However weary, a spark of will
Not to be trampled out.   105

VIII

Strange, that the mind, when fraught
With a passion so intense

One would think that it well
Might drown all life in the eye,—
That it should, by being so overwrought,　110
Suddenly strike on a sharper sense
For a shell, or a flower, little things
Which else would have been past by!
And now I remember, I,
When he lay dying there,　115
I noticed one of his many rings
(For he had many, poor worm) and thought
It is his mother's hair.

IX

Who knows if he be dead?
Whether I need have fled?　120
Am I guilty of blood?
However this may be,
Comfort her, comfort her, all things good,
While I am over the sea!
Let me and my passionate love go by,　125
But speak to her all things holy and high,
Whatever may happen to me!
Me and my harmful love go by;
But come to her waking, find her asleep,
Powers of the height, Powers of the deep,　130
And comfort her tho' I die.

III

Courage, poor heart of stone!
I will not ask thee why
Thou canst not understand
That thou art left for ever alone:　135
Courage, poor stupid heart of stone.—
Or if I ask thee why,
Care not thou to reply:
She is but dead, and the time is at hand
When thou shalt more than die.　140

IV

I

O that 'twere possible
After long grief and pain
To find the arms of my true love
Round me once again!

II

When I was wont to meet her   145
In the silent woody places
By the home that gave me birth,
We stood tranced in long embraces
Mixt with kisses sweeter sweeter
Than any thing on earth.   150

III

A shadow flits before me,
Not thou, but like to thee;
Ah Christ, that it were possible
For one short hour to see
The souls we loved, that they might tell us
What and where they be.   156

IV

It leads me forth at evening,
It lightly winds and steals
In a cold white robe before me,
When all my spirit reels   160
At the shouts, the leagues of lights,
And the roaring of the wheels.

V

Half the night I waste in sighs,
Half in dreams I sorrow after
The delight of early skies;   165
In a wakeful doze I sorrow

For the hand, the lips, the eyes,
For the meeting of the morrow,
The delight of happy laughter,
The delight of low replies.　　　　170

VI

'Tis a morning pure and sweet,
And a dewy splendour falls
On the little flower that clings
To the turrets and the walls;
'Tis a morning pure and sweet,　　　175
And the light and shadow fleet;
She is walking in the meadow,
And the woodland echo rings;
In a moment we shall meet;
She is singing in the meadow,　　　180
And the rivulet at her feet
Ripples on in light and shadow
To the ballad that she sings.

VII

Do I hear her sing as of old,
My bird with the shining head,　　　185
My own dove with the tender eye?
But there rings on a sudden a passionate
　　cry,
There is some one dying or dead,
And a sullen thunder is roll'd;
For a tumult shakes the city,　　　190
And I wake, my dream is fled;
In the shuddering dawn, behold,
Without knowledge, without pity,
By the curtains of my bed
That abiding phantom cold.　　　195

VIII

Get thee hence, nor come again,
Mix not memory with doubt,

Pass, thou deathlike type of pain,
Pass and cease to move about!
'Tis the blot upon the brain   200
That *will* show itself without.

IX

Then I rise, the eavedrops fall,
And the yellow vapours choke
The great city sounding wide;
The day comes, a dull red ball   205
Wrapt in drifts of lurid smoke
On the misty river-tide.

X

Thro' the hubbub of the market
I steal, a wasted frame,
It crosses here, it crosses there,   210
Thro' all that crowd confused and loud,
The shadow still the same;
And on my heavy eyelids
My anguish hangs like shame.

XI

Alas for her that met me,   215
That heard me softly call,
Came glimmering thro' the laurels
At the quiet evenfall,
In the garden by the turrets
Of the old manorial hall.   220

XII

Would the happy spirit descend,
From the realms of light and song,
In the chamber or the street,
As she looks among the blest,
Should I fear to greet my friend   225
Or to say 'forgive the wrong,'
Or to ask her, 'take me, sweet,
To the regions of thy rest'?

XIII

But the broad light glares and beats,
And the shadow flits and fleets   230
And will not let me be;
And I loathe the squares and streets,
And the faces that one meets,
Hearts with no love for me:
Always I long to creep   235
Into some still cavern deep,
There to weep, and weep, and weep,
My whole soul out to thee.

V

I

Dead, long dead,
Long dead!   240
And my heart is a handful of dust,
And the wheels go over my head,
And my bones are shaken with pain,
For into a shallow grave they are thrust,
Only a yard beneath the street,   245
And the hoofs of the horses beat, beat,
The hoofs of the horses beat,
Beat into my scalp and my brain,
With never an end to the stream of passing feet,
Driving, hurrying, marrying, burying,   250
Clamour and rumble, and ringing and clatter,
And here beneath it is all as bad,
For I thought the dead had peace, but it is not so;
To have no peace in the grave, is that not sad?
But up and down and to and fro,   255
Ever about me the dead men go;
And then to hear a dead man chatter
Is enough to drive one mad.

II

Wretchedest age, since Time began,
They cannot even bury a man;   260

And tho' we paid our tithes in the days that are gone,
Not a bell was rung, not a prayer was read;
It is that which makes us loud in the world of the
    dead;
There is none that does his work, not one;
A touch of their office might have sufficed,   265
But the churchmen fain would kill their church,
As the churches have kill'd their Christ.

III

See, there is one of us sobbing,
No limit to his distress;
And another, a lord of all things, praying   270
To his own great self, as I guess;
And another, a statesman there, betraying
His party-secret, fool, to the press;
And yonder a vile physician, blabbing
The case of his patient—all for what?   275
To tickle the maggot born in an empty head,
And wheedle a world that loves him not,
For it is but a world of the dead.

IV

Nothing but idiot gabble!
For the prophecy given of old   280
And then not understood,
Has come to pass as foretold;
Not let any man think for the public good,
But babble, merely for babble.
For I never whisper'd a private affair   285
Within the hearing of cat or mouse,
No, not to myself in the closet alone,
But I heard it shouted at once from the top of the
    house;
Everything came to be known:
Who told *him* we were there?   290

V

Not that grey old wolf, for he came not back
From the wilderness, full of wolves, where he used to
        lie;
He has gather'd the bones for his o'ergrown whelp to
        crack,
Crack them now for yourself, and howl, and die.

VI

Prophet, curse me the blabbing lip,   29c
And curse me the British vermin, the rat;
I know not whether he came in the Hanover ship,
But I know that he lies and listens mute
In an ancient mansion's crannies and holes:
Arsenic, arsenic, sure, would do it,   300
Except that now we poison our babes, poor souls!
It is all used up for that.

VII

Tell him now: she is standing here at my head;
Not beautiful now, not even kind;
He may take her now; for she never speaks her mind,
But is ever the one thing silent here.   306
She is not of us, as I divine;
She comes from another stiller world of the dead,
Stiller, not fairer than mine.

VIII

But I know where a garden grows,   310
Fairer than aught in the world beside,
All made up of the lily and the rose
That blow by night, when the season is good,
To the sound of dancing music and flutes:
It is only flowers, they had no fruits,   315
And I almost fear they are not roses, but blood;
For the keeper was one, so full of pride,
He linkt a dead man there to a spectral bride;

For he, if he had not been a Sultan of brutes,
Would he have that hole in his side? 320

IX

But what will the old man say?
He laid a cruel snare in a pit
To catch a friend of mine one stormy day;
Yet now I could even weep to think of it;
For what will the old man say 325
When he comes to the second corpse in the pit?

X

Friend, to be struck by the public foe,
Then to strike him and lay him low,
That were a public merit, far,
Whatever the Quaker holds, from sin; 330
But the red life spilt for a private blow—
I swear to you, lawful and lawless war
Are scarcely even akin.

XI

O me, why have they not buried me deep enough?
Is it kind to have made me a grave so rough, 335
Me, that was never a quiet sleeper?
Maybe still I am but half-dead;
Then I cannot be wholly dumb;
I will cry to the steps above my head,
And somebody, surely, some kind heart will come
To bury me, bury me 341
Deeper, ever so little deeper.

PART III

VI

I

My life has crept so long on a broken wing
Thro' cells of madness, haunts of horror and fear,
That I come to be grateful at last for a little thing:

My mood is changed, for it fell at a time of year   346
When the face of night is fair on the dewy downs,
And the shining daffodil dies, and the Charioteer
And starry Gemini hang like glorious crowns
Over Orion's grave low down in the west,   350
That like a silent lightning under the stars
She seem'd to divide in a dream from a band of the
    blest,
And spoke of a hope for the world in the coming
    wars—
'And in that hope, dear soul, let trouble have rest,
Knowing I tarry for thee,' and pointed to Mars   355
As he glow'd like a ruddy shield on the Lion's breast.

II

And it was but a dream, yet it yielded a dear delight
To have look'd, tho' but in a dream, upon eyes so fair,
That had been in a weary world my one thing bright;
And it was but a dream, yet it lighten'd my despair
When I thought that a war would arise in defence of
    the right,   361
That an iron tyranny now should bend or cease,
The glory of manhood stand on his ancient height,
Nor Britain's one sole God be the millionaire:
No more shall commerce be all in all, and Peace   365
Pipe on her pastoral hillock a languid note,
And watch her harvest ripen, her herd increase,
Nor the cannon-bullet rust on a slothful shore,
And the cobweb woven across the cannon's throat
Shall shake its threaded tears in the wind no more.

III

And as months ran on and rumour of battle grew,
'It is time, it is time, O passionate heart,' said I   372
(For I cleaved to a cause that I felt to be pure and
    true),
'It is time, O passionate heart and morbid eye,
That old hysterical mock-disease should die.'   375

And I stood on a giant deck and mix'd my breath
With a loyal people shouting a battle cry,
Till I saw the dreary phantom arise and fly
Far into the North, and battle, and seas of death.

IV

Let it go or stay, so I wake to the higher aims 380
Of a land that has lost for a little her lust of gold,
And love of a peace that was full of wrongs and
    shames,
Horrible, hateful, monstrous, not to be told;
And hail once more to the banner of battle unroll'd!
Tho' many a light shall darken, and many shall weep
For those that are crush'd in the clash of jarring
    claims, 386
Yet God's just wrath shall be wreak'd on a giant liar;
And many a darkness into the light shall leap,
And shine in the sudden making of splendid names,
And noble thought be freër under the sun, 390
And the heart of a people beat with one desire;
For the peace, that I deem'd no peace, is over and
    done,
And now by the side of the Black and the Baltic deep,
And deathful-grinning mouths of the fortress, flames
The blood-red blossom of war with a heart of fire.

V

Let it flame or fade, and the war roll down like a
    wind, 396
We have proved we have hearts in a cause, we are
    noble still,
And myself have awaked, as it seems, to the better
    mind;
It is better to fight for the good, than to rail at the ill;
I have felt with my native land, I am one with my
    kind, 400
I embrace the purpose of God, and the doom assign'd.

Morte d'Arthur

So all day long the noise of battle roll'd
Among the mountains by the winter sea;
Until King Arthur's table, man by man,
Had fall'n in Lyonnesse about their Lord,
King Arthur: then, because his wound was deep,   6
The bold Sir Bedivere uplifted him,
Sir Bedivere, the last of all his knights,
And bore him to a chapel nigh the field,
A broken chancel with a broken cross,
That stood on a dark strait of barren land.   10
On one side lay the Ocean, and on one
Lay a great water, and the moon was full.
    Then spake King Arthur to Sir Bedivere:
'The sequel of to-day unsolders all
The goodliest fellowship of famous knights   15
Whereof this world holds record. Such a sleep
They sleep—the men I loved. I think that we
Shall never more, at any future time,
Delight our souls with talk of knightly deeds,
Walking about the gardens and the halls   20
Of Camelot, as in the days that were.
I perish by this people which I made,—
Tho' Merlin sware that I should come again
To rule once more—but let what will be, be,
I am so deeply smitten thro' the helm   25
That without help I cannot last till morn.
Thou therefore take my brand Excalibur,
Which was my pride: for thou rememberest how
In those old days, one summer noon, an arm
Rose up from out the bosom of the lake,   30
Clothed in white samite, mystic, wonderful,
Holding the sword—and how I row'd across
And took it, and have worn it, like a king:
And, wheresoever I am sung or told
In aftertime, this also shall be known: 35
But now delay not: take Excalibur,

And fling him far into the middle mere:
Watch what thou seëst, and lightly bring me word.'
    To him replied the bold Sir Bedivere:
'It is not meet, Sir King, to leave thee thus,   40
Aidless, alone, and smitten thro' the helm.
A little thing may harm a wounded man.
Yet I thy hest will all perform at full,
Watch what I see, and lightly bring thee word.'
    So saying, from the ruin'd shrine he stept   45
And in the moon athwart the place of tombs,
Where lay the mighty bones of ancient men,
Old knights, and over them the sea-wind sang
Shrill, chill, with flakes of foam. He, stepping down
By zig-zag paths, and juts of pointed rock,   50
Came on the shining levels of the lake.
    There drew he forth the brand Excalibur,
And o'er him, drawing it, the winter moon,
Brightening the skirts of a long cloud, ran forth
And sparkled keen with frost against the hilt: 55
For all the haft twinkled with diamond sparks,
Myriads of topaz-lights, and jacinth-work
Of subtlest jewellery. He gazed so long
That both his eyes were dazzled, as he stood,
This way and that dividing the swift mind,   60
In act to throw: but at the last it seem'd
Better to leave Excalibur conceal'd
There in the many-knotted waterflags,
That whistled stiff and dry about the marge.
So strode he back slow to the wounded King.   65
    Then spake King Arthur to Sir Bedivere:
'Hast thou perform'd my mission which I gave?
What is it thou hast seen? or what hast heard?'
    And answer made the bold Sir Bedivere:
'I heard the ripple washing in the reeds,   70
And the wild water lapping on the crag.'
    To whom replied King Arthur, faint and pale:
'Thou hast betray'd thy nature and thy name,
Not rendering true answer, as beseem'd
Thy fëalty, nor like a noble knight: 75

For surer sign had follow'd, either hand,
Or voice, or else a motion of the mere.
This is a shameful thing for men to lie.
Yet now, I charge thee, quickly go again
As thou art lief and dear, and do the thing   80
I bad thee, watch, and lightly bring me word.'

   Then went Sir Bedivere the second time
Across the ridge, and paced beside the mere,
Counting the dewy pebbles, fix'd in thought;
But when he saw the wonder of the hilt,   85
How curiously and strangely chased, he smote
His palms together, and he cried aloud:

   'And if indeed I cast the brand away,
Surely a precious thing, one worthy note,
Should thus be lost for ever from the earth,   90
Which might have pleased the eyes of many men.
What good should follow this, if this were done?
What harm, undone? deep harm to disobey,
Seeing obedience is the bond of rule.
Were it well to obey then, if a king demand   95
An act unprofitable, against himself?
The King is sick, and knows not what he does.
What record, or what relic of my lord
Should be to aftertime, but empty breath
And rumours of a doubt? but were this kept,   100
Stored in some treasure-house of mighty kings,
Some one might show it at a joust of arms,
Saying, "King Arthur's sword, Excalibur,
Wrought by the lonely maiden of the Lake.
Nine years she wrought it, sitting in the deeps   105
Upon the hidden bases of the hills."
So might some old man speak in the aftertime
To all the people, winning reverence.
But now much honour and much fame were lost.'

   So spake he, clouded with his own conceit,   110
And hid Excalibur the second time,
And so strode back slow to the wounded King.

   Then spoke King Arthur, breathing heavily:
'What is it thou hast seen? or what hast heard?'

 And answer made the bold Sir Bedivere: 115
'I heard the water lapping on the crag,
And the long ripple washing in the reeds.'
 To whom replied King Arthur, much in wrath:
'Ah, miserable and unkind, untrue,
Unknightly, traitor-hearted! Woe is me! 120
Authority forgets a dying king,
Laid widow'd of the power in his eye
That bow'd the will. I see thee what thou art,
For thou, the latest-left of all my knights,
In whom should meet the offices of all, 125
Thou wouldst betray me for the precious hilt;
Either from lust of gold, or like a girl
Valuing the giddy pleasure of the eyes.
Yet, for a man may fail in duty twice,
And the third time may prosper, get thee hence: 130
But, if thou spare to fling Excalibur,
I will arise and slay thee with my hands.'
 Then quickly rose Sir Bedivere, and ran,
And, leaping down the ridges lightly, plunged
Among the bulrush-beds, and clutch'd the sword,
And strongly wheel'd and threw it. The great brand
Made lightnings in the splendour of the moon, 137
And flashing round and round, and whirl'd in an
 arch,
Shot like a streamer of the northern morn,
Seen where the moving isles of winter shock 140
By night, with noises of the northern sea.
So flash'd and fell the brand Excalibur:
But ere he dipt the surface, rose an arm
Clothed in white samite, mystic, wonderful,
And caught him by the hilt, and brandish'd him 145
Three times, and drew him under in the mere.
And lightly went the other to the King.
 Then spoke King Arthur, drawing thicker breath:
'Now see I by thine eyes that this is done.
Speak out: what is it thou hast heard, or seen?' 150
 And answer made the bold Sir Bedivere:
'Sir King, I closed mine eyelids, lest the gems

Should blind my purpose, for I never saw,
Nor shall see, here or elsewhere, till I die,
Not tho' I live three lives of mortal men,   155
So great a miracle as yonder hilt.
Then with both hands I flung him, wheeling him;
But when I look'd again, behold an arm,
Clothed in white samite, mystic, wonderful,
That caught him by the hilt, and brandish'd him
Three times, and drew him under in the mere.'   161

     And answer made King Arthur, breathing hard:
'My end draws nigh; 'tis time that I were gone.
Make broad thy shoulders to receive my weight,
And bear me to the margin; yet I fear   165
My wound hath taken cold, and I shall die.'

     So saying, from the pavement he half rose,
Slowly, with pain, reclining on his arm,
And looking wistfully with wide blue eyes
As in a picture. Him Sir Bedivere   170
Remorsefully regarded thro' his tears,
And would have spoken, but he found not words,
Then took with care, and kneeling on one knee,
O'er both his shoulders drew the languid hands,
And rising bore him thro' the place of tombs.   175

     But, as he walk'd, King Arthur panted hard,
Like one that feels a nightmare on his bed
When all the house is mute. So sigh'd the King,
Muttering and murmuring in his ear, 'Quick, quick!
I fear it is too late, and I shall die.'   180
But the other swiftly strode from ridge to ridge,
Clothed with his breath, and looking, as he walk'd,
Larger than human on the frozen hills.
He heard the deep behind him, and a cry
Before. His own thought drove him like a goad.   185
Dry clash'd his harness in the icy caves
And barren chasms, and all to left and right
The bare black cliff clang'd round him, as he based
His feet on juts of slippery crag that rang
Sharp-smitten with the dint of armed heels—   190
And on a sudden, lo! the level lake,

And the long glories of the winter moon.

Then saw they how there hove a dusky barge,
Dark as a funeral scarf from stem to stern,
Beneath them; and descending they were ware   195
That all the decks were dense with stately forms
Black-stoled, black-hooded, like a dream—by these
Three Queens with crowns of gold—and from them
    rose
A cry that shiver'd to the tingling stars,
And, as it were one voice, an agony   200
Of lamentation, like a wind, that shrills
All night in a waste land, where no one comes,
Or hath come, since the making of the world.

Then murmur'd Arthur, 'Place me in the barge,'
And to the barge they came. There those three
    Queens   205
Put forth their hands, and took the King, and wept.
But she, that rose the tallest of them all
And fairest, laid his head upon her lap,
And loosed the shatter'd casque, and chafed his
    hands,
And call'd him by his name, complaining loud,   210
And dropping bitter tears against his brow
Striped with dark blood: for all his face was white
And colourless, and like the wither'd moon
Smote by the fresh beam of the springing east;
And all his greaves and cuisses dash'd with drops
Of onset; and the light and lustrous curls—   216
That made his forehead like a rising sun
High from the daïs-throne—were parch'd with dust;
Or, clotted into points and hanging loose,
Mix'd with the knightly growth that fringed his lips.
So like a shatter'd column lay the King;   221
Not like that Arthur who, with lance in rest,
From spur to plume a star of tournament,
Shot thro' the lists at Camelot, and charged
Before the eyes of ladies and of kings.   225

Then loudly cried the bold Sir Bedivere,
'Ah! my Lord Arthur, whither shall I go?

Where shall I hide my forehead and my eyes?
For now I see the true old times are dead,
When every morning brought a noble chance,   230
And every chance brought out a noble knight.
Such times have been not since the light that led
The holy Elders with the gift of myrrh.
But now the whole ROUND TABLE is dissolved
Which was an image of the mighty world;   235
And I, the last, go forth companionless,
And the days darken round me, and the years,
Among new men, strange faces, other minds.'
    And slowly answered Arthur from the barge:
'The old order changeth, yielding place to new,   240
And God fulfils Himself in many ways,
Lest one good custom should corrupt the world.
Comfort thyself: what comfort is in me?
I have lived my life, and that which I have done
May He within Himself make pure! but thou,   245
If thou shouldst never see my face again,
Pray for my soul. More things are wrought by prayer
Than this world dreams of. Wherefore, let thy voice
Rise like a fountain for me night and day.
For what are men better than sheep or goats   250
That nourish a blind life within the brain,
If, knowing God, they lift not hands of prayer
Both for themselves and those who call them friend?
For so the whole round earth is every way
Bound by gold chains about the feet of God.   255
But now farewell. I am going a long way
With these thou seëst—if indeed I go—
(For all my mind is clouded with a doubt)
To the island-valley of Avilion;
Where falls not hail, or rain, or any snow,   260
Nor ever wind blows loudly; but it lies
Deep-meadow'd, happy, fair with orchard-lawns
And bowery hollows crown'd with summer sea,
Where I will heal me of my grievous wound.'
    So said he, and the barge with oar and sail   265
Moved from the brink, like some full-breasted swan

That, fluting a wild carol ere her death,
Ruffles her pure cold plume, and takes the flood
With swarthy webs. Long stood Sir Bedivere
Revolving many memories, till the hull   270
Look'd one black dot against the verge of dawn,
And one the mere the wailing died away.

ROBERT BROWNING
1812–1889

The Italian in England

That second time they hunted me
From hill to plain, from shore to sea,
And Austria, hounding far and wide
Her blood-hounds through the country-side
Breathed hot and instant on my trace,—   5
I made six days a hiding-place
Of that dry green old aqueduct
Where I and Charles, when boys, have plucked
The fire-flies from the roof above,   9
Bright creeping through the moss they love.
—How long it seems since Charles was lost!
Six days the soldiers crossed and crossed
The country in my very sight;
And when that peril ceased at night,
The sky broke out in red dismay   15
With signal-fires; well, there I lay
Close covered o'er in my recess,
Up to the neck in ferns and cress,
Thinking on Metternich our friend,
And Charles's miserable end,   20
And much beside, two days; the third,
Hunger o'ercame me when I heard
The peasants from the village go
To work among the maize; you know,
With us in Lombardy, they bring   25
Provisions packed on mules, a string

With little bells that cheer their task,
And casks, and boughs on every cask
To keep the sun's heat from the wine;
These I let pass in jingling line,   30
And, close on them, dear noisy crew,
The peasants from the village, too;
For at the very rear would troop
Their wives and sisters in a group
To help, I knew; when these had passed,   35
I threw my glove to strike the last,
Taking the chance: she did not start,
Much less cry out, but stooped apart
One instant, rapidly glanced round,
And saw me beckon from the ground: 40
A wild bush grows and hides my crypt;
She picked my glove up while she stripped
A branch off, then rejoined the rest
With that; my glove lay in her breast:
Then I drew breath: they disappeared: 45
It was for Italy I feared.

An hour, and she returned alone
Exactly where my glove was thrown.
Meanwhile came many thoughts; on me
Rested the hopes of Italy;   50
I had devised a certain tale
Which, when 'twas told her, could not fail
Persuade a peasant of its truth;
I meant to call a freak of youth
This hiding, and give hopes of pay,   55
And no temptation to betray.
But when I saw that woman's face,
Its calm simplicity of grace,
Our Italy's own attitude
In which she walked thus far, and stood,   60
Planting each naked foot so firm,
To crush the snake and spare the worm—
At first sight of her eyes, I said,
'I am that man upon whose head

They fix the price, because I hate   65
The Austrians over us: the State
Will give you gold—oh, gold so much,
If you betray me to their clutch
And be your death, for aught I know,
If once they find you saved their foe.   70
Now, you must bring me food and drink,
And also paper, pen and ink,
And carry safe what I shall write
To Padua, which you'll reach at night
Before the Duomo shuts; go in,   75
And wait till Tenebrae begin;
Walk to the Third Confessional,
Between the pillar and the wall,
And kneeling whisper, *Whence comes peace?*
Say it a second time, then cease;   80
And if the voice inside returns,
*From Christ and freedom; what concerns
The cause of Peace?*—for answer, slip
My letter where you placed your lip;
Then come back happy we have done   85
Our mother service—I, the son,
As you the daughter of our land!'

Three mornings more, she took her stand
In the same place, with the same eyes:
I was no surer of sun-rise   90
Than of her coming: we conferred
Of her own prospects, and I heard
She had a lover—stout and tall,
She said—then let her eyelids fall,
'He could do much'—as if some doubt   95
Entered her heart,—then, passing out,
'She could not speak for others who
Had other thoughts; herself she knew:'
And so she brought me drink and food.
After four days, the scouts pursued   100
Another path; at last arrived
The help my Paduan friends contrived

To furnish me: she brought the news.
For the first time I could not choose
But kiss her hand, and lay my own   105
Upon her head—'This faith was shown
To Italy, our mother; she
Uses my hand and blesses thee!'
She followed down to the sea-shore;
I left and never saw her more.   110

How very long since I have thought
Concerning—much less wished for—aught
Beside the good of Italy,
For which I live and mean to die!
I never was in love; and since   115
Charles proved false, nothing could convince
My inmost heart I had a friend.
However, if it pleased to spend
Real wishes on myself—say, three—
I know at least what one should be;   120
I would grasp Metternich until
I felt his red wet throat distil
In blood thro' these two hands: and next,
—Nor much for that am I perplexed—
Charles, perjured traitor, for his part,   125
Should die slow of a broken heart
Under his new employers: last
—Ah, there, what should I wish? For fast
Do I grow old and out of strength.
If I resolved to seek at length   130
My father's house again, how scared
They all would look, and unprepared!
My brothers live in Austria's pay
—Disowned me long ago, men say;
And all my early mates who used   135
To praise me so—perhaps induced
More than one early step of mine—
Are turning wise; while some opine
'Freedom grows Licence,' some suspect
'Haste breeds Delay,' and recollect   140

They always said, such premature
Beginnings never could endure!
So, with a sullen 'All 's for best,'
The land seems settling to its rest.
I think, then, I should wish to stand   145
This evening in that dear, lost land,
Over the sea the thousand miles,
And know if yet that woman smiles
With the calm smile; some little farm
She lives in there, no doubt; what harm   150
If I sat on the door-side bench,
And, while her spindle made a trench
Fantastically in the dust,
Inquired of all her fortunes—just
Her children's ages and their names,   155
And what may be the husband's aims
For each of them. I'd talk this out,
And sit there, for an hour about,
Then kiss her hand once more, and lay
Mine on her head, and go my way.   160

So much for idle wishing—how
It steals the time! To business now!

'Childe Roland to the Dark Tower Came'

(See Edgar's song in *Lear*)

I

My first thought was, he lied in every word,
　　That hoary cripple, with malicious eye
　　Askance to watch the working of his lie
On mine, and mouth scarce able to afford
Suppression of the glee that pursed and scored   5
　　Its edge at one more victim gained thereby.

II

What else should he be set for, with his staff?
　　What, save to waylay with his lies, ensnare
　　All travellers that might find him posted there,

And ask the road? I guessed what skull-like laugh
Would break, what crutch 'gin write my epitaph   11
   For pastime in the dusty thoroughfare,

III

If at his counsel I should turn aside
   Into that ominous tract which, all agree,
   Hides the Dark Tower. Yet acquiescingly   15
I did turn as he pointed; neither pride
Nor hope rekindling at the end descried,
   So much as gladness that some end might be.

IV

For, what with my whole world-wide wandering,
   What with my search drawn out thro' years, my hope   20
   Dwindled into a ghost not fit to cope
With that obstreperous joy success would bring,—
I hardly tried now to rebuke the spring
   My heart made, finding failure in its scope.

V

As when a sick man very near to death   25
   Seems dead indeed, and feels begin and end
   The tears, and takes the farewell of each friend,
And hears one bid the other go, draw breath
Freelier outside, ('since all is o'er,' he saith,
   'And the blow fallen no grieving can amend;')   30

VI

While some discuss if near the other graves
   Be room enough for this, and when a day
   Suits best for carrying the corpse away,
With care about the banners, scarves and staves,—
And still the man hears all, and only craves   35
   He may not shame such tender love and stay.

VII

Thus, I had so long suffered in this quest,
   Heard failure prophesied so oft, been writ

So many times among 'The Band!'—to wit,
 The knights who to the Dark Tower's search ad-
  dressed   40
Their steps—that just to fail as they, seemed best.
 And all the doubt was now—should I be fit.

VIII

So, quiet as despair, I turned from him,
 That hateful cripple, out of his highway
 Into the path he pointed. All the day   45
Had been a dreary one at best, and dim
Was settling to its close, yet shot one grim
 Red leer to see the plain catch its estray.

IX

For mark! no sooner was I fairly found
 Pledged to the plain, after a pace or two,   50
 Than, pausing to throw backward a last view
To the safe road, 'twas gone; grey plain all round:
Nothing but plain to the horizon's bound.
 I might go on; nought else remained to do.

X

So, on I went. I think I never saw   55
 Such starved ignoble nature; nothing throve:
 For flowers—as well expect a cedar grove!
But cockle, spurge, according to their law
Might propagate their kind, with none to awe,
 You'd think; a burr had been a treasure-trove.   60

XI

No! penury, inertness and grimace,
 In some strange sort, were the land's portion. 'See
 Or shut your eyes,' said Nature peevishly,
'It nothing skills: I cannot help my case:
'Tis the Last Judgement's fire must cure this place,
 Calcine its clods and set my prisoners free.'   66

XII

If there pushed any ragged thistle-stalk
   Above its mates, the head was chopped—the bents
   Were jealous else. What made those holes and rents
In the dock's harsh swarth leaves—bruised as to baulk
All hope of greenness? 'tis a brute must walk   71
   Pashing their life out, with a brute's intents.

XIII

As for the grass, it grew as scant as hair
   In leprosy; thin dry blades pricked the mud
   Which underneath looked kneaded up with blood.
One stiff blind horse, his every bone a-stare,   76
Stood stupefied, however he came there:
   Thrust out past service from the devil's stud!

XIV

Alive? he might be dead for aught I know,
   With that red, gaunt and colloped neck a-strain,
   And shut eyes underneath the rusty mane;   81
Seldom went such grotesqueness with such woe;
I never saw a brute I hated so;
   He must be wicked to deserve such pain.

XV

I shut my eyes and turned them on my heart.   85
   As a man calls for wine before he fights,
   I asked one draught of earlier, happier sights,
Ere fitly I could hope to play my part.
Think first, fight afterwards—the soldier's art:
   One taste of the old time sets all to rights!   90

XVI

Not it! I fancied Cuthbert's reddening face
   Beneath its garniture of curly gold,
   Dear fellow, till I almost felt him fold
An arm in mine to fix me to the place,
That way he used. Alas! one night's disgrace!   95
   Out went my heart's new fire and left it cold.

XVII

Giles, then, the soul of honour—there he stands
  Frank as ten years ago when knighted first.
  What honest men should dare (he said) he durst.
Good—but the scene shifts—faugh! what hangman's
    hands   100
Pin to his breast a parchment? his own bands
  Read it. Poor traitor, spit upon and curst!

XVIII

Better this Present than a Past like that;
  Back therefore to my darkening path again.
  No sound, no sight as far as eye could strain.   105
Will the night send a howlet or a bat?
I asked: when something on the dismal flat
  Came to arrest my thoughts and change their train.

XIX

A sudden little river crossed my path
  As unexpected as a serpent comes.   110
  No sluggish tide congenial to the glooms—
This, as it frothed by, might have been a bath
For the fiend's glowing hoof—to see the wrath
  Of its black eddy bespate with flakes and spumes.

XX

So petty yet so spiteful! all along,   115
  Low scrubby alders kneeled down over it;
  Drenched willows flung them headlong in a fit
Of mute despair, a suicidal throng:
The river which had done them all the wrong,   119
  Whate'er that was, rolled by, deterred no whit.

XXI

Which, while I forded,—good saints, how I feared
  To set my foot upon a dead man's cheek,
  Each step, or feel the spear I thrust to seek
For hollows, tangled in his hair or beard!
—It may have been a water-rat I speared,   125
  But, ugh! it sounded like a baby's shriek.

XXII

Glad was I when I reached the other bank.
　　Now for a better country. Vain presage!
　　Who were the strugglers, what war did they wage,
Whose savage trample thus could pad the dank　　130
Soil to a plash? toads in a poisoned tank,
　　Or wild cats in a red-hot iron cage—

XXIII

The fight must so have seemed in that fell cirque.
　　What penned them there, with all the plain to
　　　choose?
　　No footprint leading to that horrid mews,　　135
None out of it. Mad brewage set to work
Their brains, no doubt, like galley-slaves the Turk
　　Pits for his pastime, Christians against Jews.

XXIV

And more than that—a furlong on—why, there!
　　What bad use was that engine for, that wheel,　　140
　　Or brake, not wheel—that harrow fit to reel
Men's bodies out like silk? with all the air
Of Tophet's tool, on earth left unaware,
　　Or brought to sharpen its rusty teeth of steel.　　144

XXV

Then came a bit of stubbed ground, once a wood,
　　Next a marsh, it would seem, and now mere earth
　　Desperate and done with; (so a fool finds mirth,
Makes a thing and then mars it, till his mood
Changes and off he goes!) within a rood—
　　Bog, clay and rubble, sand and stark black dearth.

XXVI

Now blotches rankling, coloured gay and grim,　　151
　　Now patches where some leanness of the soil's
　　Broke into moss or substances like boils;

Then came some palsied oak, a cleft in him
Like a distorted mouth that splits its rim　　155
　　Gaping at death, and dies while it recoils.

XXVII

And just as far as ever from the end!
　　Nought in the distance but the evening, nought
　　To point my footsteps further! At the thought,
A great black bird, Apollyon's bosom-friend,　　160
Sailed past, nor beat his wide wing dragon-penned
　　That brushed my cap—perchance the guide I
　　sought.

XXVIII

For, looking up, aware I somehow grew,
　　'Spite of the dusk, the plain had given place
　　All round to mountains—with such name to grace
Mere ugly heights and heaps now stolen in view.　　166
How thus they had surprised me,—solve it, you!
　　How to get from them was no clearer case.

XXIX

Yet half I seemed to recognize some trick
　　Of mischief happened to me, God knows when—
　　In a bad dream perhaps. Here ended, then,　　171
Progress this way. When, in the very nick
Of giving up, one time more, came a click
　　As when a trap shuts—you're inside the den!

XXX

Burningly it came on me all at once,　　175
　　This was the place! those two hills on the right,
　　Crouched like two bulls locked horn in horn in
　　fight;
While to the left, a tall scalped mountain . . . Dunce,
Fool, to be dozing at the very nonce,
　　After a life spent training for the sight!　　180

XXXI

What in the midst lay but the Tower itself?
  The round squat turret, blind as the fool's heart,
  Built of brown stone, without a counterpart
In the whole world. The tempest's mocking elf
Points to the shipman thus the unseen shelf   185
  He strikes on, only when the timbers start.

XXXII

Not see? because of night perhaps?—Why, day
  Came back again for that! before it left,
  The dying sunset kindled through a cleft:
The hills, like giants at a hunting, lay,   190
Chin upon hand, to see the game at bay,—
  'Now stab and end the creature—to the heft!'

XXXIII

Not hear? when noise was everywhere! it tolled
  Increasing like a bell. Names in my ears,
  Of all the lost adventurers my peers,—   195
How such a one was strong, and such was bold,
And such was fortunate, yet each of old
  Lost, lost! one moment knelled the woe of years.

XXXIV

There they stood, ranged along the hillsides, met
  To view the last of me, a living frame   200
  For one more picture! in a sheet of flame
I saw them and I knew them all. And yet
Dauntless the slug-horn to my lips I set,
  And blew. '*Childe Roland to the Dark Tower came.*'

The Glove

(PETER RONSARD *loquitur*.)

'Heigho,' yawned one day King Francis,
  'Distance all value enhances!
When a man's busy, why, leisure

Strikes him as wonderful pleasure:
'Faith, and at leisure once is he? 5
Straightway he wants to be busy.
Here we've got peace; and aghast I'm
Caught thinking war the true pastime!
Is there a reason in metre?
Give us your speech, master Peter!' 10
I who, if mortal dare say so,
Ne'er am at loss with my Naso,
'Sire,' I replied, 'joys prove cloudlets:
Men are the merest Ixions'—
Here the King whistled aloud, 'Let's 15
... Heigho ... go look at our lions!'
Such are the sorrowful chances
If you talk fine to King Francis.

And so, to the courtyard proceeding,
Our company, Francis was leading, 20
Increased by new followers tenfold
Before he arrived at the penfold;
Lords, ladies, like clouds which bedizen
At sunset the western horizon.
And Sir De Lorge pressed 'mid the foremost 25
With the dame he professed to adore most—
Oh, what a face! One by fits eyed
Her, and the horrible pitside;
For the penfold surrounded a hollow
Which led where the eye scarce dared follow, 30
And shelved to the chamber secluded
Where Bluebeard, the great lion, brooded.
The King hailed his keeper, an Arab
As glossy and black as a scarab,
And bade him make sport and at once stir 35
Up and out of his den the old monster.
They opened a hole in the wire-work
Across it, and dropped there a firework,
And fled: one's heart's beating redoubled;
A pause, while the pit's mouth was troubled, 40
The blackness and silence so utter,

By the firework's slow sparkling and sputter;
Then earth in a sudden contortion
Gave out to our gaze her abortion!
Such a brute! Were I friend Clement Marot   45
(Whose experience of nature's but narrow,
And whose faculties move in no small mist
When he versifies David the Psalmist)
I should study that brute to describe you
Illum Juda Leonem de Tribu!   50
One's whole blood grew curdling and creepy
To see the black mane, vast and heapy,
The tail in the air stiff and straining,
The wide eyes, nor waxing nor waning,
As over the barrier which bounded   55
His platform, and us who surrounded
The barrier, they reached and they rested
On the space that might stand him in best stead:
For who knew, he thought, what the amazement,
The eruption of clatter and blaze meant,   60
And if, in this minute of wonder,
No outlet, 'mid lightning and thunder,
Lay broad, and, his shackles all shivered,
The lion at last was delivered?
Aye, that was the open sky o'erhead!   65
And you saw by the flash on his forehead,
By the hope in those eyes wide and steady,
He was leagues in the desert already,
Driving the flocks up the mountain,
Or catlike couched hard by the fountain   70
To waylay the date-gathering negress:
So guarded he entrance or egress.
'How he stands!' quoth the King: 'we may well
                                        swear,
(No novice, we've won our spurs elsewhere,
And so can afford the confession,)   75
We exercise wholesome discretion
In keeping aloof from his threshold;
Once hold you, those jaws want no fresh hold,
Their first would too pleasantly purloin

The visitor's brisket or sirloin: 80
But who's he would prove so foolhardy?
Not the best man of Marignan, pardie!'

The sentence no sooner was uttered,
Than over the rails a glove fluttered,
Fell close to the lion, and rested: 85
The dame 'twas who flung it and jested
With life so, De Lorge had been wooing
For months past; he sat there pursuing
His suit, weighing out with nonchalance
Fine speeches like gold from a balance.   90
Sound the trumpet, no true knight's a tarrier!
De Lorge made one leap at the barrier,
Walked straight to the glove,—while the lion
Ne'er moved, kept his far-reaching eye on
The palm-tree-edged desert-spring's sapphire,   95
And the musky oiled skin of the Kaffir,—
Picked it up, and as calmly retreated,
Leaped back where the lady was seated,
And full in the face of its owner
Flung the glove.

'Your heart's queen, you dethrone her?   100
So should I!'—cried the King—''twas mere vanity,
Not love, set that task to humanity!'
Lords and ladies alike turned with loathing
From such a proved wolf in sheep's clothing.
Not so, I; for I caught an expression   105
In her brow's undisturbed self-possession
Amid the Court's scoffing and merriment,—
As if from no pleasing experiment
She rose, yet of pain not much heedful
So long as the process was needful,—   110
As if she had tried in a crucible,
To what 'speeches like gold' were reducible,
And, finding the finest prove copper,
Felt the smoke in her face was but proper;
To know what she had *not* to trust to,   115

Was worth all the ashes and dust too.
She went out 'mid hooting and laughter;
Clement Marot stayed: I followed after,
And asked, as a grace, what it all meant?
If she wished not the rash deed's recalment? 120
'For I'—so I spoke—'am a Poet:
Human nature,—behoves that I know it!'
She told me, 'Too long had I heard
Of the deed proved alone by the word:
For my love—what De Lorge would not dare! 125
With my scorn—what De Lorge could compare!
And the endless descriptions of death
He would brave when my lip formed a breath,
I must reckon as braved, or, of course,
Doubt his word—and moreover, perforce, 130
For such gifts as no lady could spurn,
Must offer my love in return.
When I looked on your lion, it brought
All the dangers at once to my thought,
Encountered by all sorts of men, 135
Before he was lodged in his den,—
From the poor slave whose club or bare hands
Dug the trap, set the snare on the sands,
With no King and no Court to applaud,
By no shame, should he shrink, over-awed, 140
Yet to capture the creature made shift,
That his rude boys might laugh at the gift,
—To the page who last leaped o'er the fence
Of the pit, on no greater pretence 145
Than to get back the bonnet he dropped,
Lest his pay for a week should be stopped.
So, wiser I judged it to make
One trial what "death for my sake"
Really meant, while the power was yet mine, 150
Than to wait until time should define
Such a phrase not so simply as I,
Who took it to mean just "to die".
The blow a glove gives is but weak:
Does the mark yet discolour my cheek?

But when the heart suffers a blow,   155
Will the pain pass so soon, do you know?'
I looked, as away she was sweeping,
And saw a youth eagerly keeping
As close as he dared to the doorway;
No doubt that a noble should more weigh   160
His life than befits a plebeian;
And yet, had our brute been Nemean—
(I judge by a certain calm fervour
The youth stepped with, forward to serve her)
—He'd have scarce thought you did him the worst
    turn   165
If you whispered 'Friend, what you'd get, first earn!'
And when, shortly after, she carried
Her shame from the Court, and they married,
To that marriage some happiness, maugre
The voice of the Court, I dared augur.   170
For De Lorge, he made women with men vie,
Those in wonder and praise, these in envy;
And in short stood so plain a head taller
That he wooed and won . . . how do you call her?
The Beauty, that rose in the sequel   175
To the King's love, who loved her a week well.
And 'twas noticed he never would honour
De Lorge (who looked daggers upon her)
With the easy commission of stretching
His legs in the service, and fetching   180
His wife, from her chamber, those straying
Sad gloves she was always mislaying,
While the King took the closet to chat in,—
But of course this adventure came pat in.
And never the King told the story,   185
How bringing a glove brought such glory,
But the wife smiled,—'His nerves are grown firmer:
Mine he brings now and utters no murmur!'
Venienti occurrite morbo!
With which moral I drop my theorbo.   190

MATTHEW ARNOLD

1822–1888

Sohrab and Rustum

AN EPISODE

And the first grey of morning fill'd the east,
And the fog rose out of the Oxus stream.
But all the Tartar camp along the stream
Was hush'd, and still the men were plunged in sleep:
Sohrab alone, he slept not: all night long   5
He had lain wakeful, tossing on his bed;
But when the grey dawn stole into his tent,
He rose, and clad himself, and girt his sword,
And took his horseman's cloak, and left his tent,
And went abroad into the cold wet fog,   10
Through the dim camp to Peran-Wisa's tent.
   Through the black Tartar tents he pass'd, which stood
Clustering like bee-hives on the low flat strand
Of Oxus, where the summer floods o'erflow
When the sun melts the snows in high Pamere: 15
Through the black tents he pass'd, o'er that low strand,
And to a hillock came, a little back
From the stream's brink, the spot where first a boat,
Crossing the stream in summer, scrapes the land.
The men of former times had crown'd the top   20
With a clay fort: but that was fall'n; and now
The Tartars built there Peran-Wisa's tent,
A dome of laths, and o'er it felts were spread.
And Sohrab came there, and went in, and stood
Upon the thick-pil'd carpets in the tent,   25
And found the old man sleeping on his bed
Of rugs and felts, and near him lay his arms.
And Peran-Wisa heard him, though the step
Was dull'd; for he slept light, an old man's sleep;

And he rose quickly on one arm, and said:—   30
  'Who art thou? for it is not yet clear dawn.
Speak! is there news, or any night alarm?'
  But Sohrab came to the bedside, and said:—
'Thou know'st me Peran-Wisa: it is I.
The sun is not yet risen, and the foe   35
Sleep; but I sleep not; all night long I lie
Tossing and wakeful, and I come to thee.
For so did King Afrasiab bid me seek
Thy counsel, and to heed thee as thy son,
In Samarcand, before the army march'd;   40
And I will tell thee what my heart desires.
Thou know'st if, since from Ader-baijan first
I came among the Tartars, and bore arms,
I have still serv'd Afrasiab well, and shown,
At my boy's years, the courage of a man.   45
This too thou know'st, that, while I still bear on
The conquering Tartar ensigns through the world,
And beat the Persians back on every field,
I seek one man, one man, and one alone—
Rustum, my father; who, I hop'd, should greet,   50
Should one day greet, upon some well-fought field,
His not unworthy, not inglorious son.
So I long hop'd, but him I never find.
Come then, hear now, and grant me what I ask.
Let the two armies rest to-day: but I   55
Will challenge forth the bravest Persian lords
To meet me, man to man: if I prevail,
Rustum will surely hear it; if I fall—
Old man, the dead need no one, claim no kin.
Dim is the rumour of a common fight,   60
Where host meets host, and many names are sunk:
But of a single combat Fame speaks clear.'
  He spoke: and Peran-Wisa took the hand
Of the young man in his, and sigh'd, and said:—
'O Sohrab, an unquiet heart is thine!   65
Canst thou not rest among the Tartar chiefs,
And share the battle's common chance with us
Who love thee, but must press for ever first,

In single fight incurring single risk,
To find a father thou hast never seen?   70
That were far best, my son, to stay with us
Unmurmuring; in our tents, while it is war,
And when 'tis truce, then in Afrasiab's towns.
But, if this one desire indeed rules all,
To seek out Rustum—seek him not through fight:
Seek him in peace, and carry to his arms,   76
O Sohrab, carry an unwounded son!
But far hence seek him, for he is not here.
For now it is not as when I was young,
When Rustum was in front of every fray: 80
But now he keeps apart, and sits at home,
In Seistan, with Zal, his father old.
Whether that his own mighty strength at last
Feels the abhorr'd approaches of old age;
Or in some quarrel with the Persian King.   85
There go:—Thou wilt not? Yet my heart forebodes
Danger or death awaits thee on this field.
Fain would I know thee safe and well, though lost
To us: fain therefore send thee hence, in peace
To seek thy father, not seek single fights   90
In vain:—but who can keep the lion's cub
From ravening? and who govern Rustum's son?
Go: I will grant thee what thy heart desires.'

    So said he, and dropp'd Sohrab's hand, and left
His bed, and the warm rugs whereon he lay,   95
And o'er his chilly limbs his woollen coat
He pass'd, and tied his sandals on his feet,
And threw a white cloak round him, and he took
In his right hand a ruler's staff, no sword;
And on his head he plac'd his sheep-skin cap,   100
Black, glossy, curl'd, the fleece of Kara-Kul;
And rais'd the curtain of his tent, and call'd
His herald to his side, and went abroad.

    The sun, by this, had risen, and clear'd the fog
From the broad Oxus and the glittering sands: 105
And from their tents the Tartar horsemen fil'd
Into the open plain; so Haman bade;

Haman, who next to Peran-Wisa rul'd
The host, and still was in his lusty prime.
From their black tents, long files of horse, they
    stream'd: 110
As when, some grey November morn, the files,
In marching order spread, of long-neck'd cranes
Stream over Casbin, and the southern slopes
Of Elburz, from the Aralian estuaries,   114
Or some frore Caspian reed-bed, southward bound
For the warm Persian sea-board: so they stream'd
The Tartars of the Oxus, the King's guard,
First, with black sheep-skin caps and with long spears;
Large men, large steeds; who from Bokhara come
And Khiva, and ferment the milk of mares.   120
Next the more temperate Toorkmuns of the south,
The Tukas, and the lances of Salore,
And those from Attruck and the Caspian sands;
Light men, and on light steeds, who only drink
The acrid milk of camels, and their wells.   125
And then a swarm of wandering horse, who came
From far, and a more doubtful service own'd;
The Tartars of Ferghana, from the banks
Of the Jaxartes, men with scanty beards   129
And close-set skull-caps; and those wilder hordes
Who roam o'er Kipchak and the northern waste,
Kalmuks and unkemp'd Kuzzaks, tribes who stray
Nearest the Pole, and wandering Kirghizzes,
Who come on shaggy ponies from Pamere.
These all fil'd out from camp into the plain.   135
And on the other side the Persians form'd:
First a light cloud of horse, Tartars they seem'd,
The Ilyats of Khorassan: and behind,
The royal troops of Persia, horse and foot,
Marshall'd battalions bright in burnish'd steel.
But Peran-Wisa with his herald came   141
Threading the Tartar squadrons to the front,
And with his staff kept back the foremost ranks.
And when Ferood, who led the Persians, saw
That Peran-Wisa kept the Tartars back,   145

He took his spear, and to the front he came,
And check'd his ranks, and fix'd them where they
    stood.
And the old Tartar came upon the sand
Betwixt the silent hosts, and spake, and said:—
   'Ferood, and ye, Persians and Tartars, hear!   150
Let there be truce between the hosts to-day.
But choose a champion from the Persian lords
To fight our champion Sohrab, man to man.'
   As, in the country, on a morn in June,
When the dew glistens on the pearled ears,   155
A shiver runs through the deep corn for joy—
So, when they heard what Peran-Wisa said,
A thrill through all the Tartar squadrons ran
Of pride and hope for Sohrab, whom they lov'd.
   But as a troop of pedlars from Cabool,   160
Cross underneath the Indian Caucasus,
That vast sky-neighbouring mountain of milk snow;
Winding so high, that, as they mount, they pass
Long flocks of travelling birds dead on the snow, 164
Chok'd by the air, and scarce can they themselves
Slake their parch'd throats with sugar'd mulberries—
In single file they move, and stop their breath,
For fear they should dislodge the o'erhanging snows—
So the pale Persians held their breath with fear.
   And to Ferood his brother Chiefs came up   170
To counsel: Gudurz and Zoarrah came,
And Feraburz, who rul'd the Persian host
Second, and was the uncle of the King:
These came and counsell'd; and then Gudurz said:—
   'Ferood, shame bids us take their challenge up,
Yet champion have we none to match this youth.
He has the wild stag's foot, the lion's heart.   177
But Rustum came last night; aloof he sits
And sullen, and has pitch'd his tents apart:
Him will I seek, and carry to his ear   180
The Tartar challenge, and this young man's name.
Haply he will forget his wrath, and fight.
Stand forth the while, and take the challenge up.'

So spake he; and Ferood stood forth and said:—   185
'Old man, be it agreed as thou hast said.
Let Sohrab arm, and we will find a man.'
  He spoke; and Peran-Wisa turn'd, and strode
Back through the opening squadrons to his tent.
But through the anxious Persians Gudurz ran,
And cross'd the camp which lay behind, and reach'd,
Out on the sands beyond it, Rustum's tents.   191
Of scarlet cloth they were, and glittering gay,
Just pitch'd: the high pavilion in the midst
Was Rustum's, and his men lay camp'd around.
And Gudurz enter'd Rustum's tent, and found   195
Rustum: his morning meal was done, but still
The table stood beside him charg'd with food;
A side of roasted sheep, and cakes of bread,
And dark green melons; and there Rustum sate
Listless, and held a falcon on his wrist,   200
And play'd with it; but Gudurz came and stood
Before him; and he look'd, and saw him stand;
And with a cry sprang up, and dropp'd the bird,
And greeted Gudurz with both hands, and said:—
  'Welcome! these eyes could see no better sight.
What news? but sit down first, and eat and drink.'
  But Gudurz stood in the tent door, and said:—
'Not now: a time will come to eat and drink,
But not to-day: to-day has other needs.
The armies are drawn out, and stand at gaze: 210
For from the Tartars is a challenge brought
To pick a champion from the Persian lords
To fight their champion—and thou know'st his name—
Sohrab men call him, but his birth is hid.
O Rustum, like thy might is this young man's!   215
He has the wild stag's foot, the lion's heart.
And he is young, and Iran's Chiefs are old,
Or else too weak; and all eyes turn to thee.
Come down and help us, Rustum, or we lose.'
  He spoke: but Rustum answer'd with a smile:—
'Go to! if Iran's Chiefs are old, then I   221

Am older: if the young are weak, the King
Errs strangely: for the King, for Kai-Khosroo,
Himself is young, and honours younger men,
And lets the agèd moulder to their graves.   225
Rustum he loves no more, but loves the young—
The young may rise at Sohrab's vaunts, not I.
For what care I, though all speak Sohrab's fame?
For would that I myself had such a son,
And not that one slight helpless girl I have,   230
A son so fam'd, so brave, to send to war,
And I to tarry with the snow-hair'd Zal,
My father, whom the robber Afghans vex,
And clip his borders short, and drive his herds,
And he has none to guard his weak old age.   235
There would I go, and hang my armour up,
And with my great name fence that weak old man,
And spend the goodly treasures I have got,
And rest my age, and hear of Sohrab's fame,
And leave to death the hosts of thankless kings,   240
And with these slaughterous hands draw sword no
        more.'

     He spoke, and smil'd; and Gudurz made reply:—
'What then, O Rustum, will men say to this,
When Sohrab dares our bravest forth, and seeks
Thee most of all, and thou, whom most he seeks,   245
Hidest thy face? Take heed, lest men should say,
*Like some old miser, Rustum hoards his fame,
And shuns to peril it with younger men.'*

     And, greatly mov'd, then Rustum made reply:—
'O Gudurz, wherefore dost thou say such words?
Thou knowest better words than this to say.   251
What is one more, one less, obscure or fam'd,
Valiant or craven, young or old, to me?
Are not they mortal, am not I myself?
But who for men of naught would do great deeds?
Come, thou shalt see how Rustum hoards his fame.
But I will fight unknown, and in plain arms;   257
Let not men say of Rustum, he was match'd
In single fight with any mortal man.'

He spoke, and frown'd; and Gudurz turn'd, and
ran   260
Back quickly through the camp in fear and joy,
Fear at his wrath, but joy that Rustum came.
But Rustum strode to his tent door, and call'd
His followers in, and bade them bring his arms,
And clad himself in steel: the arms he chose   265
Were plain, and on his shield was no device,
Only his helm was rich, inlaid with gold,
And from the fluted spine atop a plume
Of horsehair wav'd, a scarlet horsehair plume.
So arm'd he issued forth; and Ruksh, his horse, 270
Follow'd him, like a faithful hound, at heel,
Ruksh, whose renown was nois'd through all the earth,
The horse, whom Rustum on a foray once
Did in Bokhara by the river find
A colt beneath its dam, and drove him home,   275
And rear'd him; a bright bay, with lofty crest;
Dight with a saddle-cloth of broider'd green
Crusted with gold, and on the ground were work'd
All beasts of chase, all beasts which hunters know:
So follow'd, Rustum left his tents, and cross'd 280
The camp, and to the Persian host appear'd.
And all the Persians knew him, and with shouts
Hail'd; but the Tartars knew not who he was.
And dear as the wet diver to the eyes
Of his pale wife who waits and weeps on shore,   285
By sandy Bahrein, in the Persian Gulf,
Plunging all day in the blue waves, at night,
Having made up his tale of precious pearls,
Rejoins her in their hut upon the sands—
So dear to the pale Persians Rustum came.   290
   And Rustum to the Persian front advanc'd,
And Sohrab arm'd in Haman's tent, and came.
And as afield the reapers cut a swathe
Down through the middle of a rich man's corn,
And on each side are squares of standing corn,   295
And in the midst a stubble, short and bare;
So on each side were squares of men, with spears

Bristling, and in the midst, the open sand.
And Rustum came upon the sand, and cast
His eyes towards the Tartar tents, and saw   300
Sohrab come forth, and ey'd him as he came.

As some rich woman, on a winter's morn,
Eyes through her silken curtains the poor drudge
Who with numb blacken'd fingers makes her fire—
At cock-crow, on a starlit winter's morn,   305
When the frost flowers the whiten'd window panes—
And wonders how she lives, and what the thoughts
Of that poor drudge may be; so Rustum ey'd
The unknown adventurous Youth, who from afar
Came seeking Rustum, and defying forth   310
All the most valiant chiefs: long he perus'd
His spirited air, and wonder'd who he was.
For very young he seem'd, tenderly rear'd;
Like some young cypress, tall, and dark, and straight,
Which in a queen's secluded garden throws   315
Its slight dark shadow on the moonlit turf,
By midnight, to a bubbling fountain's sound—
So slender Sohrab seem'd, so softly rear'd.
And a deep pity enter'd Rustum's soul
As he beheld him coming; and he stood,   320
And beckon'd to him with his hand, and said:
    'O thou young man, the air of Heaven is soft,
And warm and pleasant; but the grave is cold.
Heaven's air is better than the cold dead grave.
Behold me: I am vast, and clad in iron,   325
And tried; and I have stood on many a field
Of blood, and I have fought with many a foe:
Never was that field lost, or that foe sav'd.
O Sohrab, wherefore wilt thou rush on death?
Be govern'd: quit the Tartar host, and come   330
To Iran, and be as my son to me,
And fight beneath my banner till I die.
There are no youths in Iran brave as thou.'
    So he spake, mildly: Sohrab heard his voice,
The mighty voice of Rustum; and he saw   335
His giant figure planted on the sand,

Sole, like some single tower, which a chief
Has builded on the waste in former years
Against the robbers; and he saw that head,
Streak'd with its first grey hairs: hope fill'd his soul;
And he ran forwards and embrac'd his knees,   341
And clasp'd his hand within his own and said:—
    'Oh, by thy father's head! by thine own soul!
Art thou not Rustum? Speak! art thou not he?'
    But Rustum ey'd askance the kneeling youth,   345
And turn'd away, and spoke to his own soul:—
    'Ah me, I muse what this young fox may mean.
False, wily, boastful, are these Tartar boys.
For if I now confess this thing he asks,
And hide it not, but say—*Rustum is here*—   350
He will not yield indeed, nor quit our foes,
But he will find some pretext not to fight,
And praise my fame, and proffer courteous gifts,
A belt or sword perhaps, and go his way.
And on a feast-tide, in Afrasiab's hall,   355
In Samarcand, he will arise and cry—
"I challeng'd once, when the two armies camp'd
Beside the Oxus, all the Persian lords
To cope with me in single fight; but they
Shrank; only Rustum dar'd: then he and I   360
Chang'd gifts, and went on equal terms away."
So will he speak, perhaps, while men applaud.
Then were the chiefs of Iran sham'd through me.'
    And then he turn'd, and sternly spake aloud:—
'Rise! wherefore dost thou vainly question thus   365
Of Rustum? I am here, whom thou hast call'd
By challenge forth: make good thy vaunt, or yield.
Is it with Rustum only thou wouldst fight?
Rash boy, men look on Rustum's face and flee.
For well I know, that did great Rustum stand   370
Before thy face this day, and were reveal'd,
There would be then no talk of fighting more.
But being what I am, I tell thee this;
Do thou record it in thy inmost soul: 374
Either thou shalt renounce thy vaunt, and yield;

Or else thy bones shall strew this sand, till winds
Bleach them, or Oxus with his summer floods,
Oxus in summer wash them all away.'
  He spoke: and Sohrab answer'd, on his feet:—
'Art thou so fierce? Thou wilt not fright me so.   380
I am no girl, to be made pale by words.
Yet this thou hast said well, did Rustum stand
Here on this field, there were no fighting then.
But Rustum is far hence, and we stand here.
Begin: thou art more vast, more dread than I,   385
And thou art prov'd, I know, and I am young—
But yet Success sways with the breath of Heaven.
And though thou thinkest that thou knowest sure
Thy victory, yet thou canst not surely know.
For we are all, like swimmers in the sea,   390
Pois'd on the top of a huge wave of Fate,
Which hangs uncertain to which side to fall.
And whether it will heave us up to land,
Or whether it will roll us out to sea,
Back out to sea, to the deep waves of death,   395
We know not, and no search will make us know:
Only the event will teach us in its hour.'
  He spoke; and Rustum answer'd not, but hurl'd
His spear: down from the shoulder, down it came,
As on some partridge in the corn a hawk   400
That long has tower'd in the airy clouds
Drops like a plummet: Sohrab saw it come,
And sprang aside, quick as a flash: the spear
Hiss'd, and went quivering down into the sand,
Which sent it flying wide:—then Sohrab threw   405
In turn, and full struck Rustum's shield: sharp rang,
The iron plates rang sharp, but turn'd the spear.
And Rustum seiz'd his club, which none but he
Could wield: an unlopp'd trunk it was, and huge,
Still rough; like those which men in treeless plains
To build them boats fish from the flooded rivers,   411
Hyphasis or Hydaspes, when, high up
By their dark springs, the wind in winter-time
Has made in Himalayan forests wrack,

And strewn the channels with torn boughs; so huge
The club which Rustum lifted now, and struck   416
One stroke; but again Sohrab sprang aside
Lithe as the glancing snake, and the club came
Thundering to earth, and leapt from Rustum's hand.
And Rustum follow'd his own blow, and fell   420
To his knees, and with his fingers clutch'd the sand:
And now might Sohrab have unsheath'd his sword,
And pierc'd the mighty Rustum while he lay
Dizzy, and on his knees, and chok'd with sand: 424
But he look'd on, and smil'd, nor bar'd his sword,
But courteously drew back, and spoke, and said:—

   'Thou strik'st too hard: that club of thine will float
Upon the summer floods, and not my bones.
But rise, and be not wroth; not wroth am I:
No, when I see thee, wrath forsakes my soul.   430
Thou say'st thou art not Rustum: be it so.
Who art thou then, that canst so touch my soul?
Boy as I am, I have seen battles too;
Have waded foremost in their bloody waves,
And heard their hollow roar of dying men;   435
But never was my heart thus touch'd before.
Are they from Heaven, these softenings of the heart?
O thou old warrior, let us yield to Heaven!
Come, plant we here in earth our angry spears,
And make a truce, and sit upon this sand,   440
And pledge each other in red wine, like friends,
And thou shalt talk to me of Rustum's deeds.
There are enough foes in the Persian host
Whom I may meet, and strike, and feel no pang;
Champions enough Afrasiab has, whom thou   445
Mayst fight; fight them, when they confront thy spear.
But oh, let there be peace 'twixt thee and me!'

   He ceas'd: but while he spake, Rustum had risen,
And stood erect, trembling with rage: his club
He left to lie, but had regain'd his spear,   450
Whose fiery point now in his mail'd right-hand
Blaz'd bright and baleful, like that autumn Star,
The baleful sign of fevers: dust has soil'd

His stately crest, and dimm'd his glittering arms.
His breast heav'd; his lips foam'd; and twice his voice
Was chok'd with rage: at last these words broke
    way:—   456
  'Girl! nimble with thy feet, not with thy hands!
Curl'd minion, dancer, coiner of sweet words!
Fight; let me hear thy hateful voice no more!
Thou art not in Afrasiab's gardens now   460
With Tartar girls, with whom thou art wont to dance;
But on the Oxus sands, and in the dance
Of battle, and with me, who make no play
Of war: I fight it out, and hand to hand.
Speak not to me of truce, and pledge, and wine! 465
Remember all thy valour: try thy feints
And cunning: all the pity I had is gone:
Because thou hast sham'd me before both the hosts
With thy light skipping tricks, and thy girl's wiles.'
  He spoke; and Sohrab kindled at his taunts,   470
And he too drew his sword: at once they rush'd
Together, as two eagles on one prey
Come rushing down together from the clouds,
One from the east, one from the west: their shields
Dash'd with a clang together, and a din   475
Rose, such as that the sinewy woodcutters
Make often in the forest's heart at morn,
Of hewing axes, crashing trees: such blows
Rustum and Sohrab on each other hail'd.
And you would say that sun and stars took part 480
In that unnatural conflict; for a cloud
Grew suddenly in Heaven, and dark'd the sun
Over the fighters' heads; and a wind rose
Under their feet, and moaning swept the plain,
And in a sandy whirlwind wrapp'd the pair.   485
In gloom they twain were wrapp'd, and they alone;
For both the on-looking hosts on either hand
Stood in broad daylight, and the sky was pure,
And the sun sparkled on the Oxus stream.   489
But in the gloom they fought, with bloodshot eyes
And labouring breath; first Rustum struck the shield

Which Sohrab held stiff out: the steel-spik'd spear
Rent the tough plates, but fail'd to reach the skin,
And Rustum pluck'd it back with angry groan. 494
Then Sohrab with his sword smote Rustum's helm,
Nor clove its steel quite through; but all the crest
He shore away, and that proud horsehair plume,
Never till now defil'd, sunk to the dust;
And Rustum bow'd his head; but then the gloom
Grew blacker: thunder rumbled in the air, 500
And lightnings rent the cloud; and Ruksh, the horse,
Who stood at hand, utter'd a dreadful cry:
No horse's cry was that, most like the roar
Of some pain'd desert lion, who all day
Has trail'd the hunter's javelin in his side, 505
And comes at night to die upon the sand:—
The two hosts heard that cry, and quak'd for fear,
And Oxus curdled as it cross'd his stream.
But Sohrab heard, and quail'd not, but rush'd on,
And struck again; and again Rustum bow'd 510
His head; but this time all the blade, like glass,
Sprang in a thousand shivers on the helm,
And in his hand the hilt remain'd alone.
Then Rustum rais'd his head: his dreadful eyes 514
Glar'd, and he shook on high his menacing spear,
And shouted, *Rustum!* Sohrab heard that shout,
And shrank amaz'd: back he recoil'd one step,
And scann'd with blinking eyes the advancing Form:
And then he stood bewilder'd; and he dropp'd 519
His covering shield, and the spear pierc'd his side.
He reel'd, and staggering back, sunk to the ground.
And then the gloom dispers'd, and the wind fell,
And the bright sun broke forth, and melted all
The cloud; and the two armies saw the pair;
Saw Rustum standing, safe upon his feet, 525
And Sohrab, wounded, on the bloody sand.
   Then, with a bitter smile, Rustum began:—
'Sohrab, thou thoughtest in thy mind to kill
A Persian lord this day, and strip his corpse,
And bear thy trophies to Afrasiab's tent. 530

Or else that the great Rustum would come down
Himself to fight, and that thy wiles would move
His heart to take a gift, and let thee go.
And then that all the Tartar host would praise
Thy courage or thy craft, and spread thy fame,   535
To glad thy father in his weak old age.
Fool! thou art slain, and by an unknown man!
Dearer to the red jackals shalt thou be,
Than to thy friends, and to thy father old.'

      And, with a fearless mien, Sohrab replied:—   540
'Unknown thou art; yet thy fierce vaunt is vain.
Thou dost not slay me, proud and boastful man!
No! Rustum slays me, and this filial heart.
For were I match'd with ten such men as thou,
And I were he who till to-day I was,   545
They should be lying here, I standing there.
But that belovèd name unnerv'd my arm—
That name, and something, I confess, in thee,
Which troubles all my heart, and made my shield
Fall; and thy spear transfix'd an unarm'd foe.   550
And now thou boastest, and insult'st my fate.
But hear thou this, fierce Man, tremble to hear!
The mighty Rustum shall avenge my death!
My father, whom I seek through all the world,
He shall avenge my death, and punish thee!'   555
      As when some hunter in the spring hath found
A breeding eagle sitting on her nest,
Upon the craggy isle of a hill lake,
And pierc'd her with an arrow as she rose,
And follow'd her to find her where she fell   560
Far off;—anon her mate comes winging back
From hunting, and a great way off descries
His huddling young left sole; at that, he checks
His pinion, and with short uneasy sweeps
Circles above his eyry, with loud screams   565
Chiding his mate back to her nest; but she
Lies dying, with the arrow in her side,
In some far stony gorge out of his ken,
A heap of fluttering feathers: never more

Shall the lake glass her, flying over it; 570
Never the black and dripping precipices
Echo her stormy scream as she sails by:—
As that poor bird flies home, nor knows his loss—
So Rustum knew not his own loss, but stood
Over his dying son, and knew him not. 575
    But with a cold, incredulous voice, he said:—
'What prate is this of fathers and revenge?
The mighty Rustum never had a son.'
    And, with a failing voice, Sohrab replied:—
'Ah yes, he had! and that lost son am I. 580
Surely the news will one day reach his ear,
Reach Rustum, where he sits, and tarries long,
Somewhere, I know not where, but far from here;
And pierce him like a stab, and make him leap
To arms, and cry for vengeance upon thee. 585
Fierce Man, bethink thee, for an only son!
What will that grief, what will that vengeance be!
Oh, could I live, till I that grief had seen!
Yet him I pity not so much, but her,
My mother, who in Ader-baijan dwells 590
With that old King, her father, who grows grey
With age, and rules over the valiant Koords.
Her most I pity, who no more will see
Sohrab returning from the Tartar camp,
With spoils and honour, when the war is done. 595
But a dark rumour will be bruited up,
From tribe to tribe, until it reach her ear;
And then will that defenceless woman learn
That Sohrab will rejoice her sight no more;
But that in battle with a nameless foe, 600
By the far-distant Oxus, he is slain.'
    He spoke; and as he ceas'd he wept aloud,
Thinking of her he left, and his own death.
He spoke; but Rustum listen'd, plung'd in thought.
Nor did he yet believe it was his son 605
Who spoke, although he call'd back names he knew;
For he had had sure tidings that the babe,
Which was in Ader-baijan born to him,

Had been a puny girl, no boy at all:
So that sad mother sent him word, for fear		610
Rustum should take the boy, to train in arms;
And so he deem'd that either Sohrab took,
By a false boast, the style of Rustum's son;
Or that men gave it him, to swell his fame.
So deem'd he; yet he listen'd, plung'd in thought;
And his soul set to grief, as the vast tide		616
Of the bright rocking Ocean sets to shore
At the full moon: tears gather'd in his eyes;
For he remember'd his own early youth,
And all its bounding rapture; as, at dawn,		620
The Shepherd from his mountain lodge descries
A far bright City, smitten by the sun,
Through many rolling clouds;—so Rustum saw
His youth; saw Sohrab's mother, in her bloom;
And that old King, her father, who lov'd well		625
His wandering guest, and gave him his fair child
With joy; and all the pleasant life they led,
They three, in that long-distant summer-time—
The castle, and the dewy woods, and hunt
And hound, and morn on those delightful hills		630
In Ader-baijan. And he saw that Youth,
Of age and looks to be his own dear son,
Piteous and lovely, lying on the sand,
Like some rich hyacinth, which by the scythe
Of an unskilful gardener has been cut,		635
Mowing the garden grass-plots near its bed,
And lies, a fragrant tower of purple bloom,
On the mown, dying grass;—so Sohrab lay,
Lovely in death, upon the common sand.
And Rustum gaz'd on him with grief, and said:—
		'O Sohrab, thou indeed art such a son		641
Whom Rustum, wert thou his, might well have lov'd!
Yet here thou errest, Sohrab, or else men
Have told thee false;—thou art not Rustum's son.
For Rustum had no son: one child he had—		645
But one—a girl: who with her mother now
Plies some light female task, nor dreams of us—

Of us she dreams not, nor of wounds, nor war.'
But Sohrab answer'd him in wrath; for now
The anguish of the deep-fix'd spear grew fierce, 650
And he desired to draw forth the steel,
And let the blood flow free, and so to die;
But first he would convince his stubborn foe—
And rising sternly on one arm, he said:—

'Man, who art thou who dost deny my words? 655
Truth sits upon the lips of dying men,
And Falsehood, while I liv'd, was far from mine.
I tell thee, prick'd upon this arm I bear
That seal which Rustum to my mother gave,
That she might prick it on the babe she bore.' 660
He spoke: and all the blood left Rustum's cheeks;
And his knees totter'd, and he smote his hand
Against his breast, his heavy mailed hand,
That the hard iron corslet clank'd aloud:
And to his heart he press'd the other hand, 665
And in a hollow voice he spake, and said:—

'Sohrab, that were a proof which could not lie.
If thou shew this, then art thou Rustum's son.'
Then, with weak hasty fingers, Sohrab loos'd
His belt, and near the shoulder bar'd his arm, 670
And shew'd a sign in faint vermilion points
Prick'd: as a cunning workman, in Pekin,
Pricks with vermilion some clear porcelain vase,
An emperor's gift—at early morn he paints, 674
And all day long, and, when night comes, the lamp
Lights up his studious forehead and thin hands:—
So delicately prick'd the sign appear'd
On Sohrab's arm, the sign of Rustum's seal.
It was that Griffin, which of old rear'd Zal,
Rustum's great father, whom they left to die 680
A helpless babe, among the mountain rocks.
Him that kind Creature found, and rear'd, and lov'd—
Then Rustum took it for his glorious sign.
And Sohrab bar'd that figure on his arm,
And himself scann'd it long with mournful eyes, 685
And then he touch'd it with his hand and said:—

'How say'st thou? Is that sign the proper sign
Of Rustum's son, or of some other man's?'

He spoke: but Rustum gaz'd, and gaz'd, and stood
Speechless; and then he utter'd one sharp cry— 690
O Boy—thy Father!—and his voice chok'd there.
And then a cloud pass'd before his eyes,
And his head swam, and he sunk down to earth.
But Sohrab crawl'd to where he lay, and cast
His arms about his neck, and kiss'd his lips. 695
And with fond faltering fingers strok'd his cheeks,
Trying to call him back to life: and life
Came back to Rustum, and he op'd his eyes,
And they stood wide with horror; and he seiz'd
In both his hands the dust which lay around, 700
And threw it on his head, and smirch'd his hair,
His hair, and face, and beard, and glittering arms:
And strong convulsive groanings shook his breast,
And his sobs chok'd him; and he clutch'd his sword,
To draw it, and for ever let life out. 705
But Sohrab saw his thought, and held his hands,
And with a soothing voice he spoke, and said:—

'Father, forbear: for I but meet to-day
The doom that at my birth was written down
In Heaven, and thou art Heaven's unconscious hand.
Surely my heart cried out that it was thou, 711
When first I saw thee; and thy heart spoke too,
I know it: but Fate trod those promptings down
Under its iron heel; Fate, Fate engag'd
The strife, and hurl'd me on my father's spear. 715
But let us speak no more of this: I find
My father; let me feel that I have found.
Come, sit beside me on this sand, and take 718
My head betwixt thy hands, and kiss my cheeks,
And wash them with thy tears, and say, *My Son!*
Quick! quick! for number'd are my sands of life,
And swift; for like the lightning to this field
I came, and like the wind I go away—
Sudden, and swift, and like a passing wind.
But it was writ in Heaven that this should be.' 725

So said he: and his voice releas'd the heart
Of Rustum, and his tears broke forth; he cast
His arms round his son's neck, and wept aloud,
And kiss'd him. And awe fell on both the hosts   729
When they saw Rustum's grief: and Ruksh, the horse,
With his head bowing to the ground, and mane
Sweeping the dust, came near, and in mute woe
First to the one then to the other mov'd
His head, as if inquiring what their grief   734
Might mean; and from his dark compassionate eyes,
The big warm tears roll'd down, and cak'd the sand.
But Rustum chid him with stern voice, and said:—

'Ruksh, now thou grievest; but, O Ruksh, thy feet
Should then have rotted on thy nimble joints,
When first they bore thy Master to this field.'   740

But Sohrab look'd upon the horse and said:—
'Is this then Ruksh? How often, in past days,
My mother told me of thee, thou brave Steed!
My terrible father's terrible horse; and said,
That I should one day find thy lord and thee.   745
Come, let me lay my hand upon thy mane.
O Ruksh, thou art more fortunate than I;
For thou hast gone where I shall never go,
And snuff'd the breezes of my father's home.
And thou hast trod the sands of Seistan,   750
And seen the River of Helmund, and the Lake
Of Zirrah; and the aged Zal himself
Has often strok'd thy neck, and given thee food,
Corn in a golden platter soak'd with wine,   754
And said—"O Ruksh! bear Rustum well!"—but I
Have never known my grandsire's furrow'd face,
Nor seen his lofty house in Seistan,
Nor slak'd my thirst at the clear Helmund stream:
But lodg'd among my father's foes, and seen
Afrasiab's cities only, Samarcand,   760
Bokhara, and lone Khiva in the waste,
And the black Toorkmun tents; and only drunk
The desert rivers, Moorghab and Tejend,
Kohik, and where the Kalmuks feed their sheep,

The northern Sir; and this great Oxus stream—   765
The yellow Oxus, by whose brink I die.'
      And with a heavy groan, Rustum replied:—
'Oh that its waves were flowing over me!
Oh that I saw its grains of yellow silt
Roll tumbling in the current o'er my head!'   770
      And with a grave mild voice, Sohrab replied:—
'Desire not that, my father; thou must live.
For some are born to do great deeds, and live,
As some are born to be obscur'd, and die.
Do thou the deeds I die too young to do,   775
And reap a second glory in thine age.
Thou art my father, and thy gain is mine.
But come: thou seest this great host of men
Which follow me; I pray thee, slay not these:
Let me entreat for them: what have they done?   780
They follow'd me, my hope, my fame, my star.
Let them all cross the Oxus back in peace.
But me thou must bear hence, not send with them,
But carry me with thee to Seistan,
And place me on a bed, and mourn for me,   785
Thou, and the snow-hair'd Zal, and all thy friends.
And thou must lay me in that lovely earth,
And heap a stately mound above my bones,
And plant a far-seen pillar over all:
That so the passing horseman on the waste   790
May see my tomb a great way off, and say—
Sohrab, the mighty Rustum's son, lies there,
Whom his great father did in ignorance kill—
And I be not forgotten in my grave.'   794
      And, with a mournful voice, Rustum replied:—
'Fear not; as thou hast said, Sohrab, my son,
So shall it be: for I will burn my tents,
And quit the host, and bear thee hence with me,
And carry thee away to Seistan,
And place thee on a bed, and mourn for thee,   800
With the snow-headed Zal, and all my friends.
And I will lay thee in that lovely earth,
And heap a stately mound above thy bones,

And plant a far-seen pillar over all:
And men shall not forget thee in thy grave.   805
And I will spare thy host: yea, let them go:
Let them all cross the Oxus back in peace.
What should I do with slaying any more?
For would that all whom I have ever slain
Might be once more alive; my bitterest foes,   810
And they who were call'd champions in their time,
And through whose death I won that fame I have;
And I were nothing but a common man,
A poor, mean soldier, and without renown,
So thou mightest live too, my Son, my Son!   815
Or rather would that I, even I myself,
Might now be lying on this bloody sand,
Near death, and by an ignorant stroke of thine,
Not thou of mine; and I might die, not thou;
And I, not thou, be borne to Seistan;   820
And Zal might weep above my grave, not thine;
And say—*O son, I weep thee not too sore,*
For willingly, I know, thou met'st thine end.—
But now in blood and battles was my youth,
And full of blood and battles is my age;   825
And I shall never end this life of blood.'
      Then, at the point of death, Sohrab replied:—
'A life of blood indeed, thou dreadful Man!
But thou shalt yet have peace; only not now:
Not yet: but thou shalt have it on that day,   830
When thou shalt sail in a high-masted Ship,
Thou and the other peers of Kai-Khosroo,
Returning home over the salt blue sea,
From laying thy dear Master in his grave.'
      And Rustum gaz'd on Sohrab's face, and said:—
'Soon be that day, my Son, and deep that sea!   836
Till then, if Fate so wills, let me endure.'
      He spoke; and Sohrab smil'd on him, and took
The spear, and drew it from his side, and eas'd
His wound's imperious anguish: but the blood   840
Came welling from the open gash, and life
Flow'd with the stream: all down his cold white side

The crimson torrent ran, dim now, and soil'd,
Like the soil'd tissue of white violets
Left, freshly gather'd, on their native bank,   845
By romping children, whom their nurses call
From the hot fields at noon: his head droop'd low,
His limbs grew slack; motionless, white, he lay—
White, with eyes closed; only when heavy gasps,
Deep, heavy gasps, quivering through all his frame,
Convuls'd him back to life, he open'd them,   851
And fix'd them feebly on his father's face:
Till now all strength was ebb'd, and from his limbs
Unwillingly the spirit fled away,
Regretting the warm mansion which it left,   855
And youth and bloom, and this delightful world.
    So, on the bloody sand, Sohrab lay dead.
And the great Rustum drew his horseman's cloak
Down o'er his face, and sate by his dead son.
As those black granite pillars, once high-rear'd   860
By Jemshid in Persepolis, to bear
His house, now, mid their broken flights of steps,
Lie prone, enormous, down the mountain side—
So in the sand lay Rustum by his son.
    And night came down over the solemn waste,   865
And the two gazing hosts, and that sole pair,
And darken'd all; and a cold fog, with night,
Crept from the Oxus. Soon a hum arose,
As of a great assembly loos'd, and fires
Began to twinkle through the fog: for now   870
Both armies mov'd to camp, and took their meal:
The Persians took it on the open sands
Southward; the Tartars by the river marge:
And Rustum and his son were left alone.
    But the majestic River floated on,   875
Out of the mist and hum of that low land,
Into the frosty starlight, and there mov'd,
Rejoicing, through the hush'd Chorasmian waste,
Under the solitary moon: he flow'd
Right for the Polar Star, past Orgunjè,   880
Brimming, and bright, and large: then sands begin

To hem his watery march, and dam his streams,
And split his currents; that for many a league
The shorn and parcell'd Oxus strains along
Through beds of sand and matted rushy isles— 885
Oxus, forgetting the bright speed he had
In his high mountain-cradle in Pamere,
A foil'd circuitous wanderer:—till at last
The long'd-for dash of waves is heard, and wide
His luminous home of waters opens, bright 890
And tranquil, from whose floor the new-bath'd stars
Emerge, and shine upon the Aral Sea.

DANTE GABRIEL ROSSETTI
1828–1882

The White Ship

HENRY I OF ENGLAND.—25th NOVEMBER 1120

By none but me can the tale be told,
The butcher of Rouen, poor Berold.
   (*Lands are swayed by a King on a throne.*)
'Twas a royal train put forth to sea,
Yet the tale can be told by none but me. 5
   (*The sea hath no King but God alone.*)

King Henry held it as life's whole gain
That after his death his son should reign.

'Twas so in my youth I heard men say,
And my old age calls it back to-day. 10

King Henry of England's realm was he,
And Henry Duke of Normandy.

The times had changed when on either coast
'Clerkly Harry' was all his boast.

Of ruthless strokes full many an one 15
He had struck himself and his son;
And his elder brother's eyes were gone.

And when to the chase his court would crowd,
The poor flung ploughshares on his road,
And shrieked: 'Our cry is from King to God!'   20

But all the chiefs of the English land
Had knelt and kissed the Prince's hand.

And next with his son he sailed to France
To claim the Norman allegiance:

And every baron in Normandy   25
Had taken the oath of fealty.

'Twas sworn and sealed, and the day had come
When the King and the Prince might journey home:

For Christmas cheer is to home hearts dear,
And Christmas now was drawing near.   30

Stout Fitz-Stephen came to the King,—
A pilot famous in seafaring;

And he held to the King, in all men's sight,
A mark of gold for his tribute's right.

'Liege Lord! my father guided the ship   35
From whose boat your father's foot did slip
When he caught the English soil in his grip,

'And cried: "By this clasp I claim command
O'er every rood of English land!"

'He was borne to the realm you rule o'er now   40
In that ship with the anchor carved at her prow:

'And thither I'll bear, an it be my due,
Your father's son and his grandson too.

The famed White Ship is mine in the bay;
From Harfleur's harbour she sails to-day,   45

'With masts fair-pennoned as Norman spears
And with fifty well-tried mariners.'

Quoth the King: 'My ships are chosen each one,
But I'll not say nay to Stephen's son.

'My son and daughter and fellowship   50
Shall cross the water in the White Ship.'

The King set sail with eve's south wind,
And soon he left that coast behind.

The Prince and all his, a princely show,
Remained in the good White Ship to go.   55

With noble knights and with ladies fair,
With courtiers and sailors gathered there,
Three hundred living souls we were:

And I Berold was the meanest hind
In all that train to the Prince assign'd.   60

The Prince was a lawless shameless youth;
From his father's loins he sprang without ruth:

Eighteen years till then he had seen,
And the devil's dues in him were eighteen.

And now he cried: 'Bring wine from below;   65
Let the sailors revel ere yet they row:

'Our speed shall o'ertake my father's flight
Though we sail from the harbour at midnight.'

The rowers made good cheer without check;
The lords and ladies obeyed his beck;   70
The night was light, and they danced on the deck.

But at midnight's stroke they cleared the bay,
And the White Ship furrowed the water-way.

The sails were set, and the oars kept tune
To the double flight of the ship and the moon: 75

Swifter and swifter the White Ship sped
Till she flew as the spirit flies from the dead:

As white as a lily glimmered she
Like a ship's fair ghost upon the sea.

And the Prince cried, 'Friends, 'tis the hour to sing!
Is a songbird's course so swift on the wing?'   81

And under the winter stars' still throng,
From brown throats, white throats, merry and strong,
The knights and the ladies raised a song.

A song,—nay, a shriek that rent the sky,   85
That leaped o'er the deep!—the grievous cry
Of three hundred living that now must die.

An instant shriek that sprang to the shock
As the ship's keel felt the sunken rock.

'Tis said that afar—a shrill strange sigh—   90
The King's ships heard it and knew not why.

Pale Fitz-Stephen stood by the helm
'Mid all those folks that the wave must whelm.

A great King's heir for the waves to whelm,
And the helpless pilot pale at the helm!   95

The ship was eager and sucked athirst,
By the stealthy stab of the sharp reef pierc'd:

And like the moil round a sinking cup
The waters against her crowded up.

A moment the pilot's senses spin,—   100
The next he snatched the Prince 'mid the din,
Cut the boat loose, and the youth leaped in.

A few friends leaped with him, standing near.
'Row! the sea's smooth and the night is clear!'

'What! none to be saved but these and I?'   105
'Row, row as you'd live! All here must die!'

Out of the churn of the choking ship,
Which the gulf grapples and the waves strip,
They struck with the strained oars' flash and dip.

'Twas then o'er the splitting bulwarks' brim   110
The Prince's sister screamed to him.

He gazed aloft, still rowing apace,
And through the whirled surf he knew her face.

To the toppling decks clave one and all
As a fly cleaves to a chamber-wall.   115

I Berold was clinging anear;
I prayed for myself and quaked with fear,
But I saw his eyes as he looked at her.

He knew her face and he heard her cry,
And he said, 'Put back! she must not die!'   120

And back with the current's force they reel
Like a leaf that's drawn to a water-wheel.

'Neath the ship's travail they scarce might float,
But he rose and stood in the rocking boat.

Low the poor ship leaned on the tide: 125
O'er the naked keel as she best might slide,
The sister toiled to the brother's side.

He reached an oar to her from below,
And stiffened his arms to clutch her so.

But now from the ship some spied the boat,   130
And 'Saved!' was the cry from many a throat.

And down to the boat they leaped and fell:
It turned as a bucket turns in a well,
And nothing was there but the surge and swell.

The Prince that was and the King to come,   135
There in an instant gone to his doom,

Despite of all England's bended knee
And maugre the Norman fealty!

He was a Prince of lust and pride;
He showed no grace till the hour he died.   140

When he should be King, he oft would vow,
He'd yoke the peasant to his own plough.
O'er him the ships score their furrows now.

God only knows where his soul did wake,
But I saw him die for his sister's sake.   145

By none but me can the tale be told,
The butcher of Rouen, poor Berold.
    (*Lands are swayed by a King on a throne.*)
'Twas a royal train put forth to sea,
Yet the tale can be told by none but me.   150
    (*The sea hath no King but God alone.*)

And now the end came o'er the waters' womb
Like the last great Day that's yet to come.

With prayers in vain and curses in vain,
The White Ship sundered on the mid-main: 155

And what were men and what was a ship
Were toys and splinters in the sea's grip.

I Berold was down in the sea;
And passing strange though the thing may be,
Of dreams then known I remember me.   160

Blithe is the shout on Harfleur's strand
When morning lights the sails to land:

And blithe is Honfleur's echoing gloam
When mothers call the children home:

And high do the bells of Rouen beat   165
When the Body of Christ goes down the street.

These things and the like were heard and shown
In a moment's trance 'neath the sea alone;

And when I rose, 'twas the sea did seem,
And not these things, to be all a dream.　170

The ship was gone and the crowd was gone,
And the deep shuddered and the moon shone,

And in a strait grasp my arms did span
The mainyard rent from the mast where it ran;
And on it with me was another man.　175

Where lands were none 'neath the dim sea-sky,
We told our names, that man and I.

'O I am Godefroy de l'Aigle hight,
And son I am to a belted knight.'

'And I am Berold the butcher's son　180
Who slays the beasts in Rouen town.'

Then cried we upon God's name, as we
Did drift on the bitter winter sea.

But lo! a third man rose o'er the wave,
And we said, 'Thank God! us three may He save!'

He clutched to the yard with panting stare,　186
And we looked and knew Fitz-Stephen there.

He clung, and 'What of the Prince?' quoth he.
'Lost, lost!' we cried. He cried, 'Woe on me!'
And loosed his hold and sank through the sea.　190

And soul with soul again in that space
We two were together face to face:

And each knew each, as the moments sped,
Less for one living than for one dead:

And every still star overhead　195
Seemed an eye that knew we were but dead.

And the hours passed; till the noble's son
Sighed, 'God be thy help! my strength's fordone!

'O farewell, friend, for I can no more!'
'Christ take thee!' I moaned; and his life was o'er.

Three hundred souls were all lost but one,   201
And I drifted over the sea alone.

At last the morning rose on the sea
Like an angel's wing that beat tow'rds me.

Sore numbed I was in my sheepskin coat;   205
Half dead I hung, and might nothing note,
Till I woke sun-warmed in a fisher-boat.

The sun was high o'er the eastern brim
As I praised God and gave thanks to Him.

That day I told my tale to a priest,   210
Who charged me, till the shrift were releas'd,
That I should keep it in mine own breast.

And with the priest I thence did fare
To King Henry's court at Winchester.

We spoke with the King's high chamberlain,   215
And he wept and mourned again and again,
As if his own son had been slain:

And round us ever there crowded fast
Great men with faces all aghast:

And who so bold that might tell the thing   220
Which now they knew to their lord the King?
Much woe I learnt in their communing.

The King had watched with a heart sore stirred
For two whole days, and this was the third:

And still to all his court would he say,   225
'What keeps my son so long away?'

And they said: 'The ports lie far and wide
That skirt the swell of the English tide;

'And England's cliffs are not more white
Than her women are, and scarce so light   230
Her skies as their eyes are blue and bright;

'And in some port that he reached from France
The Prince has lingered for his pleasaùnce.'

But once the King asked: 'What distant cry
Was that we heard 'twixt the sea and sky?'   235

And one said: 'With suchlike shouts, pardie!
Do the fishers fling their nets at sea.'

And one: 'Who knows not the shrieking quest
When the sea-mew misses its young from the nest?'

'Twas thus till now they had soothed his dread,   240
Albeit they knew not what they said:

But who should speak to-day of the thing
That all knew there except the King?

Then pondering much they found a way,
And met round the King's high seat that day: 245

And the King sat with a heart sore stirred,
And seldom he spoke and seldom heard.

'Twas then through the hall the King was 'ware
Of a little boy with golden hair,

As bright as the golden poppy is   250
That the beach breeds for the surf to kiss:

Yet pale his cheek as the thorn in Spring,
And his garb black like the raven's wing.

Nothing heard but his foot through the hall,
For now the lords were silent all.   255

And the King wondered, and said, 'Alack!
Who sends me a fair boy dressed in black?

'Why, sweet heart, do you pace through the hall
As though my court were a funeral?'

Then lowly knelt the child at the dais,   260
And looked up weeping in the King's face.

'O wherefore black, O King, ye may say,
For white is the hue of death to-day.

'Your son and all his fellowship
Lie low in the sea with the White Ship.'   265

King Henry fell as a man struck dead;
And speechless still he stared from his bed
When to him next day my rede I read.

There's many an hour must needs beguile
A King's high heart that he should smile,—   270

Full many a lordly hour, full fain
Of his realm's rule and pride of his reign:—

But this King never smiled again.

By none but me can the tale be told,
The butcher of Rouen, poor Berold.   275
     (*Lands are swayed by a King on a throne.*)
'Twas a royal train put forth to sea,
Yet the tale can be told by none but me.
     (*The sea hath no King but God alone.*)

WILLIAM MORRIS
1834–1896
Atalanta's Race

ARGUMENT

Atalanta, daughter of King Schœneus, not willing to lose her virgin's
estate, made it a law to all suitors that they should run a race with
her in the public place, and if they failed to overcome her should die
unrevenged; and thus many brave men perished. At last came
Milanion, the son of Amphidamas, who, outrunning her with the
help of Venus, gained the virgin and wedded her.

Through thick Arcadian woods a hunter went,
Following the beasts up, on a fresh spring day;
But since his horn-tipped bow but seldom bent,
Now at the noontide nought had happed to slay,

Within a vale he called his hounds away,   5
Hearkening the echoes of his lone voice cling
About the cliffs and through the beech-trees ring.

But when they ended, still awhile he stood,
And but the sweet familiar thrush could hear,
And all the day-long noises of the wood,   10
And o'er the dry leaves of the vanished year
His hounds' feet pattering as they drew anear,
And heavy breathing from their heads low hung,
To see the mighty cornel bow unstrung.

Then smiling did he turn to leave the place,   15
But with his first step some new fleeting thought
A shadow cast across his sun-burnt face;
I think the golden net that April brought
From some warm world his wavering soul had caught;
For, sunk in vague sweet longing, did he go   20
Betwixt the trees with doubtful steps and slow.

Yet howsoever slow he went, at last
The trees grew sparser, and the wood was done;
Whereon one farewell backward look he cast,
Then, turning round to see what place was won,   25
With shaded eyes looked underneath the sun,
And o'er green meads and new-turned furrows brown
Beheld the gleaming of King Schœneus' town.

So thitherward he turned, and on each side
The folk were busy on the teeming land,   30
And man and maid from the brown furrows cried,
Or midst the newly-blossomed vines did stand,
And as the rustic weapon pressed the hand
Thought of the nodding of the well-filled ear,
Or how the knife the heavy bunch should shear.   35

Merry it was: about him sung the birds,
The spring flowers bloomed along the firm dry road,
The sleek-skinned mothers of the sharp-horned herds
Now for the barefoot milking-maidens lowed;

While from the freshness of his blue abode,   40
Glad his death-bearing arrows to forget,
The broad sun blazed, nor scattered plagues as yet.

Through such fair things unto the gates he came,
And found them open, as though peace were there;
Wherethrough, unquestioned of his race or name,
He entered, and along the streets 'gan fare,   46
Which at the first of folk were well-nigh bare;
But pressing on, and going more hastily,
Men hurrying too he 'gan at last to see.

Following the last of these, he still pressed on.   50
Until an open space he came unto,
Where wreaths of fame had oft been lost and won,
For feats of strength folk there were wont to do.
And now our hunter looked for something new,
Because the whole wide space was bare, and stilled
The high seats were, with eager people filled.   56

There with the others to a seat he gat,
Whence he beheld a broidered canopy,
'Neath which in fair array King Schœneus sat
Upon his throne with councillors thereby;   60
And underneath his well-wrought seat and high,
He saw a golden image of the sun,
A silver image of the Fleet-foot One.

A brazen altar stood beneath their feet
Whereon a thin flame flickered in the wind,   65
Nigh this a herald clad in raiment meet
Made ready even now his horn to wind,
By whom a huge man held a sword, entwined
With yellow flowers; these stood a little space
From off the altar, nigh the starting-place.   70

And there two runners did the sign abide
Foot set to foot— a young man slim and fair,
Crisp-haired, well-knit, with firm limbs often tried
In places where no man his strength may spare;

Dainty his thin coat was, and on his hair 75
A golden circlet of renown he wore,
And in his hand an olive garland bore.

But on this day with whom shall he contend?
A maid stood by him like Diana clad
When in the woods she lists her bow to bend, 80
Too fair for one to look on and be glad,
Who scarcely yet has thirty summers had,
If he must still behold her from afar;
Too fair to let the world live free from war.

She seemed all earthly matters to forget; 85
Of all tormenting lines her face was clear,
Her wide grey eyes upon the goal were set
Calm and unmoved as though no soul were near;
But her foe trembled as a man in fear,
Nor from her loveliness one moment turned 90
His anxious face with fierce desire that burned.

Now through the hush there broke the trumpet's
clang
Just as the setting sun made eventide.
Then from light feet a spurt of dust there sprang,
And swiftly were they running side by side; 95
But silent did the thronging folk abide
Until the turning-post was reached at last,
And round about it still abreast they passed.

But when the people saw how close they ran,
When half-way to the starting-point they were, 100
A cry of joy broke forth, whereat the man
Headed the white-foot runner, and drew near
Unto the very end of all his fear;
And scarce his straining feet the ground could feel,
And bliss unhoped for o'er his heart 'gan steal. 105

But midst the loud victorious shouts he heard
Her footsteps drawing nearer, and the sound
Of fluttering raiment, and thereat afeard

His flushed and eager face he turned around,
And even then he felt her past him bound   110
Fleet as the wind, but scarcely saw her there
Till on the goal she laid her fingers fair.

There stood she breathing like a little child
Amid some warlike clamour laid asleep,
For no victorious joy her red lips smiled,   115
Her cheek its wonted freshness did but keep;
No glance lit up her clear grey eyes and deep,
Though some divine thought softened all her face
As once more rang the trumpet through the place.

But her late foe stopped short amidst his course,
One moment gazed upon her piteously,   121
Then with a groan his lingering feet did force
To leave the spot whence he her eyes could see;
And, changed like one who knows his time must be
But short and bitter, without any word   125
He knelt before the bearer of the sword;

Then high rose up the gleaming deadly blade,
Bared of its flowers, and through the crowded place
Was silence now, and midst of it the maid
Went by the poor wretch at a gentle pace,   130
And he to hers upturned his sad white face;
Nor did his eyes behold another sight
Ere on his soul there fell eternal night.

So was the pageant ended, and all folk
Talking of this and that familiar thing   135
In little groups from that sad concourse broke,
For now the shrill bats were upon the wing,
And soon dark night would slay the evening,
And in dark gardens sang the nightingale
Her little-heeded, oft-repeated tale.   140

And with the last of all the hunter went,
Who, wondering at the strange sight he had seen,
Prayed an old man to tell him what it meant,
Both why the vanquished man so slain had been,

And if the maiden were an earthly queen,   145
Or rather what much more she seemed to be,
No sharer in the world's mortality.

'Stranger,' said he, 'I pray she soon may die
Whose lovely youth hath slain so many an one!
King Schœneus' daughter is she verily,   150
Who when her eyes first looked upon the sun
Was fain to end her life but new begun,
For he had vowed to leave but men alone
Sprung from his loins when he from earth was gone.

'Therefore he bade one leave her in the wood,   155
And let wild things deal with her as they might,
But this being done, some cruel god thought good
To save her beauty in the world's despite:
Folk say that her, so delicate and white
As now she is, a rough root-grubbing bear   160
Amidst her shapeless cubs at first did rear.

'In course of time the woodfolk slew her nurse,
And to their rude abode the youngling brought,
And reared her up to be a kingdom's curse;
Who grown a woman, of no kingdom thought,   165
But armed and swift, 'mid beasts destruction wrought,
Nor spared two shaggy centaur kings to slay
To whom her body seemed an easy prey.

'So to this city, led by fate, she came
Whom known by signs, whereof I cannot tell,   170
King Schœneus for his child at last did claim,
Nor otherwhere since that day doth she dwell
Sending too many a noble soul to hell—
What! thine eyes glisten! what then, thinkest thou
Her shining head unto the yoke to bow?   175

'Listen, my son, and love some other maid
For she the saffron gown will never wear,
And on no flower-strewn couch shall she be laid,
Nor shall her voice make glad a lover's ear:

Yet if of Death thou hast not any fear,   180
Yea, rather, if thou lov'st him utterly,
Thou still may'st woo her ere thou com'st to die,

'Like him that on this day thou sawest lie dead;
For, fearing as I deem the sea-born one,
The maid has vowed e'en such a man to wed   185
As in the course her swift feet can outrun,
But whoso fails herein, his days are done:
He came the nighest that was slain to-day,
Although with him I deem she did but play.

'Behold, such mercy Atalanta gives   190
To those that long to win her loveliness;
Be wise! be sure that many a maid there lives
Gentler than she, of beauty little less,
Whose swimming eyes thy loving words shall bless,
When in some garden, knee set close to knee,   195
Thou sing'st the song that love may teach to thee.'

So to the hunter spake that ancient man,
And left him for his own home presently:
But he turned round, and through the moonlight wan
Reached the thick wood, and there 'twixt tree and
        tree   200
Distraught he passed the long night feverishly,
'Twixt sleep and waking, and at dawn arose
To wage hot war against his speechless foes.

There to the hart's flank seemed his shaft to grow,
As panting down the broad green glades he flew,
There by his horn the Dryads well might know   206
His thrust against the bear's heart had been true,
And there Adonis' bane his javelin slew,
But still in vain through rough and smooth he went,
For none the more his restlessness was spent.   210

So wandering, he to Argive cities came,
And in the lists with valiant men he stood,
And by great deeds he won him praise and fame,

And heaps of wealth for little-valued blood;
But none of all these things, or life, seemed good   215
Unto his heart, where still unsatisfied
A ravenous longing warred with fear and pride.

Therefore it happed when but a month had gone
Since he had left King Schœneus' city old,
In hunting-gear again, again alone   220
The forest-bordered meads did he behold,
Where still mid thoughts of August's quivering gold
Folk hoed the wheat, and clipped the vine in trust
Of faint October's purple-foaming must.

And once again he passed the peaceful gate,   225
While to his beating heart his lips did lie,
That owning not victorious love and fate,
Said, half aloud, 'And here too must I try,
To win of alien men the mastery,
And gather for my head fresh meed of fame   230
And cast new glory on my father's name.'

In spite of that, how beat his heart, when first
Folk said to him, 'And art thou come to see
That which still makes our city's name accurst
Among all mothers for its cruelty?   235
Then know indeed that fate is good to thee
Because to-morrow a new luckless one
Against the whitefoot maid is pledged to run.'

So on the morrow with no curious eyes
As once he did, that piteous sight he saw,   240
Nor did that wonder in his heart arise
As toward the goal the conquering maid 'gan draw,
Nor did he gaze upon her eyes with awe,
Too full the pain of longing filled his heart
For fear or wonder there to have a part.   245

But O, how long the night was ere it went!
How long it was before the dawn begun
Showed to the wakening birds the sun's intent

That not in darkness should the world be done!
And then, and then, how long before the sun   250
Bade silently the toilers of the earth
Get forth to fruitless cares or empty mirth!

And long it seemed that in the market-place
He stood and saw the chaffering folk go by,
Ere from the ivory throne King Schœneus' face   255
Looked down upon the murmur royally,
But then came trembling that the time was nigh
When he midst pitying looks his love must claim,
And jeering voices must salute his name.

But as the throng he pierced to gain the throne,
His alien face distraught and anxious told   261
What hopeless errand he was bound upon,
And, each to each, folk whispered to behold
His godlike limbs; nay, and one woman old
As he went by must pluck him by the sleeve   265
And pray him yet that wretched love to leave.

For sidling up she said, 'Canst thou live twice,
Fair son? canst thou have joyful youth again,
That thus thou goest to the sacrifice
Thyself the victim? nay then, all in vain   270
Thy mother bore her longing and her pain,
And one more maiden on the earth must dwell
Hopeless of joy, nor fearing death and hell.

'O, fool, thou knowest not the compact then
That with the threeformed goddess she has made
To keep her from the loving lips of men,   276
And in no saffron gown to be arrayed,
And therewithal with glory to be paid,
And love of her the moonlit river sees
White 'gainst the shadow of the formless trees. 280

'Come back, and I myself will pray for thee
Unto the sea-born framer of delights,
To give thee her who on the earth may be
The fairest stirrer up to death and fights,

To quench with hopeful days and joyous nights   285
The flame that doth thy youthful heart consume:
Come back, nor give thy beauty to the tomb.'

How should he listen to her earnest speech?
Words, such as he not once or twice had said
Unto himself, whose meaning scarce could reach
The firm abode of that sad hardihead—   291
He turned about, and through the marketstead
Swiftly he passed, until before the throne
In the cleared space he stood at last alone.

Then said the King. 'Stranger, what dost thou
here?   295
Have any of my folk done ill to thee?
Or art thou of the forest men in fear?
Or art thou of the sad fraternity
Who still will strive my daughter's mates to be,
Staking their lives to win to earthly bliss   300
The lonely maid, the friend of Artemis?'

'O King,' he said, 'thou sayest the word indeed;
Nor will I quit the strife till I have won
My sweet delight, or death to end my need.
And know that I am called Milanion,   305
Of King Amphidamas the well-loved son:
So fear not that to thy old name, O King,
Much loss or shame my victory will bring.'

'Nay Prince,' said Schœneus, 'welcome to this land
Thou wert indeed, if thou wert here to try   310
Thy strength 'gainst some one mighty of his hand;
Nor would we grudge thee well-won mastery.
But now, why wilt thou come to me to die,
And at my door lay down thy luckless head,
Swelling the band of the unhappy dead,   315

'Whose curses even now my heart doth fear?
Lo, I am old, and know what life can be,
And what a bitter thing is death anear.

O Son! be wise, and hearken unto me,
And if no other can be dear to thee,   320
At least as now, yet is the world full wide,
And bliss in seeming hopeless hearts may hide:

'But if thou losest life, then all is lost.'
'Nay, King,' Milanion said, 'thy words are vain.
Doubt not that I have counted well the cost.   325
But say, on what day wilt thou that I gain
Fulfilled delight, or death to end my pain.
Right glad were I if it could be to-day,
And all my doubts at rest for ever lay.'

'Nay,' said King Schœneus, 'thus it shall not be,
But rather thou shalt let a month go by,   331
And weary with thy prayers for victory
What god thou know'st the kindest and most nigh.
So doing, still perchance thou shalt not die:
And with my goodwill wouldst thou have the maid,
For of the equal gods I grow afraid.   336

'And until then, O Prince, be thou my guest,
And all these troublous things awhile forget.'
'Nay,' said he, 'couldst thou give my soul good rest,
And on mine head a sleepy garland set,   340
Then had I 'scaped the meshes of the net,
Nor shouldst thou hear from me another word;
But now, make sharp thy fearful heading-sword.

'Yet will I do what son of man may do,
And promise all the gods may most desire.   345
That to myself I may at least be true;
And on that day my heart and limbs so tire,
With utmost strain and measureless desire,
That, at the worst, I may but fall asleep
When in the sunlight round that sword shall sweep.

He went therewith, nor anywhere would bide,   351
But unto Argos restlessly did wend;
And there, as one who lays all hope aside,

Because the leech has said his life must end,
Silent farewell he bade to foe and friend,   355
And took his way unto the restless sea,
For there he deemed his rest and help might be.

Upon the shore of Argolis there stands
A temple to the goddess that he sought,
That, turned into the lion-bearing lands,   360
Fenced from the east, of cold winds hath no thought,
Though to no homestead there the sheaves are
          brought,
No groaning press torments the close-clipped murk,
Lonely the fane stands, far from all men's work.

Pass through a close, set thick with myrtle-trees,
Through the brass doors that guard the holy place,
And entering hear the washing of the seas   367
That twice a-day rise high above the base,
And with the south-west urging them, embrace
The marble feet of her that standeth there   370
That shrink not, naked though they be and fair.

Small is the fane through which the seawind sings
About Queen Venus' well-wrought image white,
But hung around are many precious things,
The gifts of those who, longing for delight,   375
Have hung them there within the goddess' sight,
And in return have taken at her hands
The living treasures of the Grecian lands.

And thither now has come Milanion,
And showed unto the priests' wide open eyes   380
Gifts fairer than all those that there have shone,
Silk cloths, inwrought with Indian fantasies,
And bowls inscribed with sayings of the wise
Above the deeds of foolish living things;
And mirrors fit to be the gifts of kings.   385

And now before the Sea-born One he stands,
By the sweet veiling smoke made dim and soft,

And while the incense trickles from his hands,
And while the odorous smoke-wreaths hang aloft,
Thus doth he pray to her: 'O Thou, who oft   390
Hast holpen man and maid in their distress
Despise me not for this my wretchedness!

'O goddess, among us who dwell below,
Kings and great men, great for a little while,
Have pity on the lowly heads that bow,   395
Nor hate the hearts that love them without guile;
Wilt thou be worse than these, and is thy smile
A vain device of him who set thee here,
An empty dream of some artificer?

'O, great one, some men love, and are ashamed;
Some men are weary of the bonds of love;   401
Yea, and by some men lightly art thou blamed,
That from thy toils their lives they cannot move,
And 'mid the ranks of men their manhood prove.
Alas! O goddess, if thou slayest me   405
What new immortal can I serve but thee?

'Think then, will it bring honour to thy head
If folk say, "Everything aside he cast
And to all fame and honour was he dead,
And to his one hope now is dead at last,   410
Since all unholpen he is gone and past:
Ah, the gods love not man, for certainly,
He to his helper did not cease to cry."

'Nay, but thou wilt help; they who died before
Not single-hearted as I deem came here,   415
Therefore unthanked they laid their gifts before
Thy stainless feet, still shivering with their fear,
Lest in their eyes their true thought might appear,
Who sought to be the lords of that fair town,
Dreaded of men and winners of renown.   420

'O Queen, thou knowest I pray not for this:
O set us down together in some place

Where not a voice can break our heaven of bliss,
Where nought but rocks and I can see her face,
Softening beneath the marvel of thy grace,   425
Where not a foot our vanished steps can track—
The golden age, the golden age come back!

   'O fairest, hear me now who do thy will,
Plead for thy rebel that she be not slain,
But live and love and be thy servant still;   430
Ah, give her joy and take away my pain,
And thus two long-enduring servants gain.
An easy thing this is to do for me,
What need of my vain words to weary thee.

   'But none the less, this place I will not leave   435
Until I needs must go my death to meet,
Or at thy hands some happy sign receive
That in great joy we twain may one day greet
Thy presence here and kiss thy silver feet,
Such as we deem thee, fair beyond all words,   440
Victorious o'er our servants and our lords.'

   Then from the altar back a space he drew,
But from the Queen turned not his face away,
But 'gainst a pillar leaned, until the blue
That arched the sky, at ending of the day,   445
Was turned to ruddy gold and changing grey,
And clear, but low, the nigh-ebbed windless sea
In the still evening murmured ceaselessly.

   And there he stood when all the sun was down,
Nor had he moved, when the dim golden light,   450
Like the far lustre of a godlike town,
Had left the world to seeming hopeless night,
Nor would he move the more when wan moonlight
Streamed through the pillars for a little while,
And lighted up the white Queen's changeless smile.

   Nought noted he the shallow-flowing sea   456
As step by step it set the wrack a-swim;

The yellow torchlight nothing noted he
Wherein with fluttering gown and half-bared limb
The temple damsels sung their midnight hymn;   460
And nought the doubled stillness of the fane
When they were gone and all was hushed again.

But when the waves had touched the marble base,
And steps the fish swim over twice a-day,
The dawn beheld him sunken in his place   465
Upon the floor; and sleeping there he lay,
Not heeding aught the little jets of spray
The roughened sea brought nigh, across him cast,
For as one dead all thought from him had passed.

Yet long before the sun had showed his head,   470
Long ere the varied hangings on the wall
Had gained once more their blue and green and red,
He rose as one some well-known sign doth call
When war upon the city's gates doth fall,
And scarce like one fresh risen out of sleep, 475
He 'gan again his broken watch to keep.

Then he turned round; not for the sea-gull's cry
That wheeled above the temple in his flight,
Not for the fresh south wind that lovingly
Breathed on the new-born day and dying night, 480
But some strange hope 'twixt fear and great delight
Drew round his face, now flushed, now pale and wan,
And still constrained his eyes the sea to scan.

Now a faint light lit up the southern sky,
Not sun or moon, for all the world was grey,   485
But this a bright cloud seemed, that drew anigh,
Lighting the dull waves that beneath it lay
As toward the temple still it took its way,
And still grew greater, till Milanion
Saw nought for dazzling light that round him shone.

But as he staggered with his arms outspread,   491
Delicious unnamed odours breathed around,

For languid happiness he bowed his head,
And with wet eyes sank down upon the ground,
Nor wished for aught, nor any dream he found   495
To give him reason for that happiness,
Or make him ask more knowledge of his bliss.

At last his eyes were cleared, and he could see
Through happy tears the goddess face to face
With that faint image of Divinity,   500
Whose well-wrought smile and dainty changeless
    grace
Until that morn so gladdened all the place;
Then he unwitting cried aloud her name
And covered up his eyes for fear and shame.

But through the stillness he her voice could hear
Piercing his heart with joy scarce bearable,   506
That said, 'Milanion, wherefore dost thou fear,
I am not hard to those who love me well;
List to what I a second time will tell,
And thou mayest hear perchance, and live to save
The cruel maiden from a loveless grave.   511

'See, by my feet three golden apples lie—
Such fruit among the heavy roses falls,
Such fruit my watchful damsels carefully
Store up within the best loved of my walls,   515
Ancient Damascus, where the lover calls
Above my unseen head, and faint and light
The rose-leaves flutter round me in the night.

'And note, that these are not alone most fair
With heavenly gold, but longing strange they bring
Unto the hearts of men, who will not care   521
Beholding these, for any once-loved thing
Till round the shining sides their fingers cling.
And thou shalt see thy well-girt swiftfoot maid
By sight of these amidst her glory stayed.   525

'For bearing these within a scrip with thee,
When first she heads thee from the starting-place
Cast down the first one for her eyes to see,
And when she turns aside make on apace,
And if again she heads thee in the race   530
Spare not the other two to cast aside
If she not long enough behind will bide.

'Farewell, and when has come the happy time
That she Diana's raiment must unbind
And all the world seems blessed with Saturn's clime,
And thou with eager arms about her twined   536
Beholdest first her grey eyes growing kind,
Surely, O trembler, thou shalt scarcely then
Forget the Helper of unhappy men.'

Milanion raised his head at this last word   540
For now so soft and kind she seemed to be
No longer of her Godhead was he feared;
Too late he looked; for nothing could he see
But the white image glimmering doubtfully
In that departing twilight cold and grey,   545
And those three apples on the steps that lay.

These then he caught up quivering with delight,
Yet fearful lest it all might be a dream;
And though aweary with the watchful night,
And sleepless nights of longing, still did deem   550
He could not sleep; but yet the first sunbeam
That smote the fane across the heaving deep
Shone on him laid in calm untroubled sleep.

But little ere the noontide did he rise,
And why he felt so happy scarce could tell   555
Until the gleaming apples met his eyes.
Then leaving the fair place where this befell
Oft he looked back as one who loved it well,
Then homeward to the haunts of men 'gan wend
To bring all things to a happy end.   560

Now has the lingering month at last gone by,
Again are all folk round the running place,
Nor other seems the dismal pageantry
Than heretofore, but that another face
Looks o'er the smooth course ready for the race,   565
For now, beheld of all, Milanion
Stands on the spot he twice has looked upon.

But yet—what change is this that holds the maid?
Does she indeed see in his glittering eye
More than disdain of the sharp shearing blade,   570
Some happy hope of help and victory?
The others seemed to say, 'We come to die,
Look down upon us for a little while,
That dead, we may bethink us of thy smile.'

But he—what look of mastery was this   575
He cast on her? why were his lips so red?
Why was his face so flushed with happiness?
So looks not one who deems himself but dead,
E'en if to death he bows a willing head;
So rather looks a god well pleased to find   580
Some earthly damsel fashioned to his mind.

Why must she drop her lids before his gaze,
And even as she casts adown her eyes
Redden to note his eager glance of praise,
And wish that she were clad in other guise?   585
Why must the memory to her heart arise
Of things unnoticed when they first were heard,
Some lover's song, some answering maiden's word?

What makes these longings, vague, without a name,
And this vain pity never felt before,   590
This sudden languor, this contempt of fame,
This tender sorrow for the time past o'er,
These doubts that grow each minute more and more?
Why does she tremble as the time grows near,
And weak defeat and woeful victory fear?   595

Now while she seemed to hear her beating heart,
Above their heads the trumpet blast rang out
And forth they sprang; and she must play her part.
Then flew her white feet, knowing not a doubt,
Though slackening once, she turned her head about,
But then she cried aloud and faster fled   601
Than e'er before, and all men deemed him dead.

But with no sound he raised aloft his hand,
And thence what seemed a ray of light there flew
And past the maid rolled on along the sand;   605
Then trembling she her feet together drew
And in her heart a strong desire there grew
To have the toy; some god she thought had given
That gift to her, to make of earth a heaven.

Then from the course with eager steps she ran,
And in her odorous bosom laid the gold.   611
But when she turned again, the great-limbed man,
Now well ahead she failed not to behold,
And mindful of her glory waxing cold,
Sprang up and followed him in hot pursuit   615
Though with one hand she touched the golden fruit.

Note too, the bow that she was wont to bear
She laid aside to grasp the glittering prize,
And o'er her shoulder from the quiver fair
Three arrows fell and lay before her eyes   620
Unnoticed, as amidst the people's cries
She sprang to head the strong Milanion,
Who now the turning post had well-nigh won.

But as he set his mighty hand on it
White fingers underneath his own were laid,   625
And white limbs from his dazzled eyes did flit,
Then he the second fruit cast by the maid:
She ran awhile, and then as one afraid
Wavered and stopped, and turned and made no stay,
Until the globe with its bright fellow lay.   630

Then, as a troubled glance she cast around
Now far ahead the Argive could she see,
And in her garment's hem one hand she wound
To keep the double prize, and strenuously
Sped o'er the course, and little doubt had she   635
To win the day, though now but scanty space
Was left betwixt him and the winning place.

Short was the way unto such winged feet,
Quickly she gained upon him till at last
He turned about her eager eyes to meet   640
And from his hand the third fair apple cast.
She wavered not, but turned and ran so fast
After the prize that should her bliss fulfil,
That in her hand it lay ere it was still.

Nor did she rest, but turned about to win   645
Once more, an unblest woeful victory—
And yet—and yet—why does her breath begin
To fail her, and her feet drag heavily?
Why fails she now to see if far or nigh
The goal is? why do her grey eyes grow dim?   650
Why do these tremors run through every limb?

She spreads her arms abroad some stay to find
Else must she fall, indeed, and findeth this,
A strong man's arms about her body twined.
Nor may she shudder now to feel his kiss,   655
So wrapped she is in new unbroken bliss:
Made happy that the foe the prize hath won,
She weeps glad tears for all her glory done.

Shatter the trumpet, hew adown the posts!
Upon the brazen altar break the sword,   660
And scatter incense to appease the ghosts
Of those who died here by their own award.
Bring forth the image of the mighty Lord,
And her who unseen o'er the runners hung,
And did a deed for ever to be sung.   665

Here are the gathered folk; make no delay,
Open King Schœneus' well-filled treasury,
Bring out the gifts long hid from light of day,
The golden bowls o'erwrought with imagery,
Gold chains, and unguents brought from over sea,
The saffron gown the old Phœnician brought, 671
Within the temple of the Goddess wrought.

O ye, O damsels, who shall never see
Her, that Love's servant bringeth now to you,
Returning from another victory, 675
In some cool bower do all that now is due!
Since she in token of her service new
Shall give to Venus offerings rich enow,
Her maiden zone, her arrows, and her bow.

   .   .   .   .

So when his last word's echo died away, 680
The growing wind at end of that wild day
Alone they heard, for silence bound them all;
Yea, on their hearts a weight had seemed to fall,
As unto the scarce-hoped felicity
The tale grew round—the end of life so nigh, 685
The aim so little, and the joy so vain—
For as a child's unmeasured joy brings pain
Unto a grown man holding grief at bay,
So the old fervent story of that day
Brought pain half-sweet, to these: till now the fire
Upon the hearth sent up a flickering spire 691
Of ruddy flame, as fell the burned-through logs,
And, waked by sudden silence, grey old dogs,
The friends of this or that man, rose and fawned
On hands they knew; withal once more there dawned
The light of common day on those old hearts, 696
And all were ready now to play their parts,
And take what feeble joy might yet remain
In place of all they once had hoped to gain.

Now on the second day that these did meet 700
March was a-dying through soft days and sweet,

Too hopeful for the wild days yet to be;
But in the hall that ancient company,
Not lacking younger folk that day at least,
Softened by spring were gathered at the feast,   705
And as the time drew on, throughout the hall
A horn was sounded, giving note to all
That they at last the looked-for tale should hear.

Then spake a wanderer, 'O kind hosts and dear,
Hearken a little unto such a tale   710
As folk with us will tell in every vale
About the yule-tide fire, whenas the snow
Deep in the passes, letteth men to go
From place to place: now there few great folks be,
Although we upland men have memory   715
Of ills kings did us; yet as now indeed
Few have much wealth, few are in utter need.
Like the wise ants a kingless, happy folk
We long have been, not galled by any yoke,
But the white leaguer of the winter tide   720
Whereby all men at home are bound to bide.
—Alas, my folly! how I talk of it,
As though from this place where to-day we sit
The way thereto were short—Ah, would to God
Upon the snow-freed herbage now I trod!   725
But pardon, sirs; the time goes swiftly by,
Hearken a tale of conquering destiny.'

ALGERNON CHARLES SWINBURNE

1837–1909

St. Dorothy

It hath been seen and yet it shall be seen
That out of tender mouths God's praise hath been
Made perfect, and with wood and simple string
He hath played music sweet as shawm-playing
To please himself with softness of all sound;   5

And no small thing but hath been sometime found
Full sweet of use, and no such humbleness
But God hath bruised withal the sentences
And evidence of wise men witnessing;
No leaf that is so soft a hidden thing 10
It never shall get sight of the great sun;
The strength of ten has been the strength of one,
And lowliness has waxed imperious.

There was in Rome a man Theophilus
Of right great blood and gracious ways, that had 15
All noble fashions to make people glad
And a soft life of pleasurable days;
He was a goodly man for one to praise,
Flawless and whole upward from foot to head:
His arms were a red hawk that alway fed 20
On a small bird with feathers gnawed upon,
Beaten and plucked about the bosom-bone
Whereby a small round fleck like fire there was;
They called it in their tongue lampadias;
This was the banner of the lordly man. 25
In many straits of sea and reaches wan
Full of quick wind, and many a shaken firth,
It had seen fighting days of either earth,
Westward or east of waters Gaditane
(This was the place of sea-rocks under Spain 30
Called after the great praise of Hercules)
And north beyond the washing Pontic seas,
Far windy Russian places fabulous,
And salt fierce tides of storm-swoln Bosphorus.

Now as this lord came straying in Rome town 35
He saw a little lattice open down
And after it a press of maidens' heads
That sat upon their cold small quiet beds
Talking, and played upon short-strindgèd lutes;
And other some ground perfume out of roots 40
Gathered by marvellous moons in Asia;
Saffron and aloes and wild cassia,
Coloured all through and smelling of the sun;
And over all these was a certain one

Clothed softly, with sweet herbs about her hair 45
And bosom flowerful; her face more fair
Than sudden-singing April in soft lands:
Eyed like a gracious bird, and in both hands
She held a psalter painted green and red.

This Theophile laughed at the heart, and said, 50
Now God so help me hither and St. Paul,
As by the new time of their festival
I have good will to take this maid to wife.
And herewith fell to fancies of her life
And soft half-thoughts that ended suddenly. 55
This is man's guise to please himself, when he
Shall not see one thing of his pleasant things,
Nor with outwatch of many travailings
Come to be eased of the least pain he hath
For all his love and all his foolish wrath 60
And all the heavy manner of his mind.
Thus is he like a fisher fallen blind
That casts his nets across the boat awry
To strike the sea, but lo, he striketh dry
And plucks them back all broken for his pain 65
And bites his beard and casts across again
And reaching wrong slips over in the sea.
So hath this man a strangled neck for fee,
For all his cost he chuckles in his throat.

This Theophile that little hereof wote 70
Laid wait to hear of her what she might be:
Men told him she had name of Dorothy,
And was a lady of a worthy house.
Thereat this knight grew inly glorious
That he should have a love so fair of place. 75
She was a maiden of most quiet face,
Tender of speech, and had no hardihood
But was nigh feeble of her fearful blood;
Her mercy in her was so marvellous
From her least years, that seeing her school-fellows
That read beside her stricken with a rod, 81
She would cry sore and say some word to God
That he would ease her fellow of his pain.

There is no touch of sun or fallen rain
That ever fell on a more gracious thing.   85
  In middle Rome there was in stone-working
The church of Venus painted royally.
The chapels of it were some two or three,
In each of them her tabernacle was
And a wide window of six feet in glass   90
Coloured with all her works in red and gold.
The altars had bright cloths and cups to hold
The wine of Venus for the services,
Made out of honey and crushed wood-berries
That shed sweet yellow through the thick wet red,
That on high days was borne upon the head   96
Of Venus' priest for any man to drink;
So that in drinking he should fall to think
On some fair face, and in the thought thereof
Worship, and such should triumph in his love.   100
For this soft wine that did such grace and good
Was new trans-shaped and mixed with Love's own
          blood,
That in the fighting Trojan time was bled;
For which came such a woe to Diomed
That he was stifled after in hard sea.   105
And some said that this wine-shedding should be
Made of the falling of Adonis' blood,
That curled upon the thorns and broken wood
And round the gold silk shoes on Venus' feet;
The taste thereof was as hot honey sweet,   110
And in the mouth ran soft and riotous.
This was the holiness of Venus' house.
  It was their worship, that in August days
Twelve maidens should go through those **Roman**
          ways
Naked, and having gold across their brows   115
And their hair twisted in short golden rows,
To minister to Venus in this wise:
And twelve men chosen in their companies
To match these maidens by the altar-stair,
All in one habit, crowned upon the hair.   120

Among these men was chosen Theophile.
　This knight went out and prayed a little while,
Holding queen Venus by her hands and knees;
I will give thee twelve royal images
Cut in glad gold, with marvels of wrought stone　125
For thy sweet priests to lean and pray upon,
Jasper and hyacinth and chrysopras,
And the strange Asian thalamite that was
Hidden twelve ages under heavy sea
Among the little sleepy pearls, to be　　　　　130
A shrine lit over with soft candle-flame
Burning all night red as hot brows of shame,
So thou wilt be my lady without sin.
Goddess that art all gold outside and in,
Help me to serve thee in thy holy way.　　　　135
Thou knowest, Love, that in my bearing day
There shone a laughter in the singing stars
Round the gold-ceilèd bride-bed wherein Mars
Touched thee and had thee in your kissing wise.
Now therefore, sweet, kiss thou my maiden's eyes
That they may open graciously towards me;　　141
And this new fashion of thy shrine shall be
As soft with gold as thine own happy head.
　The goddess, that was painted with face red
Between two long green tumbled sides of sea,　145
Stooped her neck sideways, and spake pleasantly:
Thou shalt have grace as thou art thrall of mine.
And with this came a savour of shed wine
And plucked-out petals from a rose's head:
And softly with slow laughs of lip she said,　　150
Thou shalt have favour all thy days of me.
　Then came Theophilus to Dorothy,
Saying: O sweet, if one should strive or speak
Against God's ways, he gets a beaten cheek
For all his wage and shame above all men.　　　155
Therefore I have no will to turn again
When God saith 'go', lest a worse thing fall out.
Then she, misdoubting lest he went about
To catch her wits, made answer somewhat thus:

I have no will, my lord Theophilus,   160
To speak against this worthy word of yours;
Knowing how God's will in all speech endures,
That save by grace there may no thing be said.
Then Theophile waxed light from foot to head,
And softly fell upon this answering.   165
It is well seen you are a chosen thing
To do God service in his gracious way.
I will that you make haste and holiday
To go next year upon the Venus stair,
Covered none else, but crowned upon your hair,   170
And do the service that a maiden doth.
She said: but I that am Christ's maid were loth
To do this thing that hath such bitter name.
Thereat his brows were beaten with sore shame
And he came off and said no other word.   175
Then his eyes chanced upon his banner-bird,
And he fell fingering at the staff of it
And laughed for wrath and stared between his feet,
And out of a chafed heart he spake as thus:
Lo how she japes at me Theophilus,   180
Feigning herself a fool and hard to love;
Yet in good time for all she boasteth of
She shall be like a little beaten bird.
And while his mouth was open in that word
He came upon the house Janiculum,   185
Where some went busily, and other some
Talked in the gate called the gate glorious.
The emperor, which was one Gabalus,
Sat over all and drank chill wine alone.
To whom is come Theophilus anon,   190
And said as thus: *Beau sire, Dieu vous aide.*
And afterward sat under him, and said
All this thing through as ye have wholly heard.
   This Gabalus laughed thickly in his beard.
Yea, this is righteousness and maiden rule.   195
Truly, he said, a maid is but a fool.
And japed at them as one full villainous,
In a lewd wise, this heathen Gabalus,

And sent his men to bind her as he bade.
Thus have they taken Dorothy the maid,　　200
And haled her forth as men hale pick-purses:
A little need God knows they had of this,
To hale her by her maiden gentle hair.
Thus went she lowly, making a soft prayer,
As one who stays the sweet wine in his mouth,　　205
Murmuring with eased lips, and is most loth
To have done wholly with the sweet of it.

　Christ king, fair Christ, that knowest all men's wit
And all the feeble fashion of my ways,
O perfect God, that from all yesterdays　　210
Abidest whole with morrows perfected,
I pray thee by thy mother's holy head
Thou help me to do right, that I not slip:
I have no speech nor strength upon my lip,
Except thou help me who art wise and sweet.　　215
Do this too for those nails that clove thy feet,
Let me die maiden after many pains.
Though I be least among thy handmaidens,
Doubtless I shall take death more sweetly thus.

　Now have they brought her to King Gabalus,　　220
Who laughed in all his throat some breathing-whiles:
By God, he said, if one should leap two miles,
He were not pained about the sides so much.
This were a soft thing for a man to touch.
Shall one so chafe that hath such little bones?　　225
And shook his throat with thick and chuckled moans
For laughter that she had such holiness.
What aileth thee, wilt thou do services?
It were good fare to fare as Venus doth.

　Then said this lady with her maiden mouth,　　230
Shamefaced, and something paler in the cheek:
Now, sir, albeit my wit and will to speak
Give me no grace in sight of worthy men,
For all my shame yet know I this again,
I may not speak, nor after downlying　　235
Rise up to take delight in lute-playing,
Nor sing nor sleep, nor sit and fold my hands,

But my soul in some measure understands
God's grace laid like a garment over me.
For this fair God that out of strong sharp sea   240
Lifted the shapely and green-coloured land,
And hath the weight of heaven in his hand
As one might hold a bird, and under him
The heavy golden planets beam by beam
Building the feasting-chambers of his house,   245
And the large world he holdeth with his brows,
And with the light of them astonisheth
All place and time and face of life and death
And motion of the north wind and the south,
And is the sound within his angel's mouth   250
Of singing words and words of thanksgiving,
And is the colour of the latter spring
And heat upon the summer and the sun,
And is beginning of all things begun
And gathers in him all things to their end,   255
And with the fingers of his hand doth bend
The stretched-out sides of heaven like a sail,
And with his breath he maketh the red pale
And fills with blood faint faces of men dead,
And with the sound between his lips are fed   260
Iron and fire and the white body of snow,
And blossom of all trees in places low,
And small bright herbs about the little hills,
And fruit pricked softly with birds' tender bills,
And flight of foam about green fields of sea,   265
And fourfold strength of the great winds that be
Moved always outward from beneath his feet,
And growth of grass and growth of sheavèd wheat
And all green flower of goodly-growing lands;
And all these things he gathers with his hands   270
And covers all their beauty with his wings;
The same, even God that governs all these things,
Hath set my feet to be upon his ways.
Now therefore for no painfulness of days
I shall put off this service bound on me.   275
Also, fair sir, ye know this certainly,

How God was in his flesh full chaste and meek
And gave his face to shame, and either cheek
Gave up to smiting of men tyrannous.
    And here with a great voice this Gabalus   280
Cried out and said: By God's blood and his bones,
This were good game betwixen night and nones
For one to sit and hearken to such saws:
I were as lief fall in some big beast's jaws
As hear these women's jaw-teeth chattering;   285
By God a woman is the harder thing,
One may not put a hook into her mouth.
Now by St. Luke I am so sore adrouth
For all these saws I must needs drink again.
But I pray God deliver all us men   290
From all such noise of women and their heat.
That is a noble scripture, well I weet,
That likens women to an empty can;
When God said that he was a full wise man.
I trow no man may blame him as for that.   295
    And herewithal he drank a draught, and spat,
And said: Now shall I make an end hereof.
Come near all men and hearken for God's love,
And ye shall hear a jest or twain, God wot.
And spake as thus with mouth full thick and hot;
But thou do this thou shalt be shortly slain.   301
Lo, sir, she said, this death and all his pain
I take in penance of my bitter sins.
Yea now, quoth Gabalus, this game begins.
Lo, without sin one shall not live a span.   305
Lo, this is she that would not look on man
Between her fingers folded in thwart wise.
See how her shame hath smitten in her eyes
That was so clean she had not heard of shame.
Certes, he said, by Gabalus my name,   310
This two years back I was not so well pleased.
This were good mirth for sick men to be eased
And rise up whole and laugh at hearing of.
I pray thee show us something of thy love,
Since thou wast maid thy gown is waxen wide.   315

Yea, maid I am, she said, and somewhat sighed,
As one who thought upon the low fair house
Where she sat working, with soft bended brows
Watching her threads, among the school-maidens.
And she thought well now God had brought her
    thence   320
She should not come to sew her gold again.
  Then cried King Gabalus upon his men
To have her forth and draw her with steel gins.
And as a man hag-ridden beats and grins
And bends his body sidelong in his bed,   325
So wagged he with his body and knave's head,
Gaping at her, and blowing with his breath.
And in good time he gat an evil death
Out of his lewdness with his cursèd wives:
His bones were hewn asunder as with knives   330
For his misliving, certes it is said.
But all the evil wrought upon this maid,
It were full hard for one to handle it.
For her soft blood was shed upon her feet,
And all her body's colour bruised and faint.   335
But she, as one abiding God's great saint,
Spake not nor wept for all this travail hard.
Wherefore the King commanded afterward
To slay her presently in all men's sight.
And it was now an hour upon the night   340
And winter-time, and a few stars began.
The weather was yet feeble and all wan
For beating of a weighty wind and snow.
And she came walking in soft wise and slow,
And many men with faces piteous.   345
Then came this heavy cursing Gabalus,
That swore full hard into his drunken beard;
And faintly after without any word
Came Theophile some paces off the king.
And in the middle of this wayfaring   350
Full tenderly beholding her he said:
  There is no word of comfort with men dead
Nor any face and colour of things sweet;

But always with lean cheeks and lifted feet
These dead men lie all aching to the blood   355
With bitter cold, their brows withouten hood
Beating for chill, their bodies swathed full thin:
Alas, what hire shall any have herein
To give his life and get such bitterness?
Also the soul going forth bodiless   360
Is hurt with naked cold, and no man saith
If there be house or covering for death
To hide the soul that is discomforted.
    Then she beholding him a little said:
Alas, fair lord, ye have no wit of this;   365
For on one side death is full poor of bliss
And as ye say full sharp of bone and lean:
But on the other side is good and green
And hath soft flower of tender-coloured hair
Grown on his head, and a red mouth as fair   370
As may be kissed with lips; thereto his face
Is as God's face, and in a perfect place
Full of all sun and colour of straight boughs
And waterheads about a painted house
That hath a mile of flowers either way   375
Outward from it, and blossom-grass of May
Thickening on many a side for length of heat,
Hath God set death upon a noble seat
Covered with green and flowered in the fold,
In likeness of a great king grown full old   380
And gentle with new temperance of blood;
And on his brows a purfled purple hood,
They may not carry any golden thing;
And plays some tune with subtle fingering
On a small cithern, full of tears and sleep   385
And heavy pleasure that is quick to weep
And sorrow with the honey in her mouth;
And for this might of music that he doth
Are all souls drawn toward him with great love
And weep for sweetness of the noise thereof   390
And bow to him with worship of their knees;
And all the field is thick with companies

Of fair-clothed men that play on shawms and lutes
And gather honey of the yellow fruits
Between the branches waxen soft and wide: 395
And all this peace endures in either side
Of the green land, and God beholdeth all.
And this is girdled with a round fair wall
Made of red stone and cool with heavy leaves
Grown out against it, and green blossom cleaves   400
To the green chinks, and lesser wall-weed sweet,
Kissing the crannies that are split with heat,
And branches where the summer draws to head.

    And Theophile burnt in the cheek, and said:
Yea, could one see it, this were marvellous.   405
I pray you, at your coming to this house,
Give me some leaf of all those tree-branches;
Seeing how so sharp and white our weather is,
There is no green nor gracious red to see.

    Yea, sir, she said, that shall I certainly.   410
And from her long sweet throat without a fleck
Undid the gold, and through her stretched-out neck
The cold axe clove, and smote away her head:
Out of her throat the tender blood full red
Fell suddenly through all her long soft hair.   415
And with good speed for hardness of the air
Each man departed to his house again.

    Lo, as fair colour in the face of men
At seed-time of their blood, or in such wise
As a thing seen increaseth in men's eyes,   420
Caught first far off by sickly fits of sight,
So a word said, if one shall hear aright,
Abides against the season of its growth.
This Theophile went slowly as one doth
That is not sure for sickness of his feet;   425
And counting the white stonework of the street,
Tears fell out of his eyes for wrath and love,
Making him weep more for the shame thereof
Than for true pain: so went he half a mile.
And women mocked him, saying: Theophile,   430
Lo, she is dead; what shall a woman have

That loveth such an one? so Christ me save,
I were as lief to love a man new-hung.
Surely this man has bitten on his tongue,
This makes him sad and writhled in his face.   435
    And when they came upon the paven place
That was called sometime the place amorous
There came a child before Theophilus
Bearing a basket, and said suddenly:
Fair sir, this is my mistress Dorothy   440
That sends you gifts; and with this he was gone.
In all this earth there is not such an one
For colour and straight stature made so fair.
The tender growing gold of his pure hair
Was as wheat growing, and his mouth as flame.   445
God called him Holy after his own name;
With gold cloth like fire burning he was clad.
But for the fair green basket that he had,
It was filled up with heavy white and red;
Great roses stained still where the first rose bled,
Burning at heart for shame their heart withholds:
And the sad colour of strong marigolds   452
That have the sun to kiss their lips for love;
The flower that Venus' hair is woven of,
The colour of fair apples in the sun,   455
Late peaches gathered when the heat was done
And the slain air got breath; and after these
The fair faint-headed poppies drunk with ease,
And heaviness of hollow lilies red.
    Then cried they all that saw these things, and said
It was God's doing, and was marvellous.   461
And in brief while this knight Theophilus
Is waxen full of faith, and witnesseth
Before the king of God and love and death,
For which the king bade hang him presently.   465
A gallows of a goodly piece of tree
This Gabalus hath made to hang him on.
Forth of this world lo Theophile is gone
With a wried neck, God give us better fare
Than his that hath a twisted throat to wear;   470

But truly for his love God hath him brought
There where his heavy body grieves him nought
Nor all the people plucking at his feet;
But in his face his lady's face is sweet,
And through his lips her kissing lips are gone: 475
God send him peace, and joy of such an one.
   This is the story of St. Dorothy.
I will you of your mercy pray for me
Because I wrote these sayings for your grace,
That I may one day see her in the face.   480

AUSTIN DOBSON

1840–1921

The Ballad of 'Beau Brocade'

'Hark! I hear the sound of coaches!'—BEGGAR's OPERA

I

Seventeen hundred and thirty-nine:—
That was the date of this tale of mine.

First great GEORGE was buried and gone;
GEORGE the Second was plodding on.

LONDON then, as the 'Guides' aver,   5
Shared its glories with *Westminster*;

And people of rank to correct their 'tone',
Went out of town to *Marybone*.

Those were the days of the War with *Spain*,
PORTO-BELLO would soon be ta'en;   10

WHITEFIELD preached to the colliers grim,
Bishops in lawn sleeves preached at him;

WALPOLE talked of 'a man and his price';
Nobody's virtue was over-nice;

Those, in fine, were the brave days when   15
Coaches were stopped by . . . *Highwaymen*!

And of all the knights of the gentle trade
Nobody bolder than 'BEAU BROCADE'.

This they knew on the whole way down;
Best,—maybe,—at the *'Oak and Crown'*.　　20

(For timorous cits on their pilgrimage
Would 'club' for a 'Guard' to ride the stage;

And the Guard that rode on more than one
Was the Host of this hostel's sister's son.)

Open we here on a March day fine,　　25
Under the oak with the hanging sign.

There was Barber DICK with his basin by;
Cobbler JOE with the patch on his eye;

Portly product of Beef and Beer,
JOHN the host, he was standing near.　　30

Straining and creaking with wheels awry,
Lumbering came the *'Plymouth Fly'*;—

Lumbering up from *Bagshot Heath*,
Guard in the basket armed to the teeth;

Passengers heavily armed inside;　　35
Not the less surely the coach had been tried!

Tried!—but a couple of miles away,
By a well-dressed man!—in the open day!

Tried successfully, never a doubt,—
Pockets of passengers all turned out!　　40

Cloak-bags rifled, and cushions ripped,—
Even an Ensign's wallet stripped!

Even a Methodist hosier's wife
Offered the choice of her Money or Life!

Highwayman's manners no less polite,　　45
Hoped that their coppers (returned) were right;—

Sorry to find the company poor,
Hoped next time they'd travel with more:—

Plucked them all at his ease, in short:—
Such was the '*Plymouth Fly's*' report.   50

Sympathy! horror! and wonderment!
'Catch the Villain!' (But nobody went.)

Hosier's wife led into the bar,
(That's where the best strong waters are!)

Followed the tale of the hundred-and-one   55
Things that Somebody ought to have done.

Ensign (of BRAGG'S) made a terrible clangour:
But for the Ladies had drawn his hanger!

Robber, of course, was 'BEAU BROCADE';
Out-spoke DOLLY the Chambermaid.   60

Devonshire DOLLY, plump and red,
Spoke from the gallery overhead;—

Spoke it out boldly, staring hard:—
'Why didn't you shoot then, GEORGE the Guard?'

Spoke it out bolder, seeing him mute:—   65
'GEORGE the Guard, why didn't you shoot?'

Portly JOHN grew pale and red,
(JOHN was afraid of her, people said);

Gasped that 'DOLLY was surely cracked'
(JOHN was afraid of her—that's a fact!)   70

GEORGE the Guard grew red and pale,
Slowly finished his quart of ale:—

'Shoot? Why—Rabbit him!—didn't he shoot?'
Muttered—'The Baggage was far too cute!'

'Shoot? Why, he'd flashed the pan in his eye!'

Muttered—'She'd pay for it by and by!' 76
Further than this made no reply.

Nor could a further reply be made,
For GEORGE *was in league with* 'BEAU BROCADE'!

And JOHN the Host, in his wakefullest state, 80
Was not—on the whole—immaculate.

But nobody's virtue was over-nice
When WALPOLE talked of 'a man and his price';

And wherever Purity found abode,
'Twas certainly *not* on a posting road. 85

II

'Forty' followed to 'Thirty-nine',
Glorious days of the *Hanover* line!

Princes were born, and drums were banged;
Now and then batches of Highwaymen hanged.

'Glorious news!'—from the *Spanish Main*; 90
PORTO-BELLO at last was ta'en.

'Glorious news!'—for the liquor trade;
Nobody dreamed of 'BEAU BROCADE'.

People were thinking of *Spanish Crowns*;
Money was coming from seaport towns! 95

Nobody dreamed of 'BEAU BROCADE',
(Only DOLLY the Chambermaid!)

Blessings on VERNON! Fill up the cans;
Money was coming in '*Flys*' and '*Vans*'.

Possibly, JOHN the Host had heard; 100
Also, certainly, GEORGE the Guard.

And DOLLY had possibly tidings, too,
That made her rise from her bed anew,

Plump as ever, but stern of eye,
With a fixed intention to warn the '*Fly*'.   105

Lingering only at JOHN his door,
Just to make sure of a jerky snore;

Saddling the grey mare, *Dumpling Star*;
Fetching the pistol out of the bar;

(The old horse-pistol that, they say,   110
Came from the battle of *Malplaquet*;)

Loading with powder that maids would use,
Even in 'Forty', to clear the flues;

And a couple of silver buttons, the Squire
Gave her, away in *Devonshire*.   115

These she wadded—for want of better—
With the B–SH–P of L–ND–N's 'Pastoral Letter';

Looked to the flint, and hung the whole,
Ready to use, at her pocket-hole.

Thus equipped and accoutred, DOLLY   120
Clattered away to '*Exciseman's Folly*';—

Such was the name of a ruined abode,
Just on the edge of the *London* road.

Thence she thought she might safely try,
As soon as she saw it, to warn the '*Fly*'.   125

But, as chance fell out, her rein she drew,
As the BEAU came cantering into the view.

By the light of the moon she could see him drest
In his famous gold-sprigged tambour vest;

And under his silver-grey surtout,   130
The laced, historical coat of blue,

That he wore when he went to *London-Spaw*,
And robbed Sir MUNGO MUCKLETHRAW.

Out-spoke DOLLY the Chambermaid,
(Trembling a little, but not afraid,)   135
'Stand and Deliver, O "BEAU BROCADE"!'

But the BEAU drew nearer, and would not speak,
For he saw by the moonlight a rosy cheek;

And a spavined mare with a rusty hide;
And a girl with her hand at her pocket-side. 140

So never a word he spake as yet,
For he thought 'twas a freak of MEG or BET;—
A freak of the '*Rose*' or the '*Rummer*' set.

Out-spoke DOLLY the Chambermaid,
(Tremulous now, and sore afraid,)   145
'Stand and Deliver, O "BEAU BROCADE"!'—

Firing then, out of sheer alarm,
Hit the BEAU in the bridle-arm.

Button the first went none knows where,
But it carried away his *solitaire*;   150

Button the second a circuit made,
Glanced in under the shoulder blade;—
Down from the saddle fell 'BEAU BROCADE'!

Down from the saddle and never stirred!—
DOLLY grew white as a *Windsor* curd.   155

Slipped not less from the mare, and bound
Strips of her kirtle about his wound.

Then, lest his Worship should rise and flee,
Fettered his ankles—tenderly.

Jumped on his chestnut, BET the fleet   160
(Called after BET of *Portugal Street*);

Came like the wind to the old Inn-door;—
Roused fat JOHN from a threefold snore;—

Vowed she'd peach if he misbehaved . . .
Briefly, the *'Plymouth Fly'* was saved!   165

Staines and *Windsor* were all on fire:—
DOLLY was wed to a *Yorkshire* squire;
Went to the Town at the K–G's desire!

But whether HIS M–J–STY saw her or not,
HOGARTH jotted her down on the spot;   170

And something of DOLLY one still may trace
In the fresh contours of his *'Milkmaid's'* face.

GEORGE the Guard fled over the sea:
JOHN had a fit—of perplexity;

Turned King's evidence, sad to state;—   175
But JOHN was never immaculate.

As for the BEAU, he was duly tried,
When his wound was healed, at *Whitsuntide*;

Served—for a day—as the last of 'sights',
To the world of *St. James's Street* and *'White's'*,

Went on his way to TYBURN TREE,   181
With a pomp befitting his high degree.

Every privilege rank confers:—
Bouquet of pinks at *St. Sepulchre's*;

Flagon of ale at *Holborn Bar*;   185
Friends (in mourning) to follow his Car—
('t' is omitted where HEROES are!)

Every one knows the speech he made;
Swore that he 'rather admired the Jade!'—

Waved to the crowd with his gold-laced hat:
Talked to the Chaplain after that;   191

Turned to the Topsman undismayed . . .
This was the finish of 'BEAU BROCADE'!

And this is the Ballad that seemed to hide
In the leaves of a dusty 'LONDONER'S GUIDE';
'Humbly Inscrib'd (with curls and tails) 196
By the Author to FREDERICK, Prince of WALES:—

'Published by FRANCIS and OLIVER PINE;
Ludgate-Hill, at the Blackmoor Sign.
Seventeen-Hundred-and-Thirty-Nine.' 200

THOMAS HARDY
1840–1928

The Sacrilege
A BALLAD-TRAGEDY (*Circa* 182-)

PART I

'I have a Love I love too well
Where Dunkery frowns on Exon Moor;
I have a Love I love too well,
    To whom, ere she was mine,
"Such is my love for you," I said, 5
"That you shall have to hood your head
A silken kerchief crimson-red
    Wove finest of the fine."

'And since this Love, for one mad moon,
On Exon Wild by Dunkery Tor, 10
Since this my Love for one mad moon
    Did clasp me as her king,
I snatched a silk-piece red and rare
From off a stall at Priddy Fair,
For handkerchief to hood her hair 15
    When we went gallanting.

'Full soon the four weeks neared their end
Where Dunkery frowns on Exon Moor;
And when the four weeks neared their end,
    And their swift sweets outwore, 20

I said, "What shall I do to own
Those beauties bright as tulips blown,
And keep you here with me alone
    As mine for evermore?"

'And as she drowsed within my van   25
On Exon Wild by Dunkery Tor—
And as she drowsed within my van,
    And dawning turned to day,
She heavily raised her sloe-black eyes
And murmured back in softest wise,   30
"One more thing, and the charms you prize
    Are yours henceforth for aye.

'"And swear I will I'll never go
While Dunkery frowns on Exon Moor
To meet the Cornish Wrestler Joe   35
    For dance and dallyings.
If you'll to yon cathedral shrine,
And finger from the chest divine
Treasure to buy me ear-drops fine,
    And richly jewelled rings."   40

'I said: "I am one who has gathered gear
From Marlbury Downs to Dunkery Tor,
Who has gathered gear for many a year
    From mansion, mart and fair;
But at God's house I've stayed my hand,   45
Hearing within me some command—
Curbed by a law not of the land
    From doing damage there!"

'Whereat she pouts, this Love of mine,
As Dunkery pouts to Exon Moor,   50
And still she pouts, this Love of mine,
    So cityward I go.
But ere I start to do the thing,
And speed my soul's imperilling
For one who is my ravishing   55
    And all the joy I know,

'I come to lay this charge to thee—
On Exon Wild by Dunkery Tor—
I come to lay this charge on thee
    With solemn speech and sign: 60
Should things go ill, and my life pay
For botchery in this rash assay,
You are to take hers likewise—yea,
    The month the law takes mine.

'For should my rival, Wrestler Joe,   65
Where Dunkery frowns on Exon Moor—
My reckless rival, Wrestler Joe,
    My Love's bedwinner be,
My rafted spirit would not rest,
But wander weary and distrest   70
Throughout the world in wild protest:
    The thought nigh maddens me!'

PART II

Thus did he speak—this brother of mine—
On Exon Wild by Dunkery Tor,
Born at my birth of mother of mine,   75
    And forthwith went his way
To dare the deed some coming night . . .
I kept the watch with shaking sight,
The moon at moments breaking bright,
    At others glooming grey.   80

For three full days I heard no sound
Where Dunkery frowns on Exon Moor,
I heard no sound at all around
    Whether his fay prevailed,
Or one more foul the master were,   85
Till some afoot did tidings bear
How that, for all his practised care,
    He had been caught and jailed.

They had heard a crash when twelve had chimed
By Mendip east of Dunkery Tor,   90

When twelve had chimed and moonlight climbed;
    They watched, and he was tracked
By arch and aisle and saint and knight
Of sculptured stonework sheeted white
In the cathedral's ghostly light,   95
    And captured in the act.

Yes; for this Love he loved too well
Where Dunkery sights the Severn shore,
All for this Love he loved too well
    He burst the holy bars,   100
Seized golden vessels from the chest
To buy her ornaments of the best,
At her ill-witchery's request
    And lure of eyes like stars ...

When blustering March confused the sky   105
In Toneborough Town by Exon Moor,
When blustering March confused the sky
    They stretched him; and he died.
Down in the crowd where I, to see
The end of him, stood silently,   110
With a set face he lipped to me—
    'Remember.' 'Ay!' I cried.

By night and day I shadowed her
From Toneborough Deane to Dunkery Tor,
I shadowed her asleep, astir,   115
    And yet I could not bear—
Till Wrestler Joe anon began
To figure as her chosen man,
And took her to his shining van—
    To doom a form so fair!   120

He made it handsome for her sake—
And Dunkery smiled to Exon Moor—
He made it handsome for her sake,
    Painting it out and in;
And on the door of apple-green   125
A bright brass knocker soon was seen,

And window-curtains white and clean
    For her to sit within.

And all could see she clave to him
As cleaves a cloud to Dunkery Tor,   130
Yea, all could see she clave to him,
    And every day I said,
'A pity it seems to part those two
That hourly grow to love more true:
Yet she's the wanton woman who   135
    Sent one to swing till dead!'

That blew to blazing all my hate,
While Dunkery frowned on Exon Moor,
And when the river swelled, her fate
    Came to her pitilessly . . .   140
I dogged her, crying: 'Across that plank
They use as bridge to reach yon bank
A coat and hat lie limp and dank;
    Your goodman's, can they be?'

She paled, and went, I close behind—   145
And Exon frowned to Dunkery Tor,
She went, and I came up behind
    And tipped the plank that bore
Her, fleetly flitting across to eye
What such might bode. She slid awry;   150
And from the current came a cry,
    A gurgle; and no more.

How that befell no mortal knew
From Marlbury Downs to Exon Moor;
No mortal knew that deed undue   155
    But he who schemed the crime,
Which night still covers . . . But in dream
Those ropes of hair upon the stream
He sees, and he will hear that scream
    Until his judgment-time.   160

ROBERT LOUIS STEVENSON

1850–1894

Ticonderoga

A LEGEND OF THE WEST HIGHLANDS[1]

This is the tale of the man
  Who heard a word in the night
In the land of the heathery hills,
  In the days of the feud and the fight.
By the sides of the rainy sea,   5
  Where never a stranger came,
On the awful lips of the dead,
  He heard the outlandish name.
It sang in his sleeping ears,
  It hummed in his waking head: 10
The name—Ticonderoga,
  The utterance of the dead.

I. *The Saying of the Name*

On the loch-sides of Appin,
  When the mist blew from the sea,
A Stewart stood with a Cameron: 15
  An angry man was he.
The blood beat in his ears,
  The blood ran hot to his head,
The mist blew from the sea,
  And there was the Cameron dead.   20

---

[1] I first heard this legend of my own country from that friend of men of letters, Mr. Alfred Nutt, 'there in roaring London's central stream,' and since the ballad first saw the light of day in *Scribner's Magazine*, Mr. Nutt and Lord Archibald Campbell have been in public controversy on the facts. Two clans, the Camerons and the Campbells, lay claim to this bracing story; and they do well: the man who preferred his plighted troth to the commands and menaces of the dead is an ancestor worth disputing. But the Campbells must rest content: they have the broad lands and the broad page of history; this appanage must be denied them; for between the name of *Cameron* and that of *Campbell* the muse will never hesitate.—R. L. S.

'O, what have I done to my friend,
O, what have I done to mysel',
That he should be cold and dead,
And I in the danger of all?

'Nothing but danger about me,   25
Danger behind and before,
Death at wait in the heather
In Appin and Mamore,
Hate at all of the ferries
And death at each of the fords,   30
Camerons priming gunlocks
And Camerons sharpening swords.'

But this was a man of counsel,
This was a man of a score,
There dwelt no pawkier Stewart   35
In Appin or Mamore.
He looked on the blowing mist,
He looked on the awful dead,
And there came a smile on his face
And there slipped a thought in his head.

Out over cairn and moss,   41
Out over scrog and scaur,
He ran as runs the clansman
That bears the cross of war.
His heart beat in his body,   45
His hair clove to his face,
When he came at last in the gloaming
To the dead man's brother's place.

The east was white with the moon,
The west with the sun was red,   50
And there, in the house-doorway,
Stood the brother of the dead.

'I have slain a man to my danger,
I have slain a man to my death.
I put my soul in your hands,'   55
The panting Stewart saith:

'I lay it bare in your hands,
      For I know your hands are leal;
And be you my targe and bulwark
      From the bullet and the steel.'   60

Then up and spoke the Cameron,
      And gave him his hand again:
'There shall never a man in Scotland
      Set faith in me in vain;
And whatever man you have slaughtered,
      Of whatever name or line,   66
By my sword and yonder mountain,
      I make your quarrel mine.[1]
I bid you in to my fireside,
      I share with you house and hall;   70
It stands upon my honour
      To see you safe from all.'

It fell in the time of midnight,
      When the fox barked in the den
And the plaids were over the faces   75
      In all the houses of men,
That as the living Cameron
      Lay sleepless on his bed,
Out of the night and the other world
      Came in to him the dead.   80

'My blood is on the heather,
      My bones are on the hill;
There is joy in the home of ravens
      That the young shall eat their fill.
My blood is poured in the dust,   85
      My soul is spilled in the air;
And the man that has undone me
      Sleeps in my brother's care.'

'I'm wae for your death, my brother,
      But if all of my house were dead,   90

---

[1] Mr. Nutt reminds me, it was 'by my sword and Ben Cruachan' the
Cameron swore.—R. L. S.

I couldnae withdraw the plighted hand
    Nor break the word once said.'

'O, what shall I say to our father,
    In the place to which I fare?
O, what shall I say to our mother,   95
    Who greets to see me there?
And to all the kindly Camerons
    That have lived and died long-syne—
Is this the word you send them,
    Fause-hearted brother mine?'   100

'It's neither fear nor duty,
    It's neither quick nor dead
Shall gar me withdraw the plighted hand,
    Or break the word once said.'

Thrice in the time of midnight,   105
    When the fox barked in the den,
And the plaids were over the faces
    In all the houses of men,
Thrice as the living Cameron
    Lay sleepless on his bed,   110
Out of the night and the other world
    Came in to him the dead,
And cried to him for vengeance
    On the man that laid him low;
And thrice the living Cameron   115
    Told the dead Cameron, no.

'Thrice have you seen me, brother,
    But now shall see me no more,
Till you meet your angry fathers
    Upon the farther shore.   120
Thrice have I spoken, and now,
    Before the cock be heard,
I take my leave for ever
    With the naming of a word.
It shall sing in your sleeping ears,   125
    It shall hum in your waking head,

The name—Ticonderoga,
    And the warning of the dead.'

Now when the night was over
    And the time of people's fears,   130
The Cameron walked abroad,
    And the word was in his ears.
'Many a name I know,
    But never a name like this;
O, where shall I find a skilly man   135
    Shall tell me what it is?'
With many a man he counselled
    Of high and low degree,
With the herdsmen on the mountains
    And the fishers of the sea.   140

And he came and went unweary,
    And read the books of yore,
And the runes that were written of old
    On stones upon the moor.
And many a name he was told,   145
    But never the name of his fears—
Never, in east or west,
    The name that rang in his ears:
Names of men and of clans;
    Names for the grass and the tree,   150
For the smallest tarn in the mountains,
    The smallest reef in the sea:
Names for the high and low
    The names of the craig and the flat;
But in all the land of Scotland,   155
    Never a name like that.

II. *The Seeking of the Name*

And now there was a speech in the south,
    And a man of the south that wise,
A periwig'd lord of London,[1]
    Called on the clans to rise.   160

[1] '*A periwig'd lord of London.*' The first Pitt.—R. L. S.

And the riders rode, and the summons
  Came to the western shore,
To the land of the sea and the heather,
  To Appin and Mamore.
It called on all to gather   165
  From every scrog and scaur,
That loved their father's tartan
  And the ancient game of war.
And down the watery valley
  And up the windy hill,   170
Once more, as in the olden,
  The pipes were sounding shrill.
Again in the highland sunshine
  The naked steel was bright;
And the lads, once more in tartan,   175
  Went forth again to fight.

'O, why should I dwell here
  With a weird upon my life,
When the clansmen shout for battle
  And the war-swords clash in strife?   180
I cannae joy at feast,
  I cannae sleep in bed,
For the wonder of the word
  And the warning of the dead.
It sings in my sleeping ears,   185
  It hums in my waking head,
The name—Ticonderoga,
  The utterance of the dead.
Then up, and with the fighting men
  To march away from here,   190
Till the cry of the great war-pipe
  Shall drown it in my ear!'

Where flew King George's ensign
  The plaided soldiers went:
They drew the sword in Germany,   195
  In Flanders pitched the tent.
The bells of foreign cities

Rang far across the plain:
They passed the happy Rhine,
　　They drank the rapid Main.   200
Through Asiatic jungles
　　The Tartans filed their way,
And the neighing of the war-pipes
　　Struck terror in Cathay.
'Many a name have I heard,' he thought,
　　'In all the tongues of men,   206
Full many a name both here and there,
　　Full many both now and then.'

'When I was at home in my father's house
　　In the land of the naked knee,   210
Between the eagles that fly in the lift
　　And the herrings that swim in the sea,
And now that I am a captain-man
　　With a braw cockade in my hat—
Many a name have I heard,' he thought,
　　'But never a name like that.'   216

III. *The Place of the Name*

There fell a war in a woody place,
　　Lay far across the sea,
A war of the march in the mirk midnight
　　And the shot from behind the tree,   220
The shaven head and the painted face,
　　The silent foot in the wood,
In a land of a strange, outlandish tongue
　　That was hard to be understood.

It fell about the gloaming   225
　　The general stood with his staff,
He stood and he looked east and west
　　With little mind to laugh.
'Far have I been and much have I seen,
　　And kent both gain and loss,   230
But here we have woods on every hand

And a kittle water to cross.
Far have I been and much have I seen,
  But never the beat of this;
And there's one must go down to that water-
     side   235
  To see how deep it is.'

It fell in the dusk of the night
  When unco things betide,
The skilly captain, the Cameron,
  Went down to that waterside.   240
Canny and soft the captain went;
  And a man of the woody land,
With the shaven head and the painted face,
  Went down at his right hand.
It fell in the quiet night,   245
  There was never a sound to ken;
But all of the woods to right and the left
  Lay filled with the painted men.

'Far have I been and much have I seen,
  Both as a man and boy,   250
But never have I set forth a foot
  On so perilous an employ.'
It fell in the dusk of the night
  When unco things betide,
That he was aware of a captain-man   255
  Drew near to the waterside.
He was aware of his coming
  Down in the gloaming alone;
And he looked in the face of the man
  And lo! the face was his own.   260
'This is my weird,' he said,
  'And now I ken the worst;
For many shall fall with the morn,
  But I shall fall with the first.
O, you of the outland tongue,   265
  You of the painted face,
This is the place of my death;
  Can you tell me the name of the place?'

'Since the Frenchmen have been here
    They have called it Sault-Marie;   270
But that is a name for priests,
    And not for you and me.
It went by another word,'
    Quoth he of the shaven head:
'It was called Ticonderoga   275
    In the days of the great dead.'

And it fell on the morrow's morning,
    In the fiercest of the fight,
That the Cameron bit the dust
    As he foretold at night;   280
And far from the hills of heather
    Far from the isles of the sea,
He sleeps in the place of the name
    As it was doomed to be.

SIR HENRY NEWBOLT

1862–1938

A Ballad of John Nicholson

It fell in the year of the Mutiny,
    At darkest of the night,
John Nicholson by Jalándhar came,
    On his way to Delhi fight.

And as he by Jalándhar came   5
    He thought what he must do,
And he sent to the Rajah fair greeting,
    To try if he were true.

'God grant your highness length of days,
    And friends when need shall be;   10
And I pray you send your Captains hither
    That they may speak with me.'

On the morrow through Jalándhar town
  The Captains rode in state;
They came to the house of John Nicholson
  And stood before the gate.   16

The chief of them was Mehtab Singh,
  He was both proud and sly;
His turban gleamed with rubies red,
  He held his chin full high.   20

He marked his fellows how they put
  Their shoes from off their feet;
'Now wherefore make ye such ado
  These fallen lords to greet?

'They have ruled us for a hundred years,   25
  In truth I know not how,
But though they be fain of mastery,
  They dare not claim it now.'

Right haughtily before them all
  The durbar hall he trod,   30
With rubies red his turban gleamed,
  His feet with pride were shod.

They had not been an hour together,
  A scanty hour or so,
When Mehtab Singh rose in his place   35
  And turned about to go.

Then swiftly came John Nicholson
  Between the door and him,
With anger smouldering in his eyes
  That made the rubies dim.   40

'You are over-hasty, Mehtab Singh,'—
  Oh, but his voice was low!
He held his wrath with a curb of iron,
  That furrowed cheek and brow.

'You are over-hasty, Mehtab Singh,   45
  When that the rest are gone,

I have a word that may not wait
  To speak with you alone.'

The Captains passed in silence forth
  And stood the door behind;   50
To go before the game was played
  Be sure they had no mind.

But there within John Nicholson
  Turned him on Mehtab Singh,
'So long as the soul is in my body   55
  You shall not do this thing.

'Have ye served us for a hundred years
  And yet ye know not why?
We brook no doubt of our mastery,
  We rule until we die.   60

'Were I the one last Englishman
  Drawing the breath of life,
And you the master-rebel of all
  That stir this land to strife—

'Were I,' he said, 'but a Corporal,   65
  And you a Rajput King,
So long as the soul was in my body
  You should not do this thing.

'Take off, take off those shoes of pride,
  Carry them whence they came;   70
Your Captains saw your insolence
  And they shall see your shame.'

When Mehtab Singh came to the door
  His shoes they burned his hand,
For there in long and silent lines   75
  He saw the Captains stand.

When Mehtab Singh rode from the gate
  His chin was on his breast:
The Captains said, 'When the strong command
  Obedience is best.'   80

RUDYARD KIPLING

1865–1936

Tomlinson

Now Tomlinson gave up the ghost at his house in
    Berkeley Square,
And a Spirit came to his bedside and gripped him by
    the hair—
A Spirit gripped him by the hair and carried him far
    away,
Till he heard as the roar of a rain-fed ford the roar of
    the Milky Way:
Till he heard the roar of the Milky Way die down
    and drone and cease,   5
And they came to the Gate within the Wall where
    Peter holds the keys.
'Stand up, stand up now, Tomlinson, and answer loud
    and high
The good that ye did for the sake of men or ever ye
    came to die—
The good that ye did for the sake of men in little
    earth so lone!'
And the naked soul of Tomlinson grew white as a
    rain-washed bone.   10
'O I have a friend on earth,' he said, 'that was my
    priest and guide,
And well would he answer all for me if he were by my
    side.'
—'For that ye strove in neighbour-love it shall be
    written fair,
But now ye wait at Heaven's Gate and not in Berkeley
    Square:
Though we called your friend from his bed this night,
    he could not speak for you,   15
For the race is run by one and one and never by two
    and two.'

Then Tomlinson looked up and down, and little gain
    was there,
For the naked stars grinned overhead, and he saw
    that his soul was bare:
The Wind that blows between the worlds, it cut him
    like a knife,
And Tomlinson took up his tale and spoke of his good
    in life.   20
'This have I read in a book,' he said, 'and that was
    told to me,
And this I have thought that another man thought
    of a Prince in Muscovy.'
The good souls flocked like homing doves and bade
    him clear the path,
And Peter twirled the jangling keys in weariness and
    wrath.
'Ye have read, ye have heard, ye have thought,' he
    said, 'and the tale is yet to run: 25
By the worth of the body that once ye had, give
    answer—what ha' ye done?'
Then Tomlinson looked back and forth, and little
    good it bore,
For the Darkness stayed at his shoulder-blade and
    Heaven's Gate before:—
'O this I have felt, and this I have guessed, and this
    I have heard men say,
And this they wrote that another man wrote of a carl
    in Norroway.'   30
'Ye have read, ye have felt, ye have guessed, good
    lack! Ye have hampered Heaven's Gate;
There's little room between the stars in idleness to
    prate!
O none may reach by hired speech of neighbour,
    priest, and kin
Through borrowed deed to God's good meed that lies
    so fair within;
Get hence, get hence to the Lord of Wrong, for doom
    has yet to run,   35

And . . . the faith that ye share with Berkeley Square
    uphold you, Tomlinson!'

    .   .   .

The Spirit gripped him by the hair, and sun by sun
    they fell
Till they came to the belt of Naughty Stars that rim
    the mouth of Hell:
The first are red with pride and wrath, the next are
    white with pain,
But the third are black with clinkered sin that cannot
    burn again: 40
They may hold their path, they may leave their path,
    with never a soul to mark,
They may burn or freeze, but they must not cease in
    the scorn of the Outer Dark.
The Wind that blows between the worlds, it nipped
    him to the bone,
And he yearned to the flare of Hell-gate there as the
    light of his own hearth-stone.
The Devil he sat behind the bars, where the desperate
    legions drew,   45
But he caught the hasting Tomlinson and would not
    let him through.
'Wot ye the price of good pit-coal that I must pay?'
    said he.
'That ye rank yoursel' so fit for Hell and ask no leave
    of me?
I am all o'er-sib to Adam's breed that ye should give
    me scorn,
For I strove with God for your First Father the day
    that he was born.   50
Sit down, sit down upon the slag, and answer loud
    and high
The harm that ye did to the Sons of Men or ever you
    came to die.'
And Tomlinson looked up and up, and saw against
    the night
The belly of a tortured star blood-red in Hell-Mouth
    light;

And Tomlinson looked down and down, and saw
    beneath his feet   55
The frontlet of a tortured star milk-white in Hell-
    Mouth heat.
'O I had a love on earth,' said he, 'that kissed me to
    my fall,
And if ye would call my love to me I know she would
    answer all.'
—'All that ye did in love forbid it shall be written
    fair,
But now ye wait at Hell-Mouth Gate and not in
    Berkeley Square: 60
Though we whistled your love from her bed to-night,
    I trow she would not run,
For the sin ye do by two and two ye must pay for
    one by one!'
The Wind that blows between the worlds, it cut him
    like a knife,
And Tomlinson took up the tale and spoke of his sin
    in life:—
'Once I ha' laughed at the power of Love and twice at
    the grip of the Grave,   65
And thrice I ha' patted my God on the head that men
    might call me brave.'
The Devil he blew on a brandered soul and set it
    aside to cool:—
'Do ye think I would waste my good pit-coal on the
    hide of a brain-sick fool?
I see no worth in the hobnailed mirth or the jolt-head
    jest ye did
That I should waken my gentlemen that are sleeping
    three on a grid.'   70
Then Tomlinson looked back and forth, and there
    was little grace,
For Hell-Gate filled the houseless Soul with the Fear
    of Naked Space.
'Nay, this I ha' heard,' quo' Tomlinson, 'and this was
    noised abroad,

And this I ha' got from a Belgian book on the word
    of a dead French lord.'
—'Ye ha' heard, ye ha' read, ye ha' got, good lack!
    and the tale begins afresh—   75
Have ye sinned one sin for the pride o' the eye or the
    sinful lust of the flesh?'
Then Tomlinson he gripped the bars and yammered,
    'Let me in—
For I mind that I borrowed my neighbour's wife to
    sin the deadly sin.'
The Devil he grinned behind the bars, and banked
    the fires high:
'Did ye read of that sin in a book?' said he; and
    Tomlinson said, 'Ay!'   80
The Devil he blew upon his nails, and the little devils
    ran,
And he said, 'Go husk this whimpering thief that
    comes in the guise of a man:
Winnow him out 'twixt star and star, and sieve his
    proper worth:
There's sore decline in Adam's line if this be spawn
    of earth.'
Empusa's crew, so naked-new they may not face the
    fire,   85
But weep that they bin too small to sin to the height
    of their desire,
Over the coal they chased the Soul, and racked it all
    abroad,
As children rifle a caddis-case or the raven's foolish
    hoard.
And back they came with the tattered Thing, as
    children after play,
And they said, 'The soul that he got from God he has
    bartered clean away.   90
We have threshed a stook of print and book, and
    winnowed a chattering wind,
And many a soul wherefrom he stole, but his we can-
    not find:

We have handled him, we have dandled him, we have
    seared him to the bone,
And sure if tooth and nail show truth he has no
    soul of his own.'
The Devil he bowed his head on his breast and
    rumbled deep and low:—   95
'I'm all o'er-sib to Adam's breed that I should bid
    him go.
Yet close we lie, and deep we lie, and if I gave him
    place,
My gentlemen that are so proud would flout me to
    my face;
They'd call my house a common stews and me a
    careless host,
And—I would not anger my gentlemen for the sake
    of a shiftless ghost.'   100
The Devil he looked at the mangled Soul that prayed
    to feel the flame,
And he thought of Holy Charity, but he thought of
    his own good name:—
'Now ye could haste my coal to waste, and sit ye down
    to fry:
Did ye think of that theft for yourself?' said he; and
    Tomlinson said, 'Ay!'
The Devil he blew an outward breath, for his heart
    was free from care:—   105
'Ye have scarce the soul of a louse,' he said, 'but the
    roots of sin are there,
And for that sin should ye come in were I the lord
    alone.
But sinful pride has rule inside—and mightier than
    my own.
Honour and Wit, fore-damned they sit, to each his
    Priest and Whore:
Nay, scarce I dare myself go there, and you they'd
    torture sore.   110
Ye are neither spirit nor spirk,' he said; 'Ye are neither
    book nor brute—

Go, get ye back to the flesh again for the sake of
    Man's repute.
I'm all o'er-sib to Adam's breed that I should mock
    your pain,
But look that ye win to worthier sin ere ye come back
    again.
Get hence, the hearse is at your door—the grim black
    stallions wait—   115
They bear your clay to place to-day. Speed, lest ye
    come too late!
Go back to Earth with a lip unsealed—go back with
    an open eye,
And carry my word to the Sons of Men or ever ye
    come to die:
That the sin they do by two and two they must pay
    for one by one—
And . . . the God that you took from a printed book
    be with you, Tomlinson!'   120

LAURENCE BINYON

1869–1943

The Battle of Stamford Bridge

'Haste thee, Harold, haste thee North!
  Norway ships in the Humber crowd.
Tall Hardrada, Sigurd's son,
For thy ruin this hath done—
  England for his own hath vowed.   5

'The earls have fought, the earls are fled.
  From Tyne to Ouse the homesteads flame.
York behind her battered wall
Waits the instant of her fall
  And the shame of England's name.   10

'Traitor Tosti's banner streams
  With the invading Raven's wing;

Black the land and red the skies
When Northumbria bleeds and cries
    For thy vengeance, England's King!'   **15**

Since that frighted summons flew
    Not twelve suns have sprung and set.
Northward marching night and day
Has King Harold kept his way.
    The hour is come, the hosts are met.   **20**

Morn through thin September mist
    Flames on moving helm and man.
On either side of Derwent's banks
Are the Northmen's shielded ranks;
    But silent stays the English van.   **25**

A rider to Earl Tosti comes:
    'Turn thee, Tosti, to thy kin!
Harold thy brother brings thee sign . . .
All Northumbria shall be thine.
    Make thy peace, ere the fray begin!'   **30**

'And if I turn me to my kin,
    And if I stay the Northmen's hand,
What will Harold give to my friend this day?
To Norway's king what price will he pay
    Out of this English land?'   **35**

That rider laughed a mighty laugh.
    'Six full feet of English soil!
Or, since he is taller than the most,
Seven feet shall he have to boast;
    This Harold gives for Norway's spoil.'   **40**

'What rider was he that spoke thee fair?'
    Harold Hardrada to Tosti cried.
'It was Harold of England spoke me fair;
But now of his bane let him beware.
    Set on, set on! we will break his pride.'   **45**

Sudden arrows flashed and flew,
  Dark lines of English leapt and rushed
With sound of storm that stung like hail,
And steel rang sharp on supple mail
  With thrust that pierced and blow that crushed.

And sullenly back in a fierce amaze   51
  The Northmen gave to the river side.
The main of their host on the further shore
Could help them nothing, pressed so sore.
  In the ooze they fought, in the wave they died.

On a narrow bridge alone one man   56
  The English mass and fury stays.
The spears press close, the timber cracks
But high he swings his dreadful axe,
  With every stroke a life he slays;   60

But pierced at last from the stream below
  He falls: the Northmen break and shout.
Forward they hurl in wild onset;
But as struggling fish in a mighty net
  The English hem them round about.   65

Now Norway's king grew battle-mad,
  Mad with joy of his strength he smote.
But as he hewed his battle-path,
And heaped the dead men for a swath,
  An arrow clove him through the throat.   70

Where he slaughtered, red he fell.
  O then was Norway's hope undone,
Doomed men were they that fought in vain,
Hardrada slain, and Tosti slain!
  The field was lost, the field was won.   75

York this night rings all her bells.
  Harold feasts within her halls.
The Captains lift their wine-cups.—Hark!
What hoofs come thudding through the dark
  And sudden stop? What silence falls?   80

Spent with riding staggers in
   One who cries: 'Fell news I bring.
Duke William has o'erpast the sea.
His host is camped at Pevensey.
   Save us, save England now, O King!'   85

Woe to Harold! Twice 'tis not
   His to conquer and to save.
Well he knows the lot is cast.
England claims him to the last.
   South he marches to his grave.   90

GILBERT KEITH CHESTERTON
1874–1936

Lepanto

White founts falling in the Courts of the sun,
And the Soldan of Byzantium is smiling as they run;
There is laughter like fountains in that face of all
   men feared,
It stirs the forest darkness, the darkness of his beard,
It curls the blood-red crescent, the crescent of his lips,
For the inmost sea of all the earth is shaken with his
   ships.   6
They have dared the white republics up the capes of
   Italy,
They have dashed the Adriatic round the Lion of the
   Sea,
And the Pope has cast his arms abroad for agony and
   loss,
And called the kings of Christendom for swords about
   the Cross.   10
The cold queen of England is looking in the glass,
The shadow of the Valois is yawning at the Mass;
From evening isles fantastical rings faint the Spanish
   gun,

And the Lord upon the Golden Horn is laughing in
    the sun.

Dim drums throbbing, in the hills half heard,   15
Where only on a nameless throne a crownless prince
    has stirred,
Where, risen from a doubtful seat and half attainted
    stall,
The last knight of Europe takes weapons from the
    wall,
The last and lingering troubadour to whom the bird
    has sung,
That once went singing southward when all the world
    was young.   20
In that enormous silence, tiny and unafraid,
Comes up along a winding road the noise of the
    Crusade.
Strong gongs groaning as the guns boom far,
Don John of Austria is going to the war,
Stiff flags straining in the night-blasts cold   25
In the gloom black-purple, in the glint old-gold,
Torchlight crimson on the copper kettle-drums,
Then the tuckets, then the trumpets, then the cannon,
    and he comes.
Don John laughing in the brave beard curled,
Spurning of his stirrups like the thrones of all the
    world,   30
Holding his head up for a flag of all the free.
Love-light of Spain—hurrah!
Deathlight of Africa!
Don John of Austria
Is riding to the sea.   35

Mahound is in his paradise above the evening star,
(Don John of Austria is going to the war.)
He moves a mighty turban on the timeless houri's
    knees,
His turban that is woven of the sunsets and the seas.
He shakes the peacock gardens as he rises from his
    ease,   40

And he strides among the tree-tops and is taller than
    the trees,
And his voice through all the garden is a thunder
    sent to bring
Black Azrael and Ariel and Ammon on the wing.
Giants and the Genii,
Multiplex of wing and eye,   45
Whose strong obedience broke the sky
When Solomon was king.

They rush in red and purple from the red clouds of
    the morn,
From temples where the yellow gods shut up their
    eyes in scorn;
They rise in green robes roaring from the green hells
    of the sea   50
Where fallen skies and evil hues and eyeless creatures
    be;
On them the sea-valves cluster and the grey sea-forests
    curl,
Splashed with a splendid sickness, the sickness of the
    pearl;
They swell in sapphire smoke out of the blue cracks
    of the ground,—
They gather and they wonder and give worship to
    Mahound.   55
And he saith, 'Break up the mountains where the
    hermit-folk can hide,
And sift the red and silver sands lest bone of saint
    abide,
And chase the Giaours flying night and day, not
    giving rest,
For that which was our trouble comes again out of
    the west.
We have set the seal of Solomon on all things under
    sun,   60
Of knowledge and of sorrow and endurance of things
    done;

But a noise is in the mountains, in the mountains, and I know
The voice that shook our palaces—four hundred years ago:
It is he that saith not 'Kismet'; it is he that knows not Fate;
It is Richard, it is Raymond, it is Godfrey in the gate!
It is he whose loss is laughter when he counts the wager worth: 66
Put down your feet upon him, that our peace be on the earth.'
For he heard drums groaning and he heard guns jar,
(*Don John of Austria is going to the war.*)
Sudden and still—hurrah! 70
Bolt from Iberia!
Don John of Austria
Is gone by Alcalar.

St. Michael's on his Mountain in the sea-roads of the north,
(*Don John of Austria is girt and going forth.*) 75
Where the grey seas glitter and the sharp tides shift
And the sea-folk labour and the red sails lift.
He shakes his lance of iron and he claps his wings of stone;
The noise is gone through Normandy; the noise is gone alone;
The North is full of tangled things and texts and aching eyes, 80
And dead is all the innocence of anger and surprise,
And Christian killeth Christian in a narrow dusty room,
And Christian dreadeth Christ that hath a newer face of doom,
And Christian hateth Mary that God kissed in Galilee,
But Don John of Austria is riding to the sea. 85
Don John calling through the blast and the eclipse,
Crying with the trumpet, with the trumpet of his lips,

Trumpet that sayeth ha!
Domino gloria!
Don John of Austria   90
Is shouting to the ships.

King Philip's in his closet with the Fleece about his
    neck,
(*Don John of Austria is armed upon the deck.*)
The walls are hung with velvet that is black and soft
    as sin,
And little dwarfs creep out of it and little dwarfs
    creep in.   95
He holds a crystal phial that has colours like the
    moon,
He touches, and it tingles, and he trembles very soon,
And his face is as a fungus of a leprous white and
    grey,
Like plants in the high houses that are shuttered
    from the day,   99
And death is the phial and the end of noble work,
But Don John of Austria has fired upon the Turk.
Don John's hunting, and his hounds have bayed—
Booms away past Italy the rumour of his raid.
Gun upon gun, ha! ha!
Gun upon gun, hurrah!   105
Don John of Austria
Has loosed the cannonade.

The Pope was in his chapel before day or battle broke,
(*Don John of Austria is hidden in the smoke.*)
The hidden room in man's house where God sits all
    the year,   110
The secret window whence the world looks small and
    very dear.
He sees as in a mirror on the monstrous twilight sea
The crescent of his cruel ships whose name is mystery;
They fling great shadows foe-wards, making Cross
    and Castle dark,
They veil the plumèd lions on the galleys of St. Mark;

And above the ships are palaces of brown, black-
    bearded chiefs,   116
And below the ships are prisons, where with multi-
    tudinous griefs,
Christian captives sick and sunless, all a labouring
    race repines
Like a race in sunken cities, like a nation in the
    mines.
They are lost like slaves that swat, and in the skies of
    morning hung   120
The stairways of the tallest gods when tyranny was
    young.
They are countless, voiceless, hopeless as those fallen
    or fleeing on
Before the high Kings' horses in the granite of
    Babylon.
And many a one grows witless in his quiet room in
    hell,
Where a yellow face looks inward through the lattice
    of his cell,   125
And he finds his God forgotten, and he seeks no more
    a sign—
(*But Don John of Austria has burst the battle line!*)
Don John pounding from the slaughter-painted poop,
Purpling all the ocean like a bloody pirate's sloop,
Scarlet running over on the silvers and the golds,
Breaking of the hatches up and bursting of the holds,
Thronging of the thousands up that labour under sea,
White for bliss and blind for sun and stunned for
    liberty.
Vivat Hispania!
Domino gloria!   135
Don John of Austria
Has set his people free!

Cervantes on his galley sets the sword back in the
    sheath,
(*Don John of Austria rides homeward with a wreath,*)

And he sees across a weary land a straggling road in
    Spain,   140
Up which a lean and foolish knight forever rides in
    vain,
And he smiles, but not as Sultans smile, and settles
    back the blade . . .
(*But Don John of Austria rides home from the
    Crusade.*)

JOHN MASEFIELD
1876–1967

The Rider at the Gate

A windy night was blowing on Rome,
The cressets guttered on Caesar's home,
The fish-boats, moored at the bridge, were breaking
The rush of the river to yellow foam.

The hinges whined to the shutters shaking,   5
When clip-clop-clep came a horse-hoof raking
The stones of the road at Caesar's gate;
The spear-butts jarred at the guard's awaking.

'Who goes there?' said the guard at the gate.
'What is the news, that you ride so late?'   10
'News most pressing, that must be spoken
To Caesar alone, and that cannot wait.'

'The Caesar sleeps; you must show a token
That the news suffice that he be awoken.
What is the news, and whence do you come?   15
For no light cause may his sleep be broken.'

'Out of the dark of the sands I come,
From the dark of death, with news for Rome.
A word so fell that it must be uttered
Though it strike the soul of the Caesar dumb.'   20

Caesar turned in his bed and muttered,
With a struggle for breath the lamp-flame guttered;
Calpurnia heard her husband moan:
 'The house is falling,
The beaten men come into their own.' 25

'Speak your word,' said the guard at the gate;
'Yes, but bear it to Caesar straight,
Say, "Your murderers' knives are honing,
Your killers' gang is lying in wait."

'Out of the wind that is blowing and moaning, 30
Through the city palace and the country loaning,
I cry, "For the world's sake, Caesar, beware,
And take this warning as my atoning.

' "Beware of the Court, of the palace stair,
Of the downcast friend who speaks so fair, 35
Keep from the Senate, for Death is going
On many men's feet to meet you there."

'I, who am dead, have ways of knowing
Of the crop of death that the quick are sowing.
I, who was Pompey, cry it aloud 40
From the dark of death, from the wind blowing.

'I, who was Pompey, once was proud,
Now I lie in the sand without a shroud;
I cry to Caesar out of my pain,
"Caesar beware, your death is vowed." ' 45

The light grew grey on the window-pane,
The windcocks swung in a burst of rain,
The window of Caesar flung unshuttered,
The horse-hoofs died into wind again.

Caesar turned in his bed and muttered, 50
With a struggle for breath the lamp-flame guttered;
Calpurnia heard her husband moan:
  'The house is falling,
The beaten men come into their own.'

ALFRED NOYES
1880–1958

The Highwayman

I

The wind was a torrent of darkness among the gusty
    trees,
The moon was a ghostly galleon tossed upon cloudy
    seas,
The road was a ribbon of moonlight over the purple
    moor,
And the highwayman came riding—
       Riding—riding—   5
The highwayman came riding, up to the old inn-door.

He'd a French cocked-hat on his forehead, a bunch
    of lace at his chin,
A coat of claret velvet, and breeches of brown doeskin;
They fitted with never a wrinkle: his boots were up to
    the thigh!
And he rode with a jewelled twinkle,   10
       His pistol butts a-twinkle,
His rapier hilt a-twinkle, under the jewelled sky.

Over the cobbles he clattered and clashed in the dark
    inn-yard,
And he tapped with his whip on the shutters, but all
    was locked and barred;
He whistled a tune to the window, and who should be
    waiting there   15
But the landlord's black-eyed daughter,
       Bess, the landlord's daughter,
Plaiting a dark red love-knot into her long black hair.

And dark in the old inn-yard a stable-wicket creaked
Where Tim the ostler listened; his face was white and
    peaked;   20

His eyes were hollows of madness, his hair like
    mouldy hay,
But he loved the landlord's daughter,
      The landlord's red-lipped daughter;—
Dumb as a dog he listened, and he heard the robber
    say—

'One kiss, my bonny sweetheart, I'm after a prize
    to-night,   25
But I shall be back with the yellow gold before the
    morning light;
Yet, if they press me sharply, and harry me through
    the day,
Then look for me by moonlight,
      Watch for me by moonlight,
I'll come to thee by moonlight, though hell should
    bar the way.'   30

He rose upright in the stirrups; he scarce could reach
    her hand,
But she loosened her hair i' the casement! His face
    burnt like a brand
As the black cascade of perfume came tumbling over
    his breast;
And he kissed its waves in the moonlight,
      (Oh, sweet black waves in the moonlight!) 35
Then he tugged at his rein in the moonlight, and
    galloped away to the West.

II

He did not come in the dawning; he did not come at
    noon;
And out o' the tawny sunset, before the rise o' the
    moon,
When the road was a gipsy's ribbon, looping the
    purple moor,
A red-coat troop came marching—   40
      Marching—marching—
King George's men came marching, up to the old
    inn-door.

They said no word to the landlord, they drank his ale
 instead,
But they gagged his daughter and bound her to the
 foot of her narrow bed;
Two of them knelt at her casement, with muskets at
 their side!   45
There was death at every window;
  And hell at one dark window;
For Bess could see, through her casement, the road
 that *he* would ride.

They had tied her up to attention, with many a
  sniggering jest;
They had bound a musket beside her, with the barrel
 beneath her breast!   50
'Now keep good watch!' and they kissed her.
  She heard the dead man say—
Look for me by moonlight;
  Watch for me by moonlight;
I'll come to thee by moonlight, though hell should
 bar the way!   55

She twisted her hands behind her; but all the knots
 held good!
She writhed her hands till her fingers were wet with
 sweat or blood!
They stretched and strained in the darkness, and the
 hours crawled by like years,
Till, now, on the stroke of midnight,
  Cold, on the stroke of midnight, 60
The tip of one finger touched it! The trigger at least
 was hers!

The tip of one finger touched it; she strove no more
 for the rest!
Up, she stood to attention, with the barrel beneath
 her breast,
She would not risk their hearing; she would not strive
 again;

For the road lay bare in the moonlight;   65
    Blank and bare in the moonlight;
And the blood of her veins in the moonlight throbbed
    to her love's refrain.

Tlot-tlot; tlot-tlot! Had they heard it? The horse-
    hoofs ringing clear;
Tlot-tlot, tlot-tlot, in the distance? Were they deaf
    that they did not hear?
Down the ribbon of moonlight, over the brow of the
    hill,   70
The highwayman came riding,
    Riding, riding!
The red-coats looked to their priming! She stood up,
    straight and still!

Tlot-tlot, in the frosty silence! *tlot-tlot,* in the echoing
    night!
Nearer he came and nearer! Her face was like a light!
Her eyes grew wide for a moment; she drew one last
    deep breath,   76
Then her finger moved in the moonlight,
    Her musket shattered the moonlight,
Shattered her breast in the moonlight and warned
    him—with her death.

He turned; he spurred to the Westward; he did not
    know who stood   80
Bowed, with her head o'er the musket, drenched with
    her own red blood!
Not till the dawn he heard it, and slowly blanched to
    hear
How Bess, the landlord's daughter,
    The landlord's black-eyed daughter,
Had watched for her love in the moonlight, and died
    in the darkness there.   85

Back, he spurred like a madman, shrieking a curse to
    the sky,
With the white road smoking behind him and his
    rapier brandished high!

Blood-red were his spurs i' the golden noon; wine-red
    was his velvet coat;·
When they shot him down on the highway,
    Down like a dog on the highway,   90
And he lay in his blood on the highway, with the
    bunch of lace at his throat.

And still of a winter's night, they say, when the wind
    is in the trees,
When the moon is a ghostly galleon tossed upon
    cloudy seas,
When the road is a ribbon of moonlight over the
    purple moor,
A highwayman comes riding—   95
    Riding—riding—
A highwayman comes riding, up to the old inn-door.

Over the cobbles he clatters and clangs in the dark
    inn-yard,
And he taps with his whip on the shutters, but all is
    locked and barred;
He whistles a tune to the window, and who should be
    waiting there   100
But the landlord's black-eyed daughter,
    Bess, the landlord's daughter,
Plaiting a dark red love-knot into her long black hair.

INDEX OF FIRST LINES